# 3rd Grade

# OREGON MATH TEST PREP

## Common Core State Standards

Send all inquiries to:

**sales@teacherstreasures, or visit us at**
**http://www.teacherstreasures.com**

# INTRODUCTION

Our 3rd Grade Math Test Prep for Common Core State Standards is an excellent resource to supplement your classroom's curriculum to assess and manage students' understanding of concepts outlined in the Common Core State Standards Initiative. This resource is divided into three sections: Diagnostic, Practice, and Assessment with multiple choice questions in each section. We recommend you use the Diagnostic section as a tool to determine the students' areas that need to be retaught. We also recommend you encourage your students to show their work to determine ***how*** and ***why*** the student arrived at an answer. The Practice section should be used to strengthen the students' knowledge by re-testing the standard to ensure comprehension of each standard. To ensure students' apply taught concepts in the classroom, we advise you use the Assessment section as a final test to verify the students' have mastered the standard.

This resource contains over 500 practice problems aligned to the Common Core State Standards. To view the standards, refer to pages *i* through *iv*.

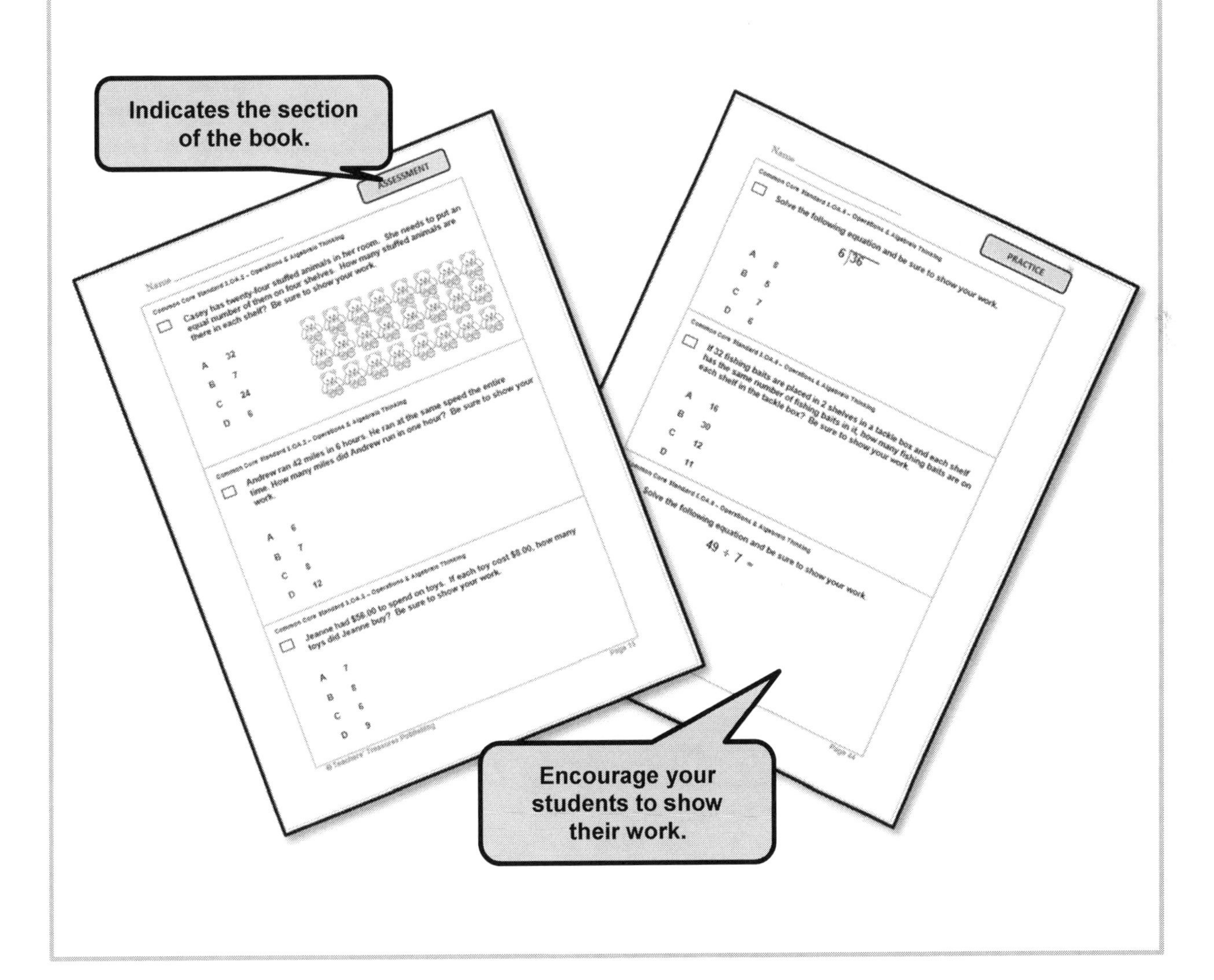

TABLE OF CONTENTS

# 3rd Grade
# Math Test Prep
FOR
# Common Core
# Standards

## COMMON CORE STATE STANDARDS

**Operations & Algebraic Thinking** **3.OA**

**Represent and solve problems involving multiplication and division.**

1. Interpret products of whole numbers, e.g., interpret 5 × 7 as the total number of objects in 5 groups of 7 objects each. *For example, describe a context in which a total number of objects can be expressed as 5 × 7.*
2. Interpret whole-number quotients of whole numbers, e.g., interpret 56 ÷ 8 as the number of objects in each share when 56 objects are partitioned equally into 8 shares, or as a number of shares when 56 objects are partitioned into equal shares of 8 objects each. *For example, describe a context in which a number of shares or a number of groups can be expressed as 56 ÷ 8.*
3. Use multiplication and division within 100 to solve word problems in situations involving equal groups, arrays, and measurement quantities, e.g., by using drawings and equations with a symbol for the unknown number to represent the problem.1
4. Determine the unknown whole number in a multiplication or division equation relating three whole numbers. *For example, determine the unknown number that makes the equation true in each of the equations 8 × ? = 48, 5 = _ ÷ 3, 6 × 6 = ?*

**Understand properties of multiplication and the relationship between multiplication and division.**

5. Apply properties of operations as strategies to multiply and divide.2 *Examples: If 6 × 4 = 24 is known, then 4 × 6 = 24 is also known. (Commutative property of multiplication.) 3 × 5 × 2 can be found by 3 × 5 = 15, then 15 × 2 = 30, or by 5 × 2 = 10, then 3 × 10 = 30. (Associative property of multiplication.) Knowing that 8 × 5 = 40 and 8 × 2 = 16, one can find 8 × 7 as 8 × (5 + 2) = (8 × 5) + (8 × 2) = 40 + 16 = 56. (Distributive property.)*
6. Understand division as an unknown-factor problem. *For example, find 32 ÷ 8 by finding the number that makes 32 when multiplied by 8.*

**Multiply and divide within 100.**

7. Fluently multiply and divide within 100, using strategies such as the relationship between multiplication and division (e.g., knowing that 8 × 5 = 40, one knows 40 ÷ 5 = 8) or properties of operations. By the end of Grade 3, know from memory all products of two one-digit numbers.
   Solve problems involving the four operations, and identify and explain patterns in arithmetic.
8. Solve two-step word problems using the four operations. Represent these problems using equations with a letter standing for the unknown quantity. Assess the reasonableness of answers using mental computation and estimation strategies including rounding.
9. Identify arithmetic patterns (including patterns in the addition table or multiplication table), and explain them using properties of operations. *For example, observe that 4*

*times a number is always even, and explain why 4 times a number can be decomposed into two equal addends.*

**Number & Operations in Base Ten** **3.NBT**

**Use place value understanding and properties of operations to perform multi-digit arithmetic.**

1. Use place value understanding to round whole numbers to the nearest 10 or 100.
2. Fluently add and subtract within 1000 using strategies and algorithms based on place value, properties of operations, and/or the relationship between addition and subtraction.
3. Multiply one-digit whole numbers by multiples of 10 in the range 10–90 (e.g., 9 × 80, 5 × 60) using strategies based on place value and properties of operations.

**Number & Operations—Fractions** **3.NF**

**Develop understanding of fractions as numbers.**

1. Understand a fraction 1/*b* as the quantity formed by 1 part when *a* whole is partitioned into *b* equal parts; understand a fraction *a*/*b* as the quantity formed by a parts of size 1/*b*.
2. Understand a fraction as a number on the number line; represent fractions on a number line diagram.
   a. Represent a fraction 1/*b* on a number line diagram by defining the interval from 0 to 1 as the whole and partitioning it into *b* equal parts. Recognize that each part has size 1/*b* and that the endpoint of the part based at 0 locates the number 1/*b* on the number line.
   b. Represent a fraction *a*/*b* on a number line diagram by marking off a lengths 1/*b* from 0. Recognize that the resulting interval has size *a*/*b* and that its endpoint locates the number *a*/*b* on the number line.

3. Explain equivalence of fractions in special cases, and compare fractions by reasoning about their size.
   a. Understand two fractions as equivalent (equal) if they are the same size, or the same point on a number line.
   b. Recognize and generate simple equivalent fractions, e.g., 1/2 = 2/4, 4/6 = 2/3). Explain why the fractions are equivalent, e.g., by using a visual fraction model.
   c. Express whole numbers as fractions, and recognize fractions that are equivalent to whole numbers. *Examples: Express 3 in the form 3 = 3/1; recognize that 6/1 = 6; locate 4/4 and 1 at the same point of a number line diagram.*
   d. Compare two fractions with the same numerator or the same denominator by reasoning about their size. Recognize that comparisons are valid only when the two fractions refer to the same whole. Record the results of comparisons with the

symbols >, =, or <, and justify the conclusions, e.g., by using a visual fraction model.

**Measurement & Data** **3.MD**

**Solve problems involving measurement and estimation of intervals of time, liquid volumes, and masses of objects.**

1. Tell and write time to the nearest minute and measure time intervals in minutes. Solve word problems involving addition and subtraction of time intervals in minutes, e.g., by representing the problem on a number line diagram.
2. Measure and estimate liquid volumes and masses of objects using standard units of grams (g), kilograms (kg), and liters (l).1 Add, subtract, multiply, or divide to solve one-step word problems involving masses or volumes that are given in the same units, e.g., by using drawings (such as a beaker with a measurement scale) to represent the problem.

**Represent and interpret data.**

3. Draw a scaled picture graph and a scaled bar graph to represent a data set with several categories. Solve one- and two-step "how many more" and "how many less" problems using information presented in scaled bar graphs. *For example, draw a bar graph in which each square in the bar graph might represent 5 pets.* 4. Generate measurement data by measuring lengths using rulers marked with halves and fourths of an inch. Show the data by making a line plot, where the horizontal scale is marked off in appropriate units— whole numbers, halves, or quarters.

**Geometric measurement: understand concepts of area and relate area to multiplication and to addition.**

5. Recognize area as an attribute of plane figures and understand concepts of area measurement.
   a. A square with side length 1 unit, called "a unit square," is said to have "one square unit" of area, and can be used to measure area.
   b. A plane figure which can be covered without gaps or overlaps by *n* unit squares is said to have an area of *n* square units.
6. Measure areas by counting unit squares (square cm, square m, square in, square ft, and improvised units).
7. Relate area to the operations of multiplication and addition.
   a. Find the area of a rectangle with whole-number side lengths by tiling it, and show that the area is the same as would be found by multiplying the side lengths.
   b. Multiply side lengths to find areas of rectangles with whole-number side lengths in the context of solving real world and mathematical problems, and represent whole-number products as rectangular areas in mathematical reasoning.

c. Use tiling to show in a concrete case that the area of a rectangle with whole-number side lengths $a$ and $b + c$ is the sum of $a \times b$ and $a \times c$. Use area models to represent the distributive property in mathematical reasoning.
d. Recognize area as additive. Find areas of rectilinear figures by decomposing them into non-overlapping rectangles and adding the areas of the non-overlapping parts, applying this technique to solve real world problems.

**Geometric measurement: recognize perimeter as an attribute of plane figures and distinguish between linear and area measures.**

8. Solve real world and mathematical problems involving perimeters of polygons, including finding the perimeter given the side lengths, finding an unknown side length, and exhibiting rectangles with the same perimeter and different areas or with the same area and different perimeters.

**Geometry** **3.G**

**Reason with shapes and their attributes.**

1. Understand that shapes in different categories (e.g., rhombuses, rectangles, and others) may share attributes (e.g., having four sides), and that the shared attributes can define a larger category (e.g., quadrilaterals). Recognize rhombuses, rectangles, and squares as examples of quadrilaterals, and draw examples of quadrilaterals that do not belong to any of these subcategories.
2. Partition shapes into parts with equal areas. Express the area of each part as a unit fraction of the whole. *For example, partition a shape into 4 parts with equal area, and describe the area of each part as 1/4 of the area of*

# MATHEMATICS CHART

## LENGTH

| Metric | Customary |
| --- | --- |
| 1 kilometer = 1000 meters | 1 yard = 3 feet |
| 1 meter = 100 centimeters | 1 foot = 12 inches |
| 1 centimeter = 10 millimeters | |

## CAPACITY & VOLUME

| Metric | Customary |
| --- | --- |
| 1 liter = 1000 milliliters | 1 gallon = 4 quarts |
| | 1 gallon = 128 ounces |
| | 1 quart = 2 pints |
| | 1 pint = 2 cups |
| | 1 cup = 8 ounces |

## MASS & WEIGHT

| Metric | Customary |
| --- | --- |
| 1 kilogram = 1000 grams | 1 ton = 2000 pounds |
| 1 gram = 1000 milligrams | 1 pound = 16 ounces |

## TIME

1 year = 365 days

1 year = 12 months

1 year = 52 weeks

1 week = 7 days

1 day = 24 hours

1 hour = 60 minutes

1 minute = 60 seconds

Name ____________________

**DIAGNOSTIC**

Common Core Standard 3.OA.1 – Operations & Algebraic Thinking

☐ **Which of the following best represents 4 × 8?**

**A**

**B**

**C**

**D**

Common Core Standard 3.OA.1 – Operations & Algebraic Thinking

☐ **Look at the diagram below. Which number sentence best represents the diagram?**

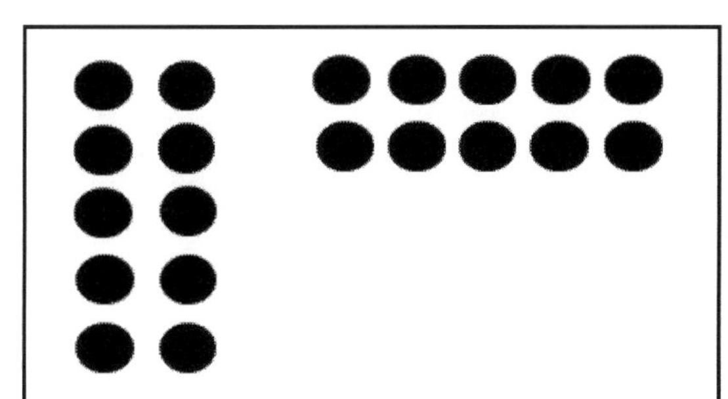

**A** 2 + 5 = 5 + 2

**B** 5 × 2 = 10

**C** 5 × 2 = 2 × 5

**D** 2 + 5 + 5 + 2 = 14

Common Core Standard 3.OA.1 – Operations & Algebraic Thinking

☐ **Which of the following best represents 5 × 3?**

**A**

**C**

**B**

**D**

Name ___________________________

DIAGNOSTIC

Common Core Standard 3.OA.1 – Operations & Algebraic Thinking

☐ **Which of the following is equal to 5 x 4?**

A 5 + 5 + 5

B 5 + 5 + 5 + 5

C 5 + 5 + 5 + 5 + 5

D 5 + 4

Common Core Standard 3.OA.1 – Operations & Algebraic Thinking

☐ **Ray had 12 balloons. If he tied the balloons together in pairs of two, how many sets of balloons does he have?**

A 5

B 4

C 6

D 3

Common Core Standard 3.OA.1 – Operations & Algebraic Thinking

☐ **Which of the following is equal to 7 + 7 + 7 + 7 + 7 + 7?**

A 7 x 7

B 7 x 5

C 7 x 6

D 7 x 4

Name ______________________

PRACTICE

Common Core Standard 3.OA.1 – Operations & Algebraic Thinking

☐ **Another way to write 9 x 9 would be which of the following?**

A 9 + 9

B 9 + 9 + 9 + 9 + 9 + 9 + 9 + 9

C 9 + 9 + 9 + 9 + 9 + 9 + 9 + 9 + 9

D 81

Common Core Standard 3.OA.1 – Operations & Algebraic Thinking

☐ **Which of the following best describes the diagram below?**

▣ ▣ ▣ ▣ ▣ ▣
▣ ▣ ▣ ▣ ▣ ▣
▣ ▣ ▣ ▣ ▣ ▣
▣ ▣ ▣ ▣ ▣ ▣

A 6 + 4 = 10

B 4 x 6 = 24

C 6 x 4 = 10

D 6 x 4 = 24

Common Core Standard 3.OA.1 – Operations & Algebraic Thinking

☐ **2 + 2 + 2 + 2 can also be represented as which of the following?**

A 2 + 4 = 6

B 6 – 2 = 4

C 2 x 4 = 8

D 4 + 2 = 8

Name ____________________

**PRACTICE**

Common Core Standard 3.OA.1 – Operations & Algebraic Thinking

☐ **Another way to write 8 x 5 is which of the following?**

**A** 8 + 5

**B** 8 + 8 + 8 + 8 + 8

**C** 5 + 5 + 5 + 5 + 5

**D** 8 - 5

Common Core Standard 3.OA.1 – Operations & Algebraic Thinking

☐ **Which of the following best represents the following multiplication problem below?**

**4 x 3**

**A** ▣ ▣ ▣ ▣<br>▣ ▣ ▣ ▣<br>▣ ▣ ▣ ▣

**C** ▣ ▣ ▣<br>▣ ▣ ▣<br>▣ ▣ ▣<br>▣ ▣ ▣

**B** ▣ ▣ ▣ ▣ ▣ ▣ ▣

**D** ▣ ▣ ▣ ▣ ▣ ▣<br>▣ ▣ ▣ ▣ ▣ ▣

Common Core Standard 3.OA.1 – Operations & Algebraic Thinking

☐ **Which of the following best represents the picture below?**

**A** 2 + 5 = 7

**B** 10 + 2 = 12

**C** 5 x 2 = 10

**D** 2 x 5 = 10

Name ______________________

**PRACTICE**

Common Core Standard 3.OA.1 – Operations & Algebraic Thinking

☐ **James had 18 lollipops. He wanted to give each of his 3 friends the same amount of lollipops. How many lollipops did each friend receive? Be sure to show your work.**

A 7

B 10

C 6

D 5

Common Core Standard 3.OA.1 – Operations & Algebraic Thinking

☐ **Complete the following multiplication problem? Be sure to show your work.**

$$5 \times \square = 35$$

A 6

B 7

C 5

D 9

Common Core Standard 3.OA.1 – Operations & Algebraic Thinking

☐ **Look at the following picture. Which answer best describes the picture below?**

A 3 x 6 = 6 x 3

B 6 x 3 = 18

C 3 + 6 = 6 + 3

D 3 x 6 = 18

Name ___________________________

**PRACTICE**

Common Core Standard 3.OA.1 – Operations & Algebraic Thinking

☐ **Look at the drawing below. Which answer best describes the drawing?**

**A** 6 + 5 = 5 + 6

**B** 5 x 6 = 6 x 5

**C** 5 x 6 = 30

**D** 6 x 5 = 30

Common Core Standard 3.OA.1 – Operations & Algebraic Thinking

☐ **Which answer best represents the following multiplication problem?**

**☐ x ☐ = 32**

**A** 6 x 4

**B** 8 + 8 + 8 + 8

**C** 8 x 3

**D** 4 + 4 + 4 + 4 + 4 + 4 + 4 +4 +4

Common Core Standard 3.OA.1 – Operations & Algebraic Thinking

☐ **Which picture best describes the following problem?**

**3 x 5 = 15**

**A**

**C**

**B**

**D**

Name ___________________________

**ASSESSMENT**

Common Core Standard 3.OA.1 – Operations & Algebraic Thinking

☐ **Complete the following multiplication problem, 8 x☐ = 72. Be sure to show your work.**

A 12

B 9

C 8

D 11

Common Core Standard 3.OA.1 – Operations & Algebraic Thinking

☐ **Which of the following best represents 2 × 6?**

A ▣ ▣ ▣ ▣ ▣ ▣<br>▣ ▣ ▣ ▣ ▣ ▣

B ▣     ▣ ▣ ▣ ▣ ▣ ▣<br>▣     ▣ ▣ ▣ ▣ ▣ ▣

C ▣ ▣ ▣ ▣ ▣ ▣ ▣ ▣

D ▣ ▣<br>▣ ▣<br>▣ ▣<br>▣ ▣<br>▣ ▣<br>▣ ▣

Common Core Standard 3.OA.1 – Operations & Algebraic Thinking

☐ **Which of the following best represents 7 × 9?**

A 7 + 9

B 9 + 9 + 9 + 9 + 9 + 9

C 7 + 7 + 7 + 7 + 7 + 7 + 7 + 7 + 7

D 16

Name ____________________________

ASSESSMENT

Common Core Standard 3.OA.1 – Operations & Algebraic Thinking

☐ **Which of the following is equal to 2 x 9?**

A 2 + 2 + 2 + 2 + 2 +2 + 2 + 2

B 9 + 9 + 9 + 9 + 9 + 9 + 9 + 9 + 9

C 9 + 9 + 9

D 2 + 2 + 2 + 2 + 2 +2 + 2 + 2 + 2

Common Core Standard 3.OA.1 – Operations & Algebraic Thinking

☐ **Which of the number sentences below best represents the drawing?**

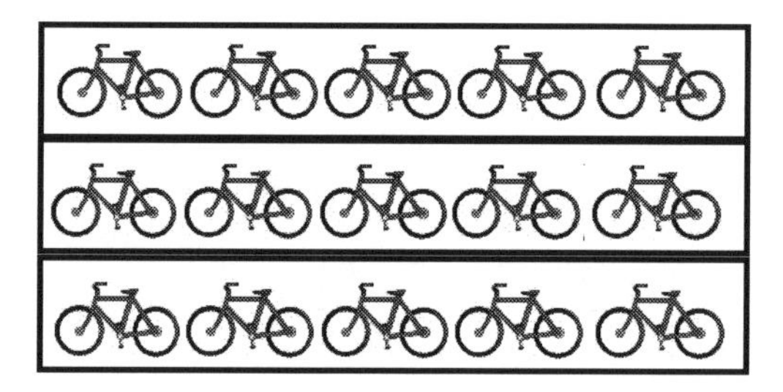

A 3 ÷ 5 = 15

B 5 + 3 = 8

C 3 x 5 = 15

D 5 x 3 = 8

Common Core Standard 3.OA.1 – Operations & Algebraic Thinking

☐ **Look at the drawing below. Which number sentence best represents the drawing?**

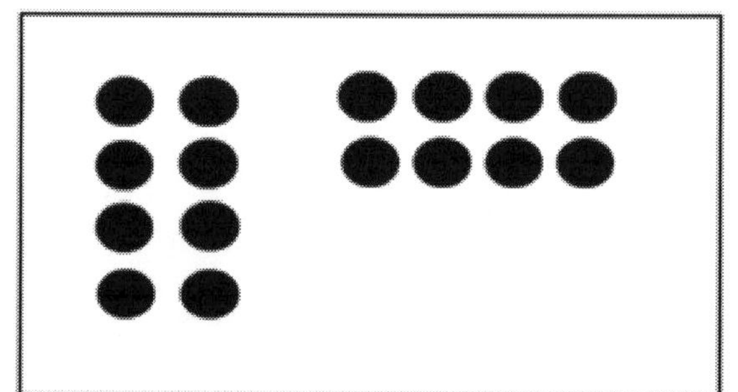

A 2 + 4 = 4 + 2

B 4 × 2 = 2 × 4

C 4 × 2 = 8

D 2 + 4 + 4 + 2 = 12

Name ____________________

**DIAGNOSTIC**

Common Core Standard 3.OA. .2 – Operations & Algebraic Thinking

☐ **Choose the picture below that shows a set that could be divided by the numeral 3.**

A

C

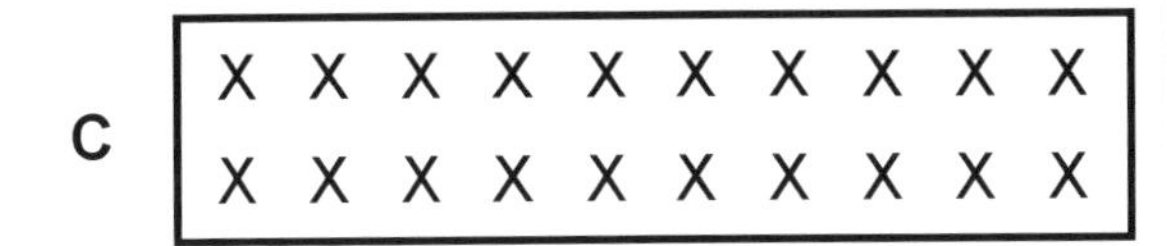


B

D

Common Core Standard 3.OA. 2 – Operations & Algebraic Thinking

☐ **Marcelle has 24 pieces of candy. He divided the candy into 2 equal sets. How many pieces of candy are in each set?**

A 48

B 8

C 10

D 12

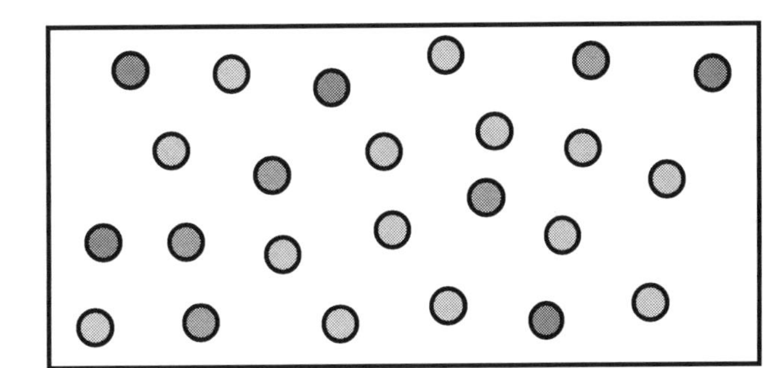

Common Core Standard 3.OA. 2 – Operations & Algebraic Thinking

☐ **How much money does Mike need to buy 3 balls and not have any money left over after his purchase?**

A $15.00

B $8.00

C $10.00

D $20.00

Each ball costs $5.00

Name ______________________

DIAGNOSTIC

Common Core Standard 3.OA. 2 – Operations & Algebraic Thinking

☐ **Which group of triangles could be equally divided into sets of 5 triangles in each set with no triangles left over?**

A ▲▲▲▲▲▲ ▲▲▲▲▲▲

B ▲▲▲▲▲▲ ▲▲▲▲▲

C ▲▲▲▲▲▲ ▲▲▲▲▲▲▲▲ ▲▲▲▲▲▲

D ▲▲▲▲▲▲

Common Core Standard 3.OA. 2 – Operations & Algebraic Thinking

☐ **Which of the following numbers could be divided by 3 and have nothing left over? Be sure to show your work.**

A 52

B 29

C 48

D 13

Common Core Standard 3.OA. 2 – Operations & Algebraic Thinking

☐ **Mack had 18 baseball cards. He wanted to divide them into several boxes. Which number could he divide into the total number of cards so that he would have an equal number of cards in each box? Be sure to show your work.**

A 5

B 2

C 4

D 7

Name ___________________________

PRACTICE

Common Core Standard 3.OA.2 – Operations & Algebraic Thinking

☐ Freddie read 35 pages in 7 days. On average, how many pages did Freddie read each day? Be sure to show your work.

A 42

B 28

C 5

D 4

Common Core Standard 3.OA.2 – Operations & Algebraic Thinking

☐ The local food bank had 24 food cans that it needed to separate into 6 boxes. How many cans were put into each box without having any cans left over? Be sure to show your work.

A 4

B 6

C 12

D 2

Common Core Standard 3.OA.2 – Operations & Algebraic Thinking

☐ Becky was helping her mother make pudding for her school party. Each cup could hold 4 ounces of pudding. If there was 48 ounces to divide from, how many cups of pudding did she make? Be sure to show your work.

A 6

B 11

C 12

D 13

Name ____________________

**PRACTICE**

Common Core Standard 3.OA.2 – Operations & Algebraic Thinking

☐ **Santa is delivering 100 gifts to 5 boys and 5 girls. If Santa gave each boy and girl the same number of gifts, how many gifts did each boy and girl receive? Be sure to show your work.**

A 10

B 6

C 11

D 9

Common Core Standard 3.OA.2 – Operations & Algebraic Thinking

☐ **After Shanelle's friends finished playing kickball, they became thirsty. Shanelle had 18 ounces of juice in her refrigerator. If she gave each of her 6 friends the same amount of juice, how many ounces of juice did each girl receive? Be sure to show your work.**

A 12 ounces

B 3 ounces

C 24 ounces

D 6 ounces

Common Core Standard 3.OA.2 – Operations & Algebraic Thinking

☐ **Jenny's father gave her $32 one dollar bills. She had four bags to put them in, how much money would each bag contain? Be sure to show your work.**

A 6

B 36

C 8

D 4

Name ____________________

**PRACTICE**

Common Core Standard 3.OA.2 – Operations & Algebraic Thinking

☐ **Henry has to pass out his Christmas cards. He has 15 cards to pass out in 3 classrooms. There are an even amount of friends in each of those classrooms. How many Christmas cards will Henry pass out to each classroom? Be sure to show your work.**

**A 4**

**B 18**

**C 6**

**D 5**

Common Core Standard 3.OA.2 – Operations & Algebraic Thinking

☐ **Arin, Aubrey, Heather, and Katherine have twenty kick balls. They want to take home an equal amount each. How many kick balls should each girl take home? Be sure to show your work.**

**A 6**

**B 4**

**C 5**

**D 9**

Common Core Standard 3.OA.2 – Operations & Algebraic Thinking

☐ **Jewel has twenty-one slices of pizza remaining. She wants to give an equal amount of pizza to each of her seven friends. How many slices of pizza should she give to each friend? Be sure to show your work.**

**A 28**

**B 6**

**C 3**

**D 4**

Name ____________________

**PRACTICE**

Common Core Standard 3.OA.2 – Operations & Algebraic Thinking

☐ **A farmer has 28 heads of cabbage. He needs to feed each of his 4 pigs. If each pig receives the same amount, how many heads of cabbage will each pig receive? Be sure to show your work.**

A 7

B 6

C 31

D 8

Common Core Standard 3.OA.2 – Operations & Algebraic Thinking

☐ **A group of 42 children were divided equally into teams for soccer. Each soccer team had 6 children on a team. How many soccer teams are there? Be sure to show your work.**

A 48

B 36

C 8

D 7

Common Core Standard 3.OA.2 – Operations & Algebraic Thinking

☐ **Anna has 48 inches of string to make friendship bracelets for her friends. If she uses 6 inches of string for each friendship bracelet, how many friends will she give the bracelets to? Be sure to show your work.**

A 42

B 8

C 6

D 52

Name ______________________

**ASSESSMENT**

Common Core Standard 3.OA.2 – Operations & Algebraic Thinking

☐ **Casey has twenty-four stuffed animals in her room. She needs to put an equal number of them on four shelves. How many stuffed animals are there in each shelf? Be sure to show your work.**

**A** 32

**B** 7

**C** 24

**D** 6

Common Core Standard 3.OA.2 – Operations & Algebraic Thinking

☐ **Andrew ran 42 miles in 6 hours. He ran at the same speed the entire time. How many miles did Andrew run in one hour? Be sure to show your work.**

**A** 6

**B** 7

**C** 8

**D** 12

Common Core Standard 3.OA.2 – Operations & Algebraic Thinking

☐ **Jeanne had $56.00 to spend on toys. If each toy cost $8.00, how many toys did Jeanne buy? Be sure to show your work.**

**A** 7

**B** 8

**C** 6

**D** 9

Name ___________________________

ASSESSMENT

Common Core Standard 3.OA.2 – Operations & Algebraic Thinking

☐ **The Fairview Baseball Association had 72 boys to play baseball for the summer. If there are 12 players on each team. How many teams will be formed? Be sure to show your work.**

**A 5**

**B 7**

**C 60**

**D 6**

Common Core Standard 3.OA.2 – Operations & Algebraic Thinking

☐ **Mr. Fernandez bought twenty five flowers for his front yard. If he divides the flowers to fit equally among five areas in his yard, how many flowers will there be in each area? Be sure to show your work.**

**A 6**

**B 5**

**C 4**

**D 20**

Common Core Standard 3.OA.2 – Operations & Algebraic Thinking

☐ **There are 96 3rd grade students in Sunshine Elementary School. There are 6 separate classrooms. How many students are in each class? Be sure to show your work.**

**A 16**

**B 20**

**C 21**

**D 12**

Name ______________________

**DIAGNOSTIC**

Common Core Standard 3.OA.3 – Operations & Algebraic Thinking

☐ **Carl has twelve army action figures. His friend Steve has five times as many action figures as Carl. How many action figures does Steve have? Be sure to show your work.**

**A** **17**

**B** **60**

**C** **7**

**D** **55**

Common Core Standard 3.OA. 3 – Operations & Algebraic Thinking

☐ **Katie has basketball games at three different locations. The basketball courts were located 10 miles away from each other. The first game starts in 1 hour. How many miles did Katie's mom have to drive? Be sure to show your work.**

**A** **10**

**B** **30**

**C** **7**

**D** **14**

Common Core Standard 3.OA. 3 – Operations & Algebraic Thinking

☐ **Anita's mother asked her to clean up her room. She has a dresser that has 5 drawers. She needs to put her 40 pairs of socks in the dresser drawers in equal amounts. How many pairs of socks will be in each drawer? Be sure to show your work.**

**A** **8**

**B** **6**

**C** **5**

**D** **4**

Name ____________________

DIAGNOSTIC

Common Core Standard 3.OA. 3 – Operations & Algebraic Thinking

☐ **Jamal has $12 dollars saved. Karrie has saved eight times as much as Jamal. How much money has Karrie saved? Be sure to show your work.**

**A** **$20**

**B** **$96**

**C** **$4**

**D** **$108**

Common Core Standard 3.OA. 3 – Operations & Algebraic Thinking

☐ **Ronaldo and his friends can build three tree houses in a week. How many tree houses can they build in half a year? Be sure to show your work.**

**A** **78**

**B** **100**

**C** **156**

**D** **18**

Common Core Standard 3.OA. 3 – Operations & Algebraic Thinking

☐ **Price Elementary School went on a field trip. There were 2 buses and 3 vans used to take 60 students. How many students were equally put into the vans and buses? Be sure to show your work.**

**A** **24**

**B** **12**

**C** **14**

**D** **36**

PRACTICE

Name ____________________

Common Core Standard 3.OA.3 – Operations & Algebraic Thinking

☐ **Shryl has 72 flowers. She wants to put the flowers into 8 vases, how many flowers are in each vase? Be sure to show your work.**

**A** 12

**B** 8

**C** 10

**D** 9

Common Core Standard 3.OA.3 – Operations & Algebraic Thinking

☐ **Juan has $48 to spend on baseball cards. If each card costs $6 each, how many cards did Juan buy? Be sure to show your work.**

**A** 42

**B** 8

**C** 7

**D** 9

Common Core Standard 3.OA.3 – Operations & Algebraic Thinking

☐ **If a dump truck can move five tons of dirt to a house and the truck has to deliver to 6 houses, how many tons of dirt did the dump truck deliver? Be sure to show your work.**

**A** 11 tons

**B** 25 tons

**C** 30 tons

**D** 36 tons

Name ______________________

PRACTICE

Common Core Standard 3.OA.3 – Operations & Algebraic Thinking

☐ **If there are 66 girls that want to play soccer and each team must have 11 girls to a team. How many soccer teams are there? Be sure to show your work.**

**A 8 teams**

**B 6 teams**

**C 5 teams**

**D 77 teams**

Common Core Standard 3.OA.3 – Operations & Algebraic Thinking

☐ **Mrs. Black baked 9 cookies. If Mr. Black ate one cookie and Jack and Suzy split the remaining cookies, how many cookies did Jack and Suzy each eat? Be sure to show your work.**

**A 6**

**B 5**

**C 4**

**D 3**

Common Core Standard 3.OA 3 – Operations & Algebraic Thinking

☐ **Mrs. Jones classroom has 3 homework assignments to take home. If there are 24 students in the class, how many total homework assignments did Mrs. Jones assign to each student? Be sure to show your work.**

**A 54**

**B 27**

**C 72**

**D 8**

Name ___________________________

**PRACTICE**

Common Core Standard 3.OA.3 – Operations & Algebraic Thinking

☐ Coach Stanford has to sort all the basketball shoes into 3 groups. If she has 36 shoes, how many shoes are in each group? Be sure to show your work.

A 12

B 10

C 33

D 11

Common Core Standard 3.OA.3 – Operations & Algebraic Thinking

☐ Rose went trick or treating on Halloween with 5 of her friends. They visited 21 houses in their neighborhood and each house gave each child 3 pieces of candy. How many pieces of candy did Rose receive? Be sure to show your work.

A 105

B 5

C 7

D 63

Common Core Standard 3.OA.3 – Operations & Algebraic Thinking

☐ Isabella wrote Christmas cards to her friends and family. If she was able to finish 6 cards in a hour and she has 54 friends and family members, how long did it take her to write all the Christmas cards? Be sure to show your work.

A 10 hours

B 9 hours

C 8 hours

D 48 hours

Name ____________________

PRACTICE

Common Core Standard 3.OA.3 – Operations & Algebraic Thinking

☐ Two girls and four boys share a large pizza together. If the total cost of the pizza was $72 and the bill was split equally, how much did each boy pay? Be sure to show your work.

A $9

B $18

C $36

D $12

Common Core Standard 3.OA.3 – Operations & Algebraic Thinking

☐ Marcos participates in his school running competion. If Marcos runs 5 miles a week, how many weeks does Marcos need to run to reach 45 miles? Be sure to show your work.

A 6 weeks

B 10 weeks

C 8 weeks

D 9 weeks

Common Core Standard 3.OA. 3 – Operations & Algebraic Thinking

☐ Chelsea has 8 dolls in her toy box. McKenna has 3 times as many dolls as Chelsea. How many dolls does McKenna have? Be sure to show your work.

A 24

B 32

C 11

D 16

Name ______________________

ASSESSMENT

Common Core Standard 3.OA.3 – Operations & Algebraic Thinking

☐ **Jeremy earned $35 last month raking leaves. If Jeremy charges $5.00 for each yard he rakes, how many yards did Jeremy rake? Be sure to show your work.**

**A 8**

**B 4**

**C 7**

**D 5**

Common Core Standard 3.OA.3 – Operations & Algebraic Thinking

☐ **Carole has received 9 cards on Valentine's Day. Sonny has 3 times as many cards as Carole. How many cards does Sonny have? Be sure to show your work.**

**A 36**

**B 3**

**C 25**

**D 27**

Common Core Standard 3.OA. 3 – Operations & Algebraic Thinking

☐ **The local museum had 84 paintings. There were twleve rooms with paintings. How many paintings were in each room? Be sure to show your work.**

**A 9**

**B 12**

**C 8**

**D 7**

Name ___________________________

ASSESSMENT

Common Core Standard 3.OA.3 – Operations & Algebraic Thinking

☐ If an egg carton has 12 eggs in it and Shanna bought 6 egg cartons, how many eggs did Shanna buy? Be sure to show your work.

A 60

B 18

C 2

D 72

Common Core Standard 3.OA.3 – Operations & Algebraic Thinking

☐ Mrs. Romano has twenty-one students in her 3rd grade class. She wants to have three equal rows of students in her classroom. How many students are on each row? Be sure to show your work.

A 9

B 6

C 7

D 18

Common Core Standard 3.OA. 3 – Operations & Algebraic Thinking

☐ Sydney reads 4 pages per day in her favorite book. How many pages will she read in one week? Be sure to show your work.

A 24

B 28

C 20

D 36

Name ____________________

**DIAGNOSTIC**

Common Core Standard 3.OA.4 – Operations & Algebraic Thinking

☐ **If 6 times a number is 30, which expression could be used to find the number? Be sure to show your work.**

**A** $30 + 6$

**B** $30 - 6$

**C** $30 \times 6$

**D** $30 \div 6$

Common Core Standard 3.OA.4 – Operations & Algebraic Thinking

☐ **If $60 \div 12 = \square$, then $60 \div \square = 12$. Which numeral would fit in both number sentences? Be sure to show your work.**

**A** 5

**B** 1

**C** 72

**D** 48

Common Core Standard 3.OA.4 – Operations & Algebraic Thinking

☐ **Which number sentence should not have a 6 in the box? Be sure to show your work.**

**A** $24 \div 4 = \square$

**B** $36 \div \square = 6$

**C** $48 \div \square = 6$

**D** $54 \div 9 = \square$

Name ____________________

DIAGNOSTIC

Common Core Standard 3.OA.4 – Operations & Algebraic Thinking

☐ **If 54 ÷ 9 = ☐, then 54 ÷ ☐ = 9. Which numeral would be correct in both number sentences? Be sure to show your work.**

**A** 7

**B** 486

**C** 6

**D** 63

Common Core Standard 3.OA.4 – Operations & Algebraic Thinking

☐ **Which number sentence should not have a 9 in the box? Be sure to show your work.**

**A** 56 ÷ ☐ = 8

**B** 36 ÷ 4 = ☐

**C** 27 ÷ ☐ = 3

**D** 54 ÷ 6 = ☐

Common Core Standard 3.OA.4 – Operations & Algebraic Thinking

☐ **If 63 ÷ 7 = ☐, then ☐ × 7 = 63. Which numeral would be correct in both number sentences? Be sure to show your work.**

**A** 441

**B** 8

**C** 56

**D** 9

Name ____________________

PRACTICE

Common Core Standard 3.OA.4 – Operations & Algebraic Thinking

☐ **If 7 times a number is 63, which expression could be used to find the number? Be sure to show your work.**

A $63 + 7$

B $63 - 7$

C $63 \times 7$

D $63 \div 7$

Common Core Standard 3.OA.4 – Operations & Algebraic Thinking

☐ **If $55 \div 11 = \square$, then $55 \div \square = 11$. Which numeral would fit in both number sentences? Be sure to show your work.**

A 5

B 44

C 6

D 4

Common Core Standard 3.OA.4 – Operations & Algebraic Thinking

☐ **Which number sentence should not have a 3 in the box? Be sure to show your work.**

A $27 \div 9 = \square$

B $36 \div \square = 12$

C $24 \div \square = 8$

D $30 \div 3 = \square$

Name ____________________

PRACTICE

Common Core Standard 3.OA.4 – Operations & Algebraic Thinking

☐ If 48 ÷ 12 = ☐, then 48 ÷ ☐ = 12. Which numeral would be correct in both number sentences? Be sure to show your work.

A 6

B 4

C 5

D 9

Common Core Standard 3.OA.4 – Operations & Algebraic Thinking

☐ Which number sentence should not have a 5 in the box? Be sure to show your work.

A 55 ÷ ☐ = 11

B 36 ÷ 7 = ☐

C 25 ÷ ☐ = 5

D 60 ÷ 12 = ☐

Common Core Standard 3.OA.4 – Operations & Algebraic Thinking

☐ If 81 ÷ 9 = ☐, then ☐ × 9 = 81. Which numeral would be correct in both number sentences? Be sure to show your work.

A 7

B 8

C 10

D 9

Name ______________________

**PRACTICE**

Common Core Standard 3.OA.4 – Operations & Algebraic Thinking

☐ **If 8 times a number is 56, which expression could be used to find the number? Be sure to show your work.**

A $56 + 8$

B $56 \div 8$

C $56 \times 8$

D $56 - 8$

Common Core Standard 3.OA.4 – Operations & Algebraic Thinking

☐ **If $27 \div 3 = \square$, then $27 \div \square = 3$. Which numeral would fit in both number sentences? Be sure to show your work.**

A 5

B 7

C 9

D 10

Common Core Standard 3.OA.4 – Operations & Algebraic Thinking

☐ **Which number sentence should not have a 7 in the box? Be sure to show your work.**

A $42 \div 6 = \square$

B $28 \div \square = 4$

C $77 \div \square = 11$

D $84 \div 7 = \square$

Name ____________________

**PRACTICE**

Common Core Standard 3.OA.4 – Operations & Algebraic Thinking

☐ **If 18 ÷ 9 = ☐, then 18 ÷ ☐ = 9. Which numeral would be correct in both number sentences? Be sure to show your work.**

A 7

B 3

C 2

D 162

Common Core Standard 3.OA.4 – Operations & Algebraic Thinking

☐ **Which number sentence should not have a 12 in the box? Be sure to s how your work.**

A 48 ÷ ☐ = 4

B 72 ÷ 8 = ☐

C 60 ÷ ☐ = 5

D 24 ÷ 2 = ☐

Common Core Standard 3.OA.4 – Operations & Algebraic Thinking

☐ **If 42 ÷ 14 = ☐, then ☐ × 14 = 42. Which numeral would be correct in both number sentences? Be sure to show your work.**

A 6

B 4

C 28

D 3

Name ____________________

ASSESSMENT

Common Core Standard 3.OA.4 – Operations & Algebraic Thinking

☐ **Which number sentence should not have a 7 in the box? Be sure to show your work.**

**A** $21 \div 3 = \square$

**B** $18 \div 3 = \square$

**C** $63 \div \square = 9$

**D** $42 \div \square = 6$

Common Core Standard 3.OA.4 – Operations & Algebraic Thinking

☐ **If $48 \div 8 = \square$, then $48 \div \square = 8$. Which numeral would be correct in both number sentences? Be sure to show your work.**

**A** 40

**B** 384

**C** 6

**D** 12

Common Core Standard 3.OA.4 – Operations & Algebraic Thinking

☐ **Which number sentence should not have a 5 in the box? Be sure to show your work.**

**A** $50 \div \square = 10$

**B** $35 \div 7 = \square$

**C** $15 \div \square = 3$

**D** $48 \div 12 = \square$

Name ______________________

**ASSESSMENT**

Common Core Standard 3.OA.4 – Operations & Algebraic Thinking

☐ **If 72 ÷ 9 = ☐, then 72 ÷ ☐ = 9. Which numeral would be correct in both number sentences?**

**A** 9

**B** 8

**C** 7

**D** 12

Common Core Standard 3.OA.4 – Operations & Algebraic Thinking

☐ **Which number sentence should not have a 7 in the box? Be sure to show your work.**

**A** 49 ÷ ☐ = 7

**B** 28 ÷ 4 = ☐

**C** 27 ÷ ☐ = 3

**D** 63 ÷ 9 = ☐

Common Core Standard 3.OA.4 – Operations & Algebraic Thinking

☐ **If 21 ÷ 7 = ☐, then ☐ × 7 = 21. Which numeral would be correct in both number sentences? Be sure to show your work.**

**A** 147

**B** 4

**C** 3

**D** 14

Name ____________________

**DIAGNOSTIC**

Common Core Standard 3.OA.5 – Operations & Algebraic Thinking

☐ **Which number sentence is in the same family of facts as $21 \div 7 = 3$? Be sure to show your work.**

A $21 - 7 = 14$

B $7 \times 3 = 21$

C $7 + 3 = 10$

D $21 \times 7 = 147$

Common Core Standard 3.OA.5 – Operations & Algebraic Thinking

☐ **One of the number sentences in the box does not belong with the others. Which number sentence is it? Be sure to show your work.**

| |
|---|
| $9 \times 4 = 36$ |
| $9 + 4 = 13$ |
| $36 \div 4 = 9$ |
| $36 \div 9 = 4$ |

A $9 \times 4 = 36$

B $36 \div 4 = 9$

C $9 + 4 = 13$

D $36 \div 9 = 4$

Common Core Standard 3.OA.5 – Operations & Algebraic Thinking

☐ **Which number sentence is in the same family of facts as $4 \times 5 = 20$? Be sure to show your work.**

A $4 + 5 = 9$

B $20 \div 5 = 4$

C $10 \times 2 = 20$

D $20 - 5 = 15$

Name ____________________

DIAGNOSTIC

Common Core Standard 3.OA.5 – Operations & Algebraic Thinking

☐ Isaac wants to help his school. He needs to place 44 mini erasers into 11 bags. Which pair of related facts would show how many erasers he can place in each bag and be correct? Be sure to show your work.

A $11 + 4 = 15; \ 15 - 11 = 4$

B $4 \times 2 = 8; \ 8 \div 2 = 4$

C $44 \div 11 = 4; \ 11 \times 4 = 44$

D $44 - 11 = 33; \ 33 + 11 = 44$

Common Core Standard 3.OA.5 – Operations & Algebraic Thinking

☐ If 8 times a number is 48, which expression could be used to find the number? Be sure to show your work.

A $8 \times 48$

B $48 \div 8$

C $8 + 48$

D $48 - 8$

Common Core Standard 3.OA.5 – Operations & Algebraic Thinking

☐ Which number sentence is in the same family of facts as $56 \div 8 = 7$? Be sure to show your work.

A $8 + 7 = 15$

B $56 - 8 = 48$

C $56 \times 7 = 392$

D $8 \times 7 = 56$

Name ____________________

**PRACTICE**

Common Core Standard 3.OA.5 – Operations & Algebraic Thinking

☐ **Which number sentence is in the same family of facts as 8 x 4 = 32? Be sure to show your work.**

A $32 - 4 = 28$

B $32 \times 8 = 256$

C $8 + 4 = 12$

D $32 \div 8 = 4$

Common Core Standard 3.OA.5 – Operations & Algebraic Thinking

☐ **The third grade students at Grover Elementary walked 96 miles to earn money for their library. It took them 12 weeks to walk that distance. Which pair of related facts would show how many miles they walked each week and be correct? Be sure to show your work.**

A $12 \times 8 = 96$; $96 - 8 = 88$

B $96 \div 12 = 8$; $12 \times 8 = 96$

C $96 \div 8 = 12$; $12 + 8 = 20$

D $96 + 12 = 108$; $108 - 12 = 98$

Common Core Standard 3.OA.5 – Operations & Algebraic Thinking

☐ 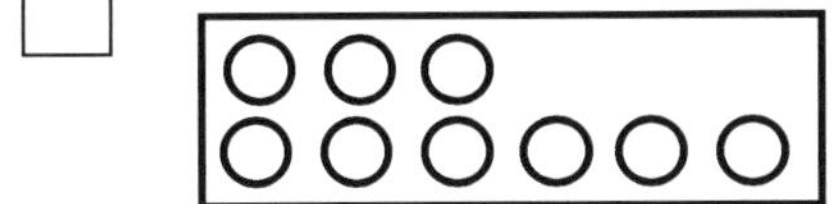 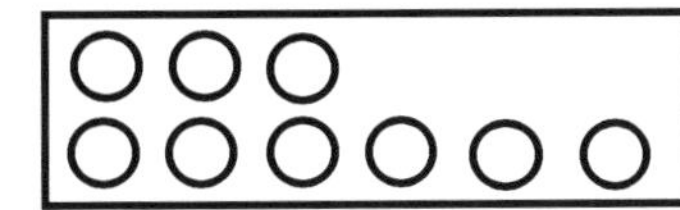 **is the same as which of the number sentences? Be sure to show your work.**

A $2 \times (3 + 6)$

B $(2 + 3) \times (2 + 6)$

C $(3 \times 6) + (3 \times 6)$

D $2 + (3 + 6)$

Name ____________________

**PRACTICE**

Common Core Standard 3.OA.5 – Operations & Algebraic Thinking

☐ **One of the number sentences in the box does not belong with the others. Which number sentence is it? Be sure to show your work.**

| $28 \div 7 = 4$ |
|---|
| $4 + 7 = 11$ |
| $28 \div 4 = 7$ |
| $4 \times 7 = 28$ |

A $4 \times 7 = 28$

B $4 + 7 = 11$

C $28 \div 7 = 4$

D $28 \div 4 = 7$

Common Core Standard 3.OA.5 – Operations & Algebraic Thinking

☐ **Which of the following best represents the drawings? Be sure to show your work.**

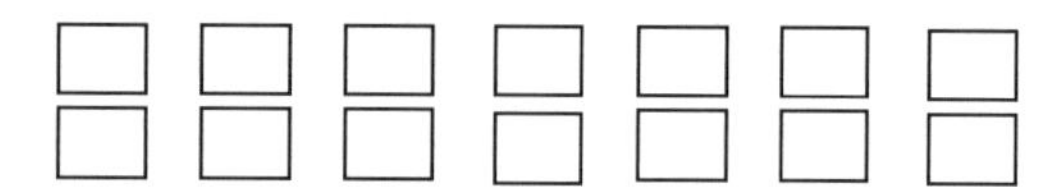

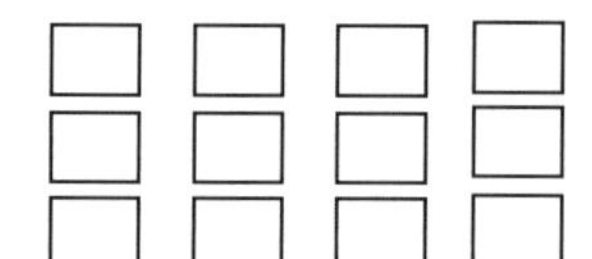

A $(2 \times 7) + (3 \times 4)$

B $(2 + 7) \times (3 + 4)$

C $2 + 7 + 3 + 4$

D $(2 \times 7) \times (3 \times 4)$

Common Core Standard 3.OA.5 – Operations & Algebraic Thinking

☐ **Which two numbers below would make the number sentence not true? Be sure to show your work.**

$$\square + 7 + \square = 9 \times 4$$

A 15, 14

B 12, 23

C 12, 17

D 10, 19

Name ______________________

PRACTICE

Common Core Standard 3.OA.5 – Operations & Algebraic Thinking

☐ **Which of the following is not equal to the number sentence below? Be sure to show your work.**

$$9 + (15 - 6)$$

A $(15 + 9) - 6$

B $(9 - 6) + 15$

C $(15 + 6) - 9$

D $15 + (9 - 6)$

Common Core Standard 3.OA.5 – Operations & Algebraic Thinking

☐ 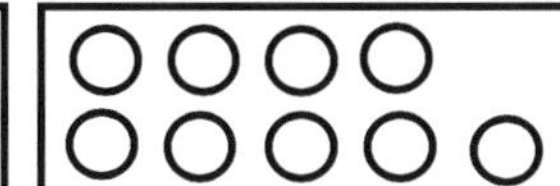 **is the same as which of the number sentences? Be sure to show your work.**

A $2 + (4 \times 5)$

B $(2 \times 4) + (2 \times 5)$

C $2 + 4 + 5$

D $(2 + 4) \times (2 + 5)$

Common Core Standard 3.OA.5 – Operations & Algebraic Thinking

☐ **What number will make this a true equation? Be sure to show your work.**

$$19 - (14 - 5) = 7 + \square$$

A 5

B 10

C 4

D 3

Name ______________________

**PRACTICE**

Common Core Standard 3.OA.5 – Operations & Algebraic Thinking

☐ **Which number below will make the number sentence true? Be sure to show your work.**

$$5 \times (4 - 2) = \square + 8$$

A 10

B 1

C 2

D 8

Common Core Standard 3.OA.5 – Operations & Algebraic Thinking

☐ **One of the number sentences in the box does not belong with the others. Which number sentence is it? Be sure to show your work.**

A $56 \div 7 = 8$

B $7 \times 8 = 56$

C $56 \div 8 = 7$

D $7 + 8 = 15$

| |
|---|
| $56 \div 7 = 8$ |
| $7 \times 8 = 56$ |
| $56 \div 8 = 7$ |
| $7 + 8 = 15$ |

Common Core Standard 3.OA.5 – Operations & Algebraic Thinking

☐ **Penny needs to clean up her room. She has to put 24 shoes into pairs. Which set of related facts would show how many shoes she can place together and be correct? Be sure to show your work.**

A $24 + 2 = 26$; $26 - 24 = 2$

B $12 \times 2 = 24$; $24 \div 2 = 12$

C $24 \times 2 = 48$; $48 \div 2 = 24$

D $35 - 11 = 24$; $24 + 11 = 35$

Name ______________________

ASSESSMENT

Common Core Standard 3.OA.5 – Operations & Algebraic Thinking

☐ **One of the number sentences in the box does not belong with the others. Which number sentence does not belong? Be sure to show your work.**

| |
|---|
| $45 \div 9 = 5$ |
| $9 \times 5 = 45$ |
| $45 - 5 = 40$ |
| $45 \div 5 = 9$ |

A $45 - 5 = 40$

B $9 \times 5 = 45$

C $45 \div 5 = 9$

D $45 \div 9 = 5$

Common Core Standard 3.OA.5 – Operations & Algebraic Thinking

☐ **Which number sentence is in the same family of facts as 2 x 12 = 24? Be sure to show your work.**

A $12 - 2 = 10$

B $24 \times 2 = 48$

C $24 \div 12 = 2$

D $24 + 12 = 36$

Common Core Standard 3.OA. 5 – Operations & Algebraic Thinking

☐ **Hailey bought 6 containers for her CDs. She has 42 CDs that she needs to store. Which pair of related facts would show how many CDs she can place in each container and be correct? Be sure to show your work.**

A $42 \times 6 = 252$; $252 \div 6 = 42$

B $42 - 7 = 35$; $7 + 35 = 42$

C $42 + 6 = 48$; $42 - 6 = 36$

D $42 \div 6 = 7$; $6 \times 7 = 42$

Name ____________________

**ASSESSMENT**

Common Core Standard 3.OA.5 – Operations & Algebraic Thinking

☐ **Which number sentence is in the same family of facts as 28 ÷ 4 = 7? Be sure to show your work.**

A $28 \times 7 = 196$

B $28 - 7 = 21$

C $4 \times 7 = 28$

D $4 + 7 = 11$

Common Core Standard 3.OA.5 – Operations & Algebraic Thinking

☐ **One of the number sentences in the box does not belong with the others. Which number sentence is it? Be sure to show your work.**

A $8 \times 9 = 72$

B $72 + 9 = 81$

C $72 \div 9 = 8$

D $9 \times 8 = 72$

| |
|---|
| $8 \times 9 = 72$ |
| $72 \div 9 = 8$ |
| $72 + 9 = 81$ |
| $9 \times 8 = 72$ |

Common Core Standard 3.OA.5 – Operations & Algebraic Thinking

☐ **Which number sentence is in the same family of facts as 132 ÷ 12 = 11? Be sure to show your work.**

A $11 + 12 = 22$

B $132 - 12 = 121$

C $12 \times 11 = 132$

D $132 \times 11 = 1452$

Name ____________________

**DIAGNOSTIC**

Common Core Standard 3.OA.6 – Operations & Algebraic Thinking

☐ **A bakery baked 108 cookies that need to be placed in 9 sacks. An equal number of cookies will be placed in each sack. How many cookies should each sack contain? Be sure to show your work.**

**A** 12

**B** 11

**C** 10

**D** 9

Common Core Standard 3.OA.6 – Operations & Algebraic Thinking

☐ **Solve the following equation and be sure to show your work.**

$$56 \div 7 =$$

**A** 8

**B** 49

**C** 7

**D** 9

Common Core Standard 3.OA.6 – Operations & Algebraic Thinking

☐ **Solve the following equation and be sure to show your work.**

$$12\overline{)72}$$

**A** 6

**B** 8

**C** 7

**D** 5

Name ______________________

**DIAGNOSTIC**

Common Core Standard 3.OA.6 – Operations & Algebraic Thinking

☐ **What is the answer when 63 is divided by 9? Be sure to show your work.**

**A** 8

**B** 7

**C** 54

**D** 72

Common Core Standard 3.OA.6 – Operations & Algebraic Thinking

☐ **Frederick saved $100 last summer. He put $10 each week in a savings account. How many weeks did it take Frederick to reach $100? Be your show your work.**

**A** 90

**B** 10

**C** 110

**D** 11

Common Core Standard 3.OA.6 – Operations & Algebraic Thinking

☐ **Solve the following equation and be sure to show your work.**

$$24 \div 8 =$$

**A** 16

**B** 3

**C** 4

**D** 32

Name ____________________

PRACTICE

Common Core Standard 3.OA.6 – Operations & Algebraic Thinking

☐ **Solve the following equation and be sure to show your work.**

$$27 \div 9 =$$

A 18

B 3

C 4

D 36

Common Core Standard 3.OA.6 – Operations & Algebraic Thinking

☐ **What is the answer when 78 is divided by 3? Be sure to show your work.**

A 26

B 24

C 75

D 30

Common Core Standard 3.OA.6 – Operations & Algebraic Thinking

☐ **Suzy picked some flowers for her mother from her yard. She picked 36 flowers and wants to put them in 3 vases. If she puts the same amount of flowers in each vase, how many flowers will be in each vase? Be sure to show your work.**

A 33

B 11

C 12

D 39

Name ______________________

**PRACTICE**

Common Core Standard 3.OA.6 – Operations & Algebraic Thinking

☐ **Solve the following equation and be sure to show your work.**

$$6\overline{)36}$$

A 8

B 5

C 7

D 6

Common Core Standard 3.OA.6 – Operations & Algebraic Thinking

☐ **If 32 fishing baits are placed in 2 shelves in a tackle box and each shelf has the same number of fishing baits in it, how many fishing baits are on each shelf in the tackle box? Be sure to show your work.**

A 16

B 30

C 12

D 11

Common Core Standard 3.OA.6 – Operations & Algebraic Thinking

☐ **Solve the following equation and be sure to show your work.**

$$49 \div 7 =$$

A 56

B 42

C 7

D 8

Name ____________________________

PRACTICE

Common Core Standard 3.OA.6 – Operations & Algebraic Thinking

☐ A used car lot has 96 cars that need to be placed in 6 rows. An equal number of cars will be placed in each row. How many cars should each row contain? Be sure to show your work.

A 12

B 16

C 14

D 90

Common Core Standard 3.OA.6 – Operations & Algebraic Thinking

☐ Solve the following equation and be sure to show your work.

$$36 \div 4 =$$

A 8

B 32

C 7

D 9

Common Core Standard 3.OA.6 – Operations & Algebraic Thinking

☐ Solve the following equation and be sure to show your work.

$$11\overline{)33}$$

A 3

B 22

C 2

D 44

Name ________________________

PRACTICE

Common Core Standard 3.OA.6 – Operations & Algebraic Thinking

☐ **What is the answer when 6 is divided by 2? Be sure to show your work.**

A 2

B 3

C 4

D 8

Common Core Standard 3.OA.6 – Operations & Algebraic Thinking

☐ **Solve the following equation and be sure to show your work.**

$$15 \div 3 =$$

A 12

B 3

C 4

D 5

Common Core Standard 3.OA.6 – Operations & Algebraic Thinking

☐ **What is the answer when 14 is divided by 7? Be sure to show your work.**

A 2

B 7

C 3

D 4

Name ______________________

**ASSESSMENT**

Common Core Standard 3.OA.6 – Operations & Algebraic Thinking

☐ **Solve the following equation and be sure to show your work**

$$30 \div 6 =$$

A 24

B 6

C 36

D 5

Common Core Standard 3.OA.6 – Operations & Algebraic Thinking

☐ **What is the answer when 22 is divided by 11? Be sure to show your work.**

A 33

B 2

C 11

D 1

Common Core Standard 3.OA.6 – Operations & Algebraic Thinking

☐ **Jake's mother is making goodie bags for his birthday party. She has 81 small pieces of candy to put into 9 bags. If she puts the same amount of candy in each bag, how many pieces of candy will be in each bag? Be sure to show your work.**

A 90

B 10

C 72

D 9

Name ____________________

**ASSESSMENT**

Common Core Standard 3.OA.6 – Operations & Algebraic Thinking

☐ **Solve the following equation and be sure to show your work.**

$$7 \overline{)14}$$

A 2

B 4

C 7

D 3

Common Core Standard 3.OA.6 – Operations & Algebraic Thinking

☐ **If 48 books are placed on 8 shelves in a library and each shelf has the same number of books on it, how many books are on each shelf? Be sure to show your work.**

A 384

B 56

C 42

D 6

Common Core Standard 3.OA.6 – Operations & Algebraic Thinking

☐ **Solve the following equation and be sure to show your work.**

$$25 \div 5 =$$

A 4

B 5

C 20

D 30

Name ____________________

**DIAGNOSTIC**

Common Core Standard 3.OA.7 – Operations & Algebraic Thinking

☐ **Solve the following equation and be sure to show your work.**

$$81 \div 9 =$$

A 72

B 8

C 90

D 9

Common Core Standard 3.OA.7 – Operations & Algebraic Thinking

☐ **Solve the following equation and be sure to show your work.**

$$7 \times 7 =$$

A 56

B 49

C 14

D 42

Common Core Standard 3.OA.7 – Operations & Algebraic Thinking

☐ **Solve the following equation and be sure to show your work.**

$$12\overline{)36}$$

A 3

B 24

C 4

D 2

Name ____________________

DIAGNOSTIC

Common Core Standard 3.OA.7 – Operations & Algebraic Thinking

☐ **Solve the following equation and be sure to show your work.**

$$\begin{array}{r} 9 \\ \times\ 6 \\ \hline \end{array}$$

A 45

B 63

C 54

D 15

Common Core Standard 3.OA.7 – Operations & Algebraic Thinking

☐ **Solve the following equation and be sure to show your work.**

$$4\overline{)24}$$

A 7

B 28

C 6

D 5

Common Core Standard 3.OA.7 – Operations & Algebraic Thinking

☐ **Solve the following equation and be sure to show your work.**

$$7 \times 3 =$$

A 10

B 28

C 14

D 21

Name ___________________________

**PRACTICE**

Common Core Standard 3.OA.7 – Operations & Algebraic Thinking

☐ **Solve the following equation and be sure to show your work.**

$$5 \times 6 =$$

A 30

B 35

C 25

D 11

Common Core Standard 3.OA.7 – Operations & Algebraic Thinking

☐ **Solve the following equation and be sure to show your work.**

$$\begin{array}{r} 3 \\ \times\ 10 \\ \hline \end{array}$$

A 7

B 13

C 30

D 33

Common Core Standard 3.OA.7 – Operations & Algebraic Thinking

☐ **Solve the following equation and be sure to show your work.**

$$18 \div 9 =$$

A 4

B 9

C 3

D 2

Name ______________________

**PRACTICE**

Common Core Standard 3.OA.7 – Operations & Algebraic Thinking

☐ **Solve the following equation and be sure to show your work.**

$$6 \times 7 =$$

A 36

B 42

C 48

D 13

Common Core Standard 3.OA.7 – Operations & Algebraic Thinking

☐ **Solve the following equation and be sure to show your work.**

$$2\overline{)10}$$

A 8

B 5

C 6

D 3

Common Core Standard 3.OA.7 – Operations & Algebraic Thinking

☐ **Solve the following equation and be sure to show your work.**

$$20 \div 10 =$$

A 3

B 4

C 10

D 2

Name ________________________

**PRACTICE**

Common Core Standard 3.OA.7 – Operations & Algebraic Thinking

☐ **Solve the following equation and be sure to show your work.**

$$90 \div 10 =$$

A 80

B 8

C 100

D 9

Common Core Standard 3.OA.7 – Operations & Algebraic Thinking

☐ **Solve the following equation and be sure to show your work.**

$$6\overline{)72}$$

A 10

B 9

C 11

D 12

Common Core Standard 3.OA.7 – Operations & Algebraic Thinking

☐ **Solve the following equation and be sure to show your work.**

$$12 \times 5 =$$

A 7

B 60

C 17

D 72

Name ____________________

**PRACTICE**

Common Core Standard 3.OA.7 – Operations & Algebraic Thinking

☐ **Solve the following equation and be sure to show your work.**

$$50 \div 2 =$$

A 30

B 25

C 48

D 20

Common Core Standard 3.OA.7 – Operations & Algebraic Thinking

☐ **Solve the following equation and be sure to show your work.**

$$\begin{array}{r} 15 \\ \times\ 4 \\ \hline \end{array}$$

A 45

B 75

C 60

D 19

Common Core Standard 3.OA.7 – Operations & Algebraic Thinking

☐ **Solve the following equation and be sure to show your work.**

$$\begin{array}{r} 26 \\ \times\ 3 \\ \hline \end{array}$$

A 78

B 52

C 96

D 29

Name ___________________________

**ASSESSMENT**

Common Core Standard 3.OA.7 – Operations & Algebraic Thinking

☐ **Solve the following equation and be sure to show your work.**

$$98 \div 7 =$$

A 92

B 12

C 13

D 14

Common Core Standard 3.OA.7 – Operations & Algebraic Thinking

☐ **Solve the following equation and be sure to show your work.**

$$\begin{array}{r} 8 \\ \times\ 7 \\ \hline \end{array}$$

A 56

B 49

C 35

D 42

Common Core Standard 3.OA.7 – Operations & Algebraic Thinking

☐ **Solve the following equation and be sure to show your work.**

$$6 \overline{)48}$$

A 7

B 8

C 42

D 6

Name ____________________

**ASSESSMENT**

Common Core Standard 3.OA.7 – Operations & Algebraic Thinking

☐ **Solve the following equation and be sure to show your work.**

$$4 \times 7 =$$

A 3

B 32

C 28

D 21

Common Core Standard 3.OA.7 – Operations & Algebraic Thinking

☐ **Solve the following equation and be sure to show your work.**

$$9\overline{)54}$$

A 6

B 5

C 45

D 7

Common Core Standard 3.OA.7 – Operations & Algebraic Thinking

☐ **Solve the following equation and be sure to show your work.**

$$5 \times 5 =$$

A 35

B 20

C 10

D 25

Name ________________________

DIAGNOSTIC

Common Core Standard 3.OA.8 – Operations & Algebraic Thinking

☐ **Laurie has 180 dolls stored in baskets. She has 30 baskets in total. The dolls are stored equally in each basket. She took one basket and gave her first friend 3 dolls and her second friend 2 dolls from that basket. How many dolls were left in <u>that</u> basket? Be sure to show your work.**

**A 0**

**B 1**

**C 2**

**D 30**

Common Core Standard 3.OA.8 – Operations & Algebraic Thinking

☐ **Cody needs to stock the barn with feed bags. He needs to put 54 feed bags on 9 shelves. From one shelf, he gave 4 feed bags to another farmer. How many feed bags are remaining on <u>that</u> shelf? Be sure to show your work.**

**A 2**

**B 3**

**C 4**

**D 1**

Common Core Standard 3.OA.8 – Operations & Algebraic Thinking

☐ **Coach Greene needs to buy 108 baseballs for practice. The baseballs come in a package containing 12 balls. He bought 3 packages from one sporting goods store and 2 packages from another. How many more packages of baseballs does he need to buy? Be sure to show your work.**

**A 3 packages**

**B 12 packages**

**C 10 packages**

**D 4 packages**

Name ______________________

DIAGNOSTIC

Common Core Standard 3.OA.8 – Operations & Algebraic Thinking

☐ **Mrs. Perez has 8 students in her dance class. Each of her students has 2 pairs of shoes; one set of tap shoes and one set of ballet shoes. How many dance shoes in total does her students have? Be sure to show your work. Be sure to show your work.**

**A 24**

**B 32**

**C 40**

**D 10**

Common Core Standard 3.OA.8 – Operations & Algebraic Thinking

☐ **Jermaine collects stamps. He has 36 stamps. He stored them equally in 3 separate boxes. From one box, he gave 5 stamps to his little brother and also gave 7 to his best friend. How many boxes of stamps does he have left? Be sure to show your work.**

**A 3**

**B 2**

**C 24**

**D 4**

Common Core Standard 3.OA.8 – Operations & Algebraic Thinking

☐ **Jamal and his friends went to buy 6 dozen toys. One dozen toys equals 12 toys. Kashawn bought 15 toys. Earl bought 17 toys. Bryson bought 13 toys. Patrick bought five toys. Jamal buys the rest of the toys. How many toys did Jamal buy? Be sure to show your work.**

**A 22**

**B 57**

**C 62**

**D 21**

PRACTICE

Name ________________________

Common Core Standard 3.OA.8 – Operations & Algebraic Thinking

☐ **Liam went to the store to buy groceries. He bought hamburger meat for $8, tomatoes for $4, and bread for $6. He gave the cashier a $20 dollar bill. How much change will Liam receive from the cashier? Be sure to show your work.**

**A $3**

**B $18**

**C $2**

**D $1**

Common Core Standard 3.OA.8 – Operations & Algebraic Thinking

☐ **Zoe painted pictures for her art project. She wanted to make 12 paintings featuring animals and 8 paintings featuring people. If she has only 13 canvasses to paint on, how many more will she need? Be sure to show your work.**

**A 7**

**B 83**

**C 9**

**D 33**

Common Core Standard 3.OA.8 – Operations & Algebraic Thinking

☐ **Sophia's piggy bank is full of money. In addition, she received $12 from her mother today. She went to the clothing store to buy a shirt for $6 and a pair of jeans for $23. At the end of the day, Sophia had $22 left over. How much money was in her piggy bank at the start of the day? Be sure to show your work.**

**A 25**

**B 5**

**C 63**

**D 39**

Name ____________________

**PRACTICE**

Common Core Standard 3.OA.8 – Operations & Algebraic Thinking

☐ **At the beginning of the scavenger race, Gabriela found 14 items. She gave 8 of those items to her friends and then found 12 more items. How many items did she have when the scavenger race was finished? Be sure to show your work.**

**A** 10

**B** 34

**C** 18

**D** 12

Common Core Standard 3.OA.8 – Operations & Algebraic Thinking

☐ **Jacob's father asked him to rake the leaves in the front yard. He put the leaves into 6 different piles. Jacob was able to bag 2 of the piles. He thought the piles were too big and split all the remaining piles in half. How many piles of leaves are there now? Be sure to show your work.**

**A** 4

**B** 8

**C** 3

**D** 12

Common Core Standard 3.OA.8 – Operations & Algebraic Thinking

☐ **Jayden wanted to buy a gaming console. He started saving his money beginning in April. He was able to save $127 in April, $183 in May, and $78 in June. He still needs $212 to by the gaming console. How much is the gaming console he wants to buy? Be sure to show your work.**

**A** 473

**B** 310

**C** 388

**D** 600

Name ______________________

PRACTICE

Common Core Standard 3.OA.8 – Operations & Algebraic Thinking

☐ Mia walked a mile to her friend's house. She and her friend took a bus and went to the museum that was 18 miles away. If Mia walked to her friend's house and took the bus to the museum and returned to her friend's house using the same bus, and then walked back home. How far did Mia travel that day? Be sure to show your work.

A 36 miles

B 19 miles

C 18 miles

D 38 miles

Common Core Standard 3.OA.8 – Operations & Algebraic Thinking

☐ Javier collects soccer jerseys. He has 36 jerseys from his favorite teams. He has 12 jerseys from Manchester United and 14 from FC Dallas. How many jerseys does he have remaining from Real Madrid? Be sure to show your work.

A 10

B 26

C 24

D 22

Common Core Standard 3.OA.8 – Operations & Algebraic Thinking

☐ Chantoya had $44. Her father gave her an additional $15 and her grandmother gave her $20. How much money does Chantoya have all together? Be sure to show your work.

A $64

B $79

C $59

D $35

Name ____________________

PRACTICE

Common Core Standard 3.OA.8 – Operations & Algebraic Thinking

☐ **Martin Luther King Elementary has to sell 80 raffle tickets. Each ticket cost $3. So far the school has collected $165 in sales. How many more tickets does the school need to sell all the tickets? Be sure to show your work.**

A 25

B 55

C 10

D 12

Common Core Standard 3.OA.8 – Operations & Algebraic Thinking

☐ **Calvin wants to sell his football card collection. He has 12 cards to sell for $6 each. To ship the cards, he will charge an additional $2 to ship each card. How much will Calvin make if he sells and ships all his football cards? Be sure to show your work.**

A $72

B $96

C $48

D $86

Common Core Standard 3.OA.8 – Operations & Algebraic Thinking

☐ **Lilli buys 2 boxes of flowers. Lusine buys 3 boxes of flowers. If each box has 18 flowers, how many flowers did the girls buy altogether? Be sure to show your work.**

A 3

B 108

C 90

D 12

Name ________________________

**ASSESSMENT**

Common Core Standard 3.OA.8 – Operations & Algebraic Thinking

☐ **Santiago wants to buy cupcakes for 4 classrooms. There are 23 students and 1 teacher in each classroom. Santiago also wants to give Principal Brown and Assistant Principal Lebowitz each a cupcake as well. How many cupcakes will Santiago need to buy? Be sure to show your work.**

**A** 96

**B** 94

**C** 92

**D** 98

Common Core Standard 3.OA.8 – Operations & Algebraic Thinking

☐ **Suzy sells cups of lemonade. At the start of the day she had 60 cups of lemonade. She has sold 20 separate cups of lemonade to her friends and 1 dozen cups to her church. How many cups did she have at the end of the day? Be sure to show your work.**

**A** 28

**B** 40

**C** 39

**D** 81

Common Core Standard 3.OA.8 – Operations & Algebraic Thinking

☐ **Kelly can jump rope 40 times in 30 seconds. If she can keep her pace, how many times will she jump the rope in two minutes? Be sure to show your work.**

**A** 140

**B** 160

**C** 20

**D** 240

Name ________________________

ASSESSMENT

Common Core Standard 3.OA.8 – Operations & Algebraic Thinking

☐ **Mrs. Lee makes 24 cakes to sell over the next week. If she sold 4 cakes on Monday, sold 9 cakes on Tuesday, and sold the rest on Thursday. How many did she sell on Thursday? Be sure to show your work.**

A 12

B 15

C 37

D 11

Common Core Standard 3.OA.8 – Operations & Algebraic Thinking

☐ **Ricki is in charge of putting away the Christmas tree ornaments. Each box holds 11 ornaments. Ricki has 7 boxes to store the ornaments. She has 99 ornaments. How many additional boxes will she need to store all the ornaments? Be sure to show your work.**

A 3

B 2

C 1

D 4

Common Core Standard 3.OA.8 – Operations & Algebraic Thinking

☐ **Trina was growing cucumbers in her garden. She planted 8 rows of 6 cucumber plants. Each plant gave one cucumber. Some pigs ate 12 of her cucumbers. How many cucumbers did Trina pick from her garden? Be sure to show your work.**

A 26

B 36

C 30

D 14

Name ____________________

DIAGNOSTIC

Common Core Standard 3.OA.9 – Operations & Algebraic Thinking

☐ **What is the missing number in the number pattern? Be sure to show your work.**

**3, 6, 9, 12, ☐, 18**

**A** 13

**B** 15

**C** 14

**D** 16

Common Core Standard 3.OA.9 – Operations & Algebraic Thinking

☐ **What is the missing number in the number pattern? Be sure to show your work.**

**1, 5, 9, ☐, 17, 21**

**A** 10

**B** 18

**C** 13

**D** 15

Common Core Standard 3.OA.9 – Operations & Algebraic Thinking

☐ **What is the next number in the number pattern? Be sure to show your work.**

**6, 9, 11, 14, 16, ☐, . . .**

**A** 18

**B** 20

**C** 21

**D** 19

Name ____________________

**DIAGNOSTIC**

Common Core Standard 3.OA.9 – Operations & Algebraic Thinking

☐ **What is the next number in the number pattern? Be sure to show your work.**

**80, 82, 77, 79, 74, 76 , ☐, . . .**

**A** 69

**B** 75

**C** 71

**D** 76

Common Core Standard 3.OA.9 – Operations & Algebraic Thinking

☐ **Look at the number patterns. In which pattern could 28 be the missing number? Be sure to show your work.**

**A** 27, ☐, 31, 33, 35.

**B** 18, 22, ☐, 30, 34

**C** 13, 18, 23, ☐, 33

**D** 21, 23, 25, ☐, 29

Common Core Standard 3.OA.9 – Operations & Algebraic Thinking

☐ **Look at the number patterns. In which pattern could 17 be the next number? Be sure to show your work.**

**A** 27, 24, 21, 18, ☐, . . .

**B** 26, 24, 22, 20, ☐, . . .

**C** 10, 12, 14, 16, ☐, . . .

**D** 41, 35, 29, 23, ☐, . . .

Name ____________________

PRACTICE

Common Core Standard 3.OA.9 – Operations & Algebraic Thinking

☐ **Look at the number patterns. In which pattern could 12 be the missing number? Be sure to show your work.**

A 2, ☐ , 14, 20, 26

B 3, 9, ☐ , 21, 27

C 4, 9, ☐ , 19, 24

D 3, 6, 9, ☐ , 15

Common Core Standard 3.OA.9 – Operations & Algebraic Thinking

☐ **Look at the number patterns. In which pattern could 22 be the next number? Be sure to show your work.**

A 15, 17, 19, 21, ☐ , . . .

B 14, 16, 18, 20, ☐ , . . .

C 7, 11, 15, 19, ☐ , . . .

D 5, 10, 15, 20, ☐ , . . .

Common Core Standard 3.OA.9 – Operations & Algebraic Thinking

☐ **Look at the number pattern. Which number comes next? Be sure to show your work.**

55, 50, 45, 40, 35, ☐

A 40

B 30

C 25

D 20

Name ____________________

**PRACTICE**

Common Core Standard 3.OA.9 – Operations & Algebraic Thinking

☐ **Look at the table. What pattern do the numbers follow? Be sure to show your work.**

| Tricycles | 2 | 4 | 6 | 8 | 10 |
|---|---|---|---|---|---|
| Wheels | 6 | 12 | 18 | 24 | 30 |

A Number of tricycles and wheels go up by 6 each time.

B Number of tricycles go up by 2 and wheels go up by 6 each time.

C Number of tricycles and wheels go up by 4 each time.

D Number of tricycles and wheels decrease each time.

Common Core Standard 3.OA.9 – Operations & Algebraic Thinking

☐ **Look at the table. What pattern do the numbers follow? Be sure to show your work.**

| Triangles | 1 | 5 | 10 | 15 | 20 |
|---|---|---|---|---|---|
| Sides | 3 | 15 | 30 | 45 | 60 |

A Number of triangles and sides decrease each time.

B This is a subtraction pattern.

C This is a division pattern.

D This is a multiplication pattern.

Common Core Standard 3.OA.9 – Operations & Algebraic Thinking

☐ **The 3 sets of numbers all follow different patterns. What is *alike* about these 3 patterns? Be sure to show your work.**

| | |
|---|---|
| Set ☺ | 3, 5, 7, 9 |
| Set ♡ | 2, 6, 10, 14 |
| Set ☆ | 1, 4, 7, 10 |

A The numbers are all even.

B The numbers decrease each time.

C The numbers increase each time.

D The numbers increase by 4 each time.

PRACTICE

Name ___________________________

Common Core Standard 3.OA.9 – Operations & Algebraic Thinking

☐ **Which set of numbers is the same as the following pattern? Be sure to show your work.**

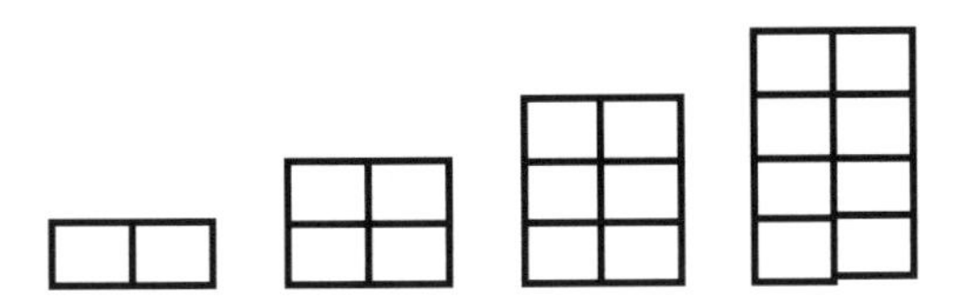

A 2, 4, 5, 6

B 2, 4, 6, 8

C 1, 2, 3, 4

D 2, 4, 8, 16

Common Core Standard 3.OA.9 – Operations & Algebraic Thinking

☐ **The teachers park their cars in a parking lot. The students wanted to find out how many car tires were in the parking lot. What are the missing numbers in the table? Be sure to show your work.**

| Cars | 3 | 6 | 9 | 12 | 15 | 18 |
|---|---|---|---|---|---|---|
| Tires | 12 | 24 | | 48 | 60 | |

A 25, 61

B 36, 70

C 35, 71

D 36, 72

Common Core Standard 3.OA.9 – Operations & Algebraic Thinking

☐ **Mrs. Tucker cut small squares to make flowers to decorate a quilt she was making. She noticed she had used 12 squares for each 3 flowers on the quilt. The chart shows the number of squares needed to make more flowers. How many squares are needed to make 8 flowers? Be sure to show your work.**

Mrs. Tucker's Flowers

| Number of Flowers | Number of Squares |
|---|---|
| 3 | 12 |
| 4 | 16 |
| 5 | 20 |
| 6 | 24 |
| | |
| | |

A 32

B 28

C 25

D 30

PRACTICE

Name ____________________

Common Core Standard 3.OA.9 – Operations & Algebraic Thinking

☐ **Greg's school played a football game Thursday night. The table shows the touchdowns they made and their final score. What number is missing in the table? Be sure to show your work.**

| Touchdowns | Score |
|---|---|
| 1 | 7 |
| 2 | 14 |
| 3 | 21 |
| 4 | ? |
| 5 | 35 |

A 27

B 23

C 28

D 34

Common Core Standard 3.OA.9 – Operations & Algebraic Thinking

☐ **Theo made a chart showing how much money he has saved. What is the rule for changing the *Out* numbers to *In* numbers? Be sure to show your work.**

Theo's Savings

| IN | 5 | 10 | 15 | 20 |
|---|---|---|---|---|
| OUT | $15 | $30 | $45 | $60 |

A Add 30

B Divide by 3

C Add 10

D Multiply by 3

Common Core Standard 3.OA.9 – Operations & Algebraic Thinking

☐ **Each IN number is paired with an OUT number. The relationship for each pair of numbers is the same. If the OUT number is 8, how will you find it's paired IN number? Be sure to show your work.**

| IN | 27 | 36 | 54 |
|---|---|---|---|
| OUT | 3 | 4 | 6 |

A Multiply 8 by 6

B Add 8 and 9

C Subtract 8 from 54

D Multiply 8 by 9

Name ______________________

ASSESSMENT

Common Core Standard 3.OA.9 – Operations & Algebraic Thinking

☐ **Look at the number pattern. Which number comes next? Be sure to show your work.**

**28, 30, 32, 34, 36, ☐**

**A** **38**

**B** **30**

**C** **37**

**D** **35**

Common Core Standard 3.OA.9 – Operations & Algebraic Thinking

☐ **Look at the number pattern. Which number comes next? Be sure to show your work.**

**76, 73, 70, 67, 64, ☐**

**A** **65**

**B** **62**

**C** **61**

**D** **60**

Common Core Standard 3.OA.9 – Operations & Algebraic Thinking

☐ **What is the missing number in the number pattern? Be sure to show your work.**

**12, 18, 24, ☐ , 36**

**A** **30**

**B** **35**

**C** **29**

**D** **25**

Name ____________________

ASSESSMENT

Common Core Standard 3.OA.9 – Operations & Algebraic Thinking

☐ **What is the missing number in the number pattern? Be sure to show your work.**

**24, 32, ☐, 48, 56**

A 34

B 33

C 40

D 47

Common Core Standard 3.OA.9 – Operations & Algebraic Thinking

☐ **What is the next number in the number pattern? Be sure to show your work.**

**15, 14, 16, 15, 17, ☐, . . .**

A 18

B 17

C 16

D 19

Common Core Standard 3.OA.9 – Operations & Algebraic Thinking

☐ **What is the next number in the number pattern? Be sure to show your work.**

**46, 52, 56, 57, 63, 67, ☐, . . .**

A 68

B 67

C 64

D 69

Name ____________________

DIAGNOSTIC

Common Core Standard 3.NBT.1 – Numbers & Operations in Base Ten

☐ **Which number best describes rounding 587,254 to the nearest tens?**

A 587,250

B 587,260

C 587,300

D 588,000

Common Core Standard 3.NBT.1 – Numbers & Operations in Base Ten

☐ **Which number best describes rounding 158 to the nearest hundreds?**

A One hundred

B Two hundred

C One hundred and sixty

D One hundred and fifty

Common Core Standard 3.NBT.1 – Numbers & Operations in Base Ten

☐ **Which number best describes rounding 1,947 to the nearest tens?**

A 1,950

B 2,000

C 1,940

D 1,910

Name ___________________________

DIAGNOSTIC

Common Core Standard 3.NBT.1 – Numbers & Operations in Base Ten

☐ **88,542 to the nearest tens.**

A 88,000

B 88,500

C 88,540

D 89,000

Common Core Standard 3.NBT.1 – Numbers & Operations in Base Ten

☐ **Round 233 to the nearest hundreds.**

A 200

B 230

C 300

D 240

Common Core Standard 3.NBT.1 – Numbers & Operations in Base Ten

☐ **Round 10,854 to the nearest hundreds.**

A 11,800

B 10,900

C 11,000

D 10,850

Name ______________________

PRACTICE

Common Core Standard 3.NBT.1 – Numbers & Operations in Base Ten

☐ **Round 895 to the nearest tens.**

A Nine hundred

B Eight hundred and ninety

C Eight hundred and ninety-six

D Nine hundred and ninety-five

Common Core Standard 3.NBT.1 – Numbers & Operations in Base Ten

☐ **Round 919 to the nearest hundreds.**

A 920

B 900

C 910

D 1000

Common Core Standard 3.NBT.1 – Numbers & Operations in Base Ten

☐ **Round 83 to the nearest tens.**

A 90

B 82

C 84

D 80

Name ____________________

PRACTICE

Common Core Standard 3.NBT.1 – Numbers & Operations in Base Ten

☐ **Round 374 to the nearest hundreds.**

A 370

B 400

C 380

D 375

Common Core Standard 3.NBT.1 – Numbers & Operations in Base Ten

☐ **Round 69 to the nearest tens.**

A 70

B 68

C 60

D 75

Common Core Standard 3.NBT.1 – Numbers & Operations in Base Ten

☐ **Round 281 to the nearest hundreds.**

A Two hundred and eighty

B Two hundred and eighty-two

C Three hundred

D Two hundred and ninety

Name ____________________

PRACTICE

Common Core Standard 3.NBT.1 – Numbers & Operations in Base Ten

☐ **Round 340 to the nearest tens.**

A 350

B 341

C 400

D 340

Common Core Standard 3.NBT.1 – Numbers & Operations in Base Ten

☐ **Round 343 to the nearest hundreds.**

A Three hundred and forty

B Three hundred

C Three hundred and forty-four

D Three hundred and fifty

Common Core Standard 3.NBT.1 – Numbers & Operations in Base Ten

☐ **Round 367 to the nearest hundreds.**

A Four hundred

B Three hundred and sixty

C Three hundred and seventy

D Three hundred and sixty-eight

Name ____________________

PRACTICE

Common Core Standard 3.NBT.1 – Numbers & Operations in Base Ten

☐ **Round 973 to the nearest hundreds.**

A 1000

B 970

C 980

D 974

Common Core Standard 3.NBT.1 – Numbers & Operations in Base Ten

☐ **Round 552 to the nearest tens.**

A 553

B 551

C 550

D 600

Common Core Standard 3.NBT.1 – Numbers & Operations in Base Ten

☐ **Round 954 to the nearest tens.**

A One thousand

B Nine hundred and sixty

C Nine hundred and fifty

D Nine hundred and fifty-three

Name ________________________

ASSESSMENT

Common Core Standard 3.NBT.1 – Numbers & Operations in Base Ten

☐ **Round 639 to the nearest tens.**

**A** Six hundred and thirty-nine

**B** Six hundred and forty

**C** Six hundred

**D** Six hundred and thirty

Common Core Standard 3.NBT.1 – Numbers & Operations in Base Ten

☐ **Round 3,154 to the nearest hundred.**

**A** Three thousand, one hundred and fifty

**B** Three thousand, one hundred

**C** Three thousand

**D** Three thousand, two hundred

Common Core Standard 3.NBT.1 – Numbers & Operations in Base Ten

☐ **Round 61 to the nearest tens.**

**A** Sixty-two

**B** Sixty

**C** Sixty-one

**D** One hundred

Name ________________________

ASSESSMENT

Common Core Standard 3.NBT.1 – Numbers & Operations in Base Ten

☐ **Round 589 to the nearest hundreds.**

A 590

B 600

C 580

D 500

Common Core Standard 3.NBT.1 – Numbers & Operations in Base Ten

☐ **Round 741 to the nearest tens.**

A 741

B 700

C 740

D 750

Common Core Standard 3.NBT.1 – Numbers & Operations in Base Ten

☐ **Round 592 to the nearest hundreds.**

A Six hundred

B Five hundred and ninety

C Five hundred and ninety-three

D Five hundred

Name ____________________________

DIAGNOSTIC

Common Core Standard 3.NBT.2 – Numbers & Operations in Base Ten

☐ Solve the following equation and be sure to show your work.

$$\begin{array}{r} 692 \\ -\ \underline{520} \end{array}$$

A 1211

B 171

C 172

D 1212

Common Core Standard 3.NBT.2 – Numbers & Operations in Base Ten

☐ Solve the following equation and be sure to show your work.

$$\begin{array}{r} 992 \\ -\ \underline{789} \end{array}$$

A 203

B 202

C 1781

D 201

Common Core Standard 3.NBT.2 – Numbers & Operations in Base Ten

☐ Solve the following equation and be sure to show your work.

$$\begin{array}{r} 224 \\ +\ \underline{487} \end{array}$$

A 712

B 285

C 911

D 711

Name ________________________

**DIAGNOSTIC**

Common Core Standard 3.NBT.2 – Numbers & Operations in Base Ten

☐ **Solve the following equation and be sure to show your work.**

$$\begin{array}{r} 846 \\ +\ 116 \\ \hline \end{array}$$

A 730

B 952

C 962

D 720

Common Core Standard 3.NBT.2 – Numbers & Operations in Base Ten

☐ **Solve the following equation and be sure to show your work.**

$$\begin{array}{r} 848 \\ -\ 692 \\ \hline \end{array}$$

A 154

B 156

C 146

D 136

Common Core Standard 3.NBT.2 – Numbers & Operations in Base Ten

☐ **Solve the following equation and be sure to show your work.**

$$\begin{array}{r} 352 \\ +\ 557 \\ \hline \end{array}$$

A 819

B 908

C 919

D 909

Name ______________________

**PRACTICE**

Common Core Standard 3.NBT.2 – Numbers & Operations in Base Ten

☐ **Solve the following equation and be sure to show your work.**

$$\begin{array}{r} 621 \\ +\ \underline{248} \end{array}$$

A 869

B 889

C 373

D 473

Common Core Standard 3.NBT.2 – Numbers & Operations in Base Ten

☐ **Solve the following equation and be sure to show your work.**

$$\begin{array}{r} 457 \\ -\ \underline{194} \end{array}$$

A 651

B 363

C 263

D 343

Common Core Standard 3.NBT.2 – Numbers & Operations in Base Ten

☐ **Solve the following equation and be sure to show your work.**

$$\begin{array}{r} 283 \\ +\ \underline{427} \end{array}$$

A 600

B 710

C 700

D 264

Name ___________________________

**PRACTICE**

Common Core Standard 3.NBT.2 – Numbers & Operations in Base Ten

☐ **Solve the following equation and be sure to show your work.**

$$\begin{array}{r} 931 \\ +\ 52 \\ \hline \end{array}$$

A 921

B 320

C 879

D 983

Common Core Standard 3.NBT.2 – Numbers & Operations in Base Ten

☐ **Solve the following equation and be sure to show your work.**

$$\begin{array}{r} 516 \\ -\ 91 \\ \hline \end{array}$$

A 585

B 425

C 607

D 505

Common Core Standard 3.NBT.2 – Numbers & Operations in Base Ten

☐ **Solve the following equation and be sure to show your work.**

$$\begin{array}{r} 734 \\ -\ 649 \\ \hline \end{array}$$

A 115

B 1383

C 86

D 85

Name ______________________

**PRACTICE**

Common Core Standard 3.NBT.2 – Numbers & Operations in Base Ten

☐ **Solve the following equation and be sure to show your work.**

$$\begin{array}{r} 811 \\ +\ \underline{187} \end{array}$$

A 776

B 624

C 998

D 887

Common Core Standard 3.NBT.2 – Numbers & Operations in Base Ten

☐ **Solve the following equation and be sure to show your work.**

$$\begin{array}{r} 692 \\ -\ \underline{359} \end{array}$$

A 951

B 334

C 347

D 333

Common Core Standard 3.NBT.2 – Numbers & Operations in Base Ten

☐ **Solve the following equation and be sure to show your work.**

$$\begin{array}{r} 212 \\ +\ \underline{636} \end{array}$$

A 848

B 424

C 852

D 858

Name ___________________________

**PRACTICE**

Common Core Standard 3.NBT.2 – Numbers & Operations in Base Ten

☐ **Solve the following equation and be sure to show your work.**

$$\begin{array}{r} 555 \\ +\ 97 \\ \hline \end{array}$$

A 458

B 652

C 552

D 542

Common Core Standard 3.NBT.2 – Numbers & Operations in Base Ten

☐ **Solve the following equation and be sure to show your work.**

$$\begin{array}{r} 999 \\ -\ 891 \\ \hline \end{array}$$

A 198

B 98

C 8

D 108

Common Core Standard 3.NBT.2 – Numbers & Operations in Base Ten

☐ **Solve the following equation and be sure to show your work.**

$$\begin{array}{r} 246 \\ -\ 84 \\ \hline \end{array}$$

A 242

B 330

C 152

D 162

Name ________________________

ASSESSMENT

Common Core Standard 3.NBT.2 – Numbers & Operations in Base Ten

☐ **Solve the following equation and be sure to show your work.**

$$\begin{array}{r} 241 \\ +\ 47 \\ \hline \end{array}$$

A 288

B 194

C 298

D 104

Common Core Standard 3.NBT.2 – Numbers & Operations in Base Ten

☐ **Solve the following equation and be sure to show your work.**

$$\begin{array}{r} 542 \\ -\ 334 \\ \hline \end{array}$$

A 208

B 209

C 876

D 207

Common Core Standard 3.NBT.2 – Numbers & Operations in Base Ten

☐ **Solve the following equation and be sure to show your work.**

$$\begin{array}{r} 601 \\ +\ 108 \\ \hline \end{array}$$

A 493

B 719

C 709

D 710

Name ________________________

ASSESSMENT

Common Core Standard 3.NBT.2 – Numbers & Operations in Base Ten

☐ **Solve the following equation and be sure to show your work.**

$$\begin{array}{r} 273 \\ +\ 47 \\ \hline \end{array}$$

A 310

B 320

C 226

D 236

Common Core Standard 3.NBT.2 – Numbers & Operations in Base Ten

☐ **Solve the following equation and be sure to show your work.**

$$\begin{array}{r} 364 \\ -\ 38 \\ \hline \end{array}$$

A 402

B 432

C 336

D 326

Common Core Standard 3.NBT.2 – Numbers & Operations in Base Ten

☐ **Solve the following equation and be sure to show your work.**

$$\begin{array}{r} 503 \\ -\ 437 \\ \hline \end{array}$$

A 134

B 940

C 166

D 66

Name ____________________

DIAGNOSTIC

Common Core Standard 3.NBT.3 – Numbers & Operations in Base Ten

☐ **Solve the following equation and be sure to show your work.**

$$8 \times 40 =$$

A 120

B 320

C 280

D 360

Common Core Standard 3.NBT.3 – Numbers & Operations in Base Ten

☐ **Solve the following equation and be sure to show your work.**

$$40 \times \square = 160$$

A 4

B 5

C 6

D 120

Common Core Standard 3.NBT.3 – Numbers & Operations in Base Ten

☐ **Solve the following equation and be sure to show your work.**

$$\begin{array}{r} 50 \\ \underline{\times\ 4} \end{array}$$

A 46

B 200

C 54

D 160

Name ____________________

DIAGNOSTIC

Common Core Standard 3.NBT.3 – Numbers & Operations in Base Ten

☐ **Solve the following equation and be sure to show your work.**

$$\begin{array}{r} 80 \\ \times\ 9 \\ \hline \end{array}$$

A 730

B 89

C 71

D 720

Common Core Standard 3.NBT.3 – Numbers & Operations in Base Ten

☐ **Solve the following equation and be sure to show your work.**

$$5 \times 20 =$$

A 25

B 120

C 80

D 100

Common Core Standard 3.NBT.3 – Numbers & Operations in Base Ten

☐ **Solve the following equation and be sure to show your work.**

$$\square \times 9 = 450$$

A 50

B 60

C 55

D 441

Name ____________________

**PRACTICE**

Common Core Standard 3.NBT.3 – Numbers & Operations in Base Ten

☐ **Solve the following equation and be sure to show your work.**

$$3 \times 50 =$$

A 53

B 150

C 120

D 180

Common Core Standard 3.NBT.3 – Numbers & Operations in Base Ten

☐ **Solve the following equation and be sure to show your work.**

$$80 \times \square = 160$$

A 3

B 80

C 2

D 4

Common Core Standard 3.NBT.3 – Numbers & Operations in Base Ten

☐ **Solve the following equation and be sure to show your work.**

$$\begin{array}{r} 40 \\ \underline{\times\ 8} \end{array}$$

A 280

B 320

C 360

D 48

Name ______________________

**PRACTICE**

Common Core Standard 3.NBT.3 – Numbers & Operations in Base Ten

☐ **Solve the following equation and be sure to show your work.**

$$\begin{array}{r} 30 \\ \times\ 7 \\ \hline \end{array}$$

A 280

B 210

C 320

D 180

Common Core Standard 3.NBT.3 – Numbers & Operations in Base Ten

☐ **Solve the following equation and be sure to show your work.**

$$6 \times 40 =$$

A 200

B 240

C 280

D 46

Common Core Standard 3.NBT.3 – Numbers & Operations in Base Ten

☐ **Solve the following equation and be sure to show your work.**

$$\square \times 6 = 300$$

A 50

B 60

C 40

D 294

Name ____________________________

**PRACTICE**

Common Core Standard 3.NBT.3 – Numbers & Operations in Base Ten

☐ **Solve the following equation and be sure to show your work.**

$$9 \times 70 =$$

A 630

B 560

C 700

D 97

Common Core Standard 3.NBT.3 – Numbers & Operations in Base Ten

☐ **Solve the following equation and be sure to show your work.**

$$20 \times \square = 180$$

A 8

B 11

C 9

D 160

Common Core Standard 3.NBT.3 – Numbers & Operations in Base Ten

☐ **Solve the following equation and be sure to show your work.**

$$\begin{array}{r} 60 \\ \underline{\times\ 8} \end{array}$$

A 420

B 540

C 480

D 68

Name ____________________

**PRACTICE**

Common Core Standard 3.NBT.3 – Numbers & Operations in Base Ten

☐ **Solve the following equation and be sure to show your work.**

$$\begin{array}{r} 70 \\ \times\ 1 \\ \hline \end{array}$$

A 71

B 70

C 69

D 0

Common Core Standard 3.NBT.3 – Numbers & Operations in Base Ten

☐ **Solve the following equation and be sure to show your work.**

$$3 \times 40 =$$

A 160

B 120

C 43

D 37

Common Core Standard 3.NBT.3 – Numbers & Operations in Base Ten

☐ **Solve the following equation and be sure to show your work.**

$$\square \times 4 = 360$$

A 356

B 85

C 90

D 80

Name ____________________

**ASSESSMENT**

Common Core Standard 3.NBT.3 – Numbers & Operations in Base Ten

☐ **Solve the following equation and be sure to show your work.**

$$90 \times 4 =$$

A 86

B 360

C 94

D 270

Common Core Standard 3.NBT.3 – Numbers & Operations in Base Ten

☐ **Solve the following equation and be sure to show your work.**

$$90 \times \square = 720$$

A 6

B 9

C 8

D 7

Common Core Standard 3.NBT.3 – Numbers & Operations in Base Ten

☐ **Solve the following equation and be sure to show your work.**

$$\begin{array}{r} 70 \\ \underline{\times\ 7} \end{array}$$

A 490

B 77

C 420

D 560

Name ____________________

ASSESSMENT

Common Core Standard 3.NBT.3 – Numbers & Operations in Base Ten

☐ **Solve the following equation and be sure to show your work.**

$$\begin{array}{r} 60 \\ \times\ 9 \\ \hline \end{array}$$

A 69

B 480

C 540

D 600

Common Core Standard 3.NBT.3 – Numbers & Operations in Base Ten

☐ **Solve the following equation and be sure to show your work.**

$$50 \times 7 =$$

A 57

B 43

C 300

D 350

Common Core Standard 3.NBT.3 – Numbers & Operations in Base Ten

☐ **Solve the following equation and be sure to show your work.**

$$\square \times 40 = 160$$

A 5

B 6

C 4

D 120

Name ____________________

DIAGNOSTIC

Common Core Standard 3.NF.1 – Numbers & Operations - Fractions

☐ **Shalonda wants to give her friends some Valentine's Cards, but her friends are in several different classes. There are 5 of her friends in Mr. Sanchez's class, 9 of her friends in Mrs. Jones class, and 6 of her friends in Mrs. Beckham's class. Which teacher has the greatest share of Shalonda's friends in his or her class? Write a fraction to represent their share. Be sure to show your work.**

A Mr. Sanchez $\frac{5}{20}$

B Mrs. Jones $\frac{6}{20}$

C Mrs. Beckham $\frac{6}{20}$

D Mrs. Jones $\frac{9}{20}$

Common Core Standard 3.NF.1 – Numbers & Operations – Fractions

☐ **The models are arranged in order. Which of the following fractions belongs in the space if a fraction were used in place of the model? Be sure to show your work.**

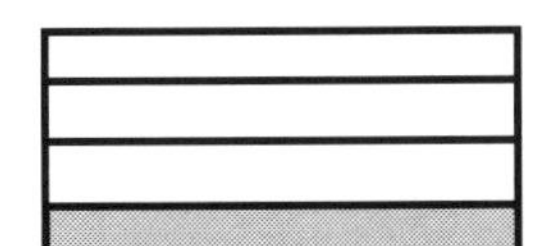

?

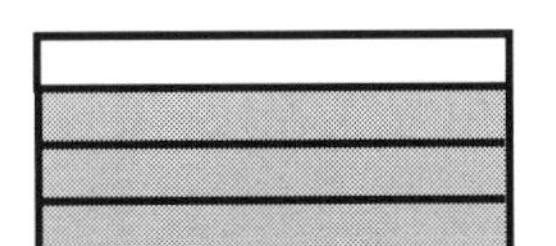

A $\frac{2}{3}$

B $\frac{3}{4}$

C $\frac{1}{3}$

D $\frac{1}{2}$

Common Core Standard 3.NF.1 – Numbers & Operations – Fractions

☐ **Which model shows the fraction $\frac{4}{10}$ below?**

A 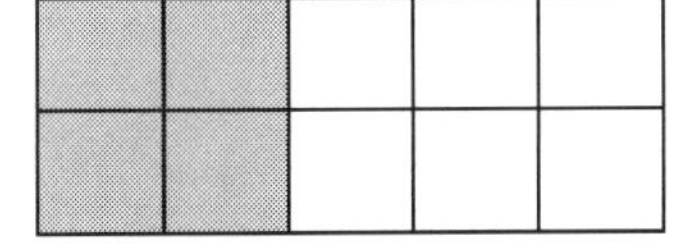

B 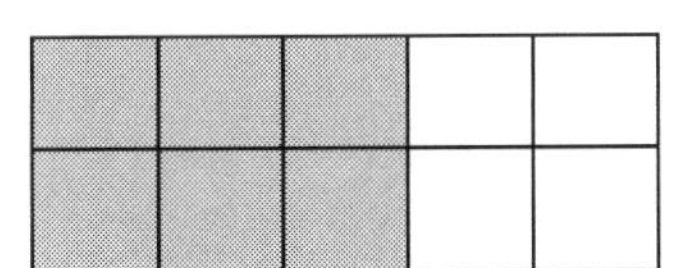

C 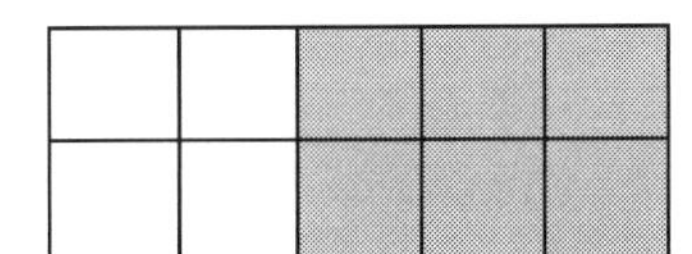

D 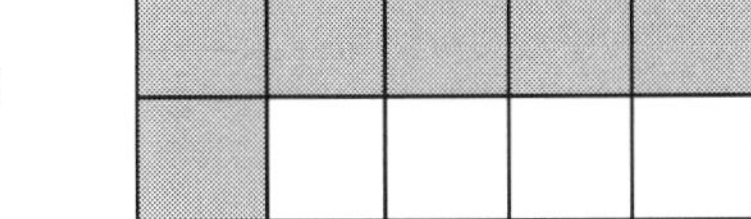

Name ____________________

**DIAGNOSTIC**

Common Core Standard 3.NF.1 – Numbers & Operations – Fractions

☐ **The figure is shaded to represent a fraction. How could this fraction be written? Be sure to show your work.**

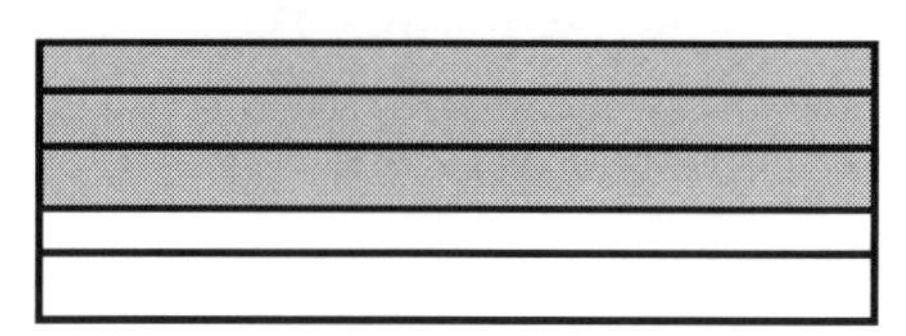

**A** Five thirds

**B** $\frac{7}{8}$

**C** Three fifths

**D** $\frac{3}{2}$

Common Core Standard 3.NF.1 – Numbers & Operations - Fractions

☐ **Which of the following fractions would come next in the series if a fraction were used instead of the model? Be sure to show your work.**

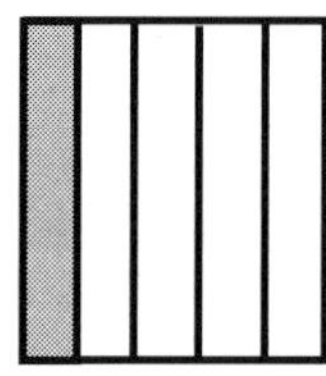

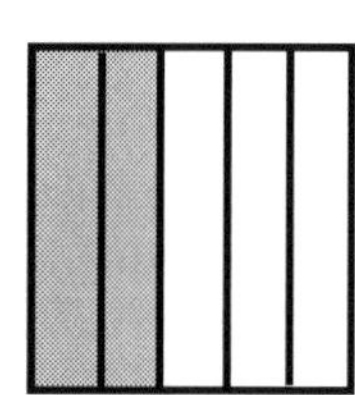

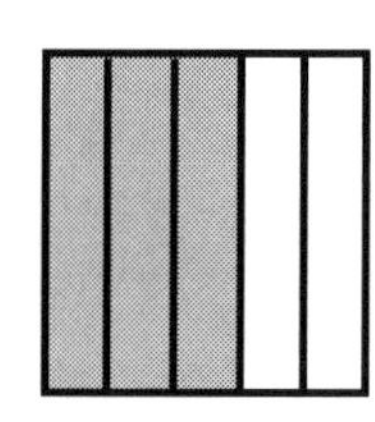

?

**A** $\frac{5}{5}$

**B** $\frac{1}{2}$

**C** $\frac{4}{5}$

**D** $\frac{1}{5}$

Common Core Standard 3.NF.1 – Numbers & Operations – Fractions

☐ **Which model shows the fraction $\frac{3}{5}$ below? Be sure to show your work.**

 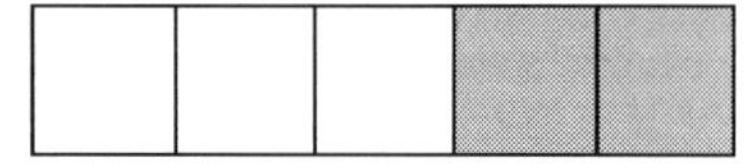

(B) 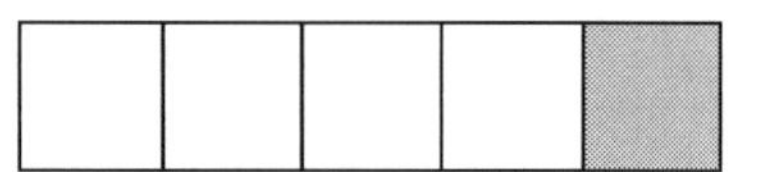

(C) 

(D) 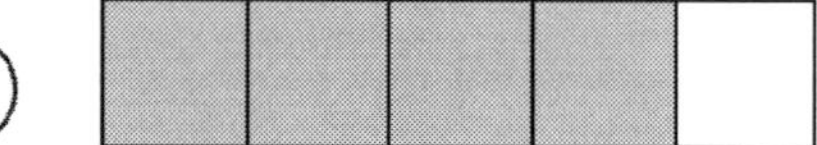

Name ______________________

**PRACTICE**

Common Core Standard 3.NF.1 – Numbers & Operations - Fractions

☐ **Noah's cat had kittens one night. His cat had 2 white kittens, 4 black kittens, and 3 mixed color kittens. Write a fraction that represents the share of kittens that were mixed color. Be sure to show your work.**

**A** 2/9

**B** 6/9

**C** 4/9

**D** 1/3

Common Core Standard 3.NF.1 – Numbers & Operations – Fractions

☐ **The diamonds are arranged in order. Which of the following fractions would be the next sequence of diamonds? Be sure to show your work.**

?

**A** $\frac{4}{5}$

**B** $\frac{5}{5}$

**C** $\frac{2}{3}$

**D** $\frac{1}{5}$

Common Core Standard 3.NF.1 – Numbers & Operations – Fractions

☐ **Which model shows the fraction $\frac{2}{6}$ below? Be sure to show your work.**

**A** 

**C** 

**B** 

**D**

Name ______________________

**PRACTICE**

Common Core Standard 3.NF.1 – Numbers & Operations – Fractions

☐ **The shapes shaded below are used to represent a fraction. How could this fraction be written? Be sure to show your work.**

A $\frac{5}{9}$

B Four ninths

C Five fourths

D $\frac{5}{4}$

Common Core Standard 3.NF.1 – Numbers & Operations - Fractions

☐ **Aggasi is going on a trip to Armenia. He has packed 3 pairs of shoes, 6 pairs of jeans, and 8 shirts. What fraction of Aggasi's clothes are jeans? Be sure to show your work.**

A 8/17

B 8/9

C 6/17

D 3/17

Common Core Standard 3.NF.1 – Numbers & Operations – Fractions

☐ **Which model shows the fraction $\frac{3}{8}$ below? Be sure to show your work.**

A

B

C

D

Name ________________________

PRACTICE

Common Core Standard 3.NF.1 – Numbers & Operations - Fractions

☐ **Elijah collects sports cards. He has 8 baseball cards, 9 football cards, 6 hockey cards, and 3 soccer cards. Write a fraction that represents the share of football cards. Be sure to show your work.**

**A** 6/26

**B** 9/26

**C** 8/26

**D** 17/26

Common Core Standard 3.NF.1 – Numbers & Operations – Frac ons

☐ **Which shaded model shows the fraction $\frac{1}{4}$ below? Be sure to show your work.**

**A**

**B**

**C**

**D**

Common Core Standard 3.NF.1 – Numbers & Operations – Fractions

☐ **Mrs. Ranjana's class went to the zoo. The class saw 5 elephants, 4 lions, 7 giraffes, and 3 zebras. Write a fraction that represents the share of lions and zebras. Be sure to show your work.**

**A** 9/19

**B** 10/19

**C** 7/19

**D** 5/19

Name ________________________

**PRACTICE**

Common Core Standard 3.NF.1 – Numbers & Operations – Fractions

☐ **Which shaded model shows the fraction $\frac{3}{5}$ below? Be sure to show your work.**

**A**

**C**

**B**

**D**

Common Core Standard 3.NF.1 – Numbers & Operations - Fractions

☐ **Sasha wanted to paint a picture for her grandmother as a present. She had 2 red markers, 9 blue markers, 5 green markers, and 8 yellow markers. What fraction of Sasha's markers are green? Be sure to show your work.**

**A** **5/24**

**C** **8/24**

B **9/24**

**D** **19/24**

Common Core Standard 3.NF.1 – Numbers & Operations – Fractions

☐ **Which shaded model shows the fraction $\frac{3}{7}$ below? Be sure to show your work.**

**A**

**C**

**B**

**D**

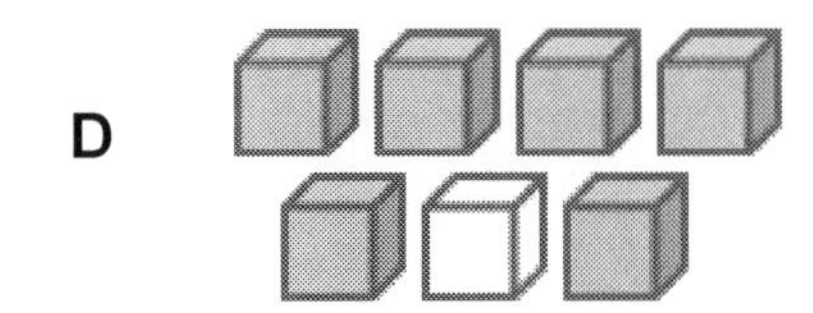

Name ____________________________

**ASSESSMENT**

Common Core Standard 3.NF.1 – Numbers & Operations - Fractions

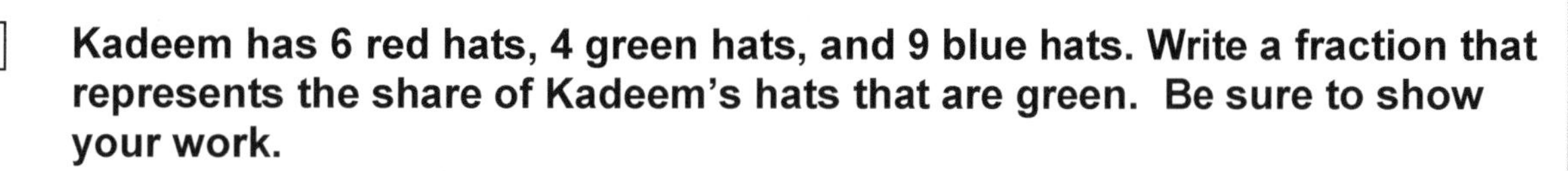

☐ **Kadeem has 6 red hats, 4 green hats, and 9 blue hats. Write a fraction that represents the share of Kadeem's hats that are green. Be sure to show your work.**

**A** **10/19**

**B** **4/19**

**C** **6/19**

**D** **9/19**

Common Core Standard 3.NF.1 – Numbers & Operations – Fractions

☐ **The models are arranged in order. Which of the following fractions belongs in the space if a fraction were used in place of the model? Be sure to show your work.**

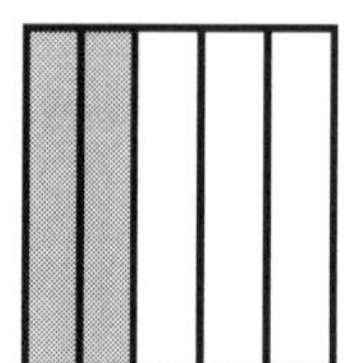 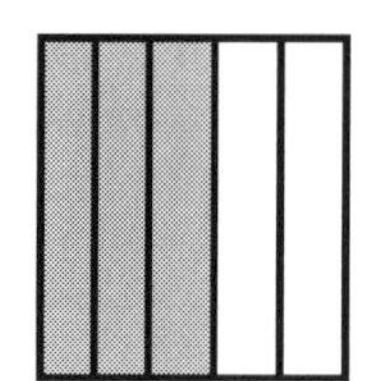  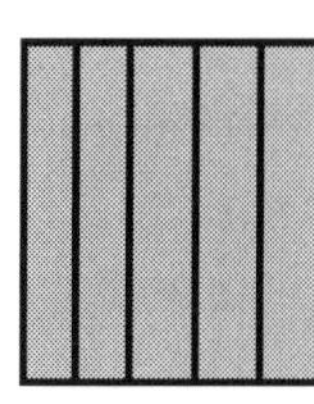

**A** $\frac{4}{5}$

**B** $\frac{5}{5}$

**C** $\frac{3}{5}$

**D** $\frac{1}{5}$

Common Core Standard 3.NF.1 – Numbers & Operati ns – Fractions

☐ **Which model shows the fraction $\frac{7}{16}$ below? Be sure to show your work.**

**A** 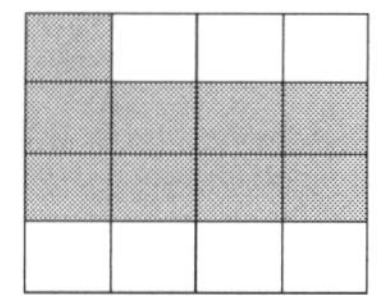

**C** 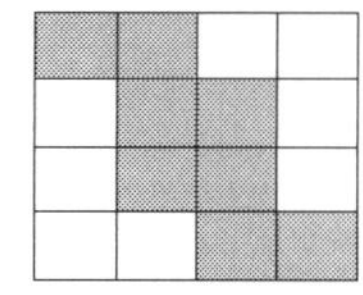

**B** 

**D**

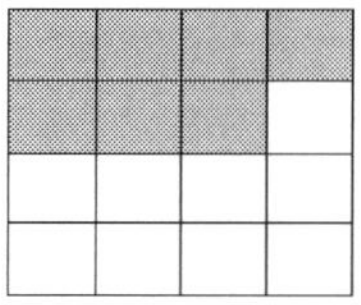

Name ____________________

**ASSESSMENT**

Common Core Standard 3.NF.1 – Numbers & Operations – Fractions

☐ **The figure is shaded to represent a fraction. How could this fraction be written? Be sure to show your work.**

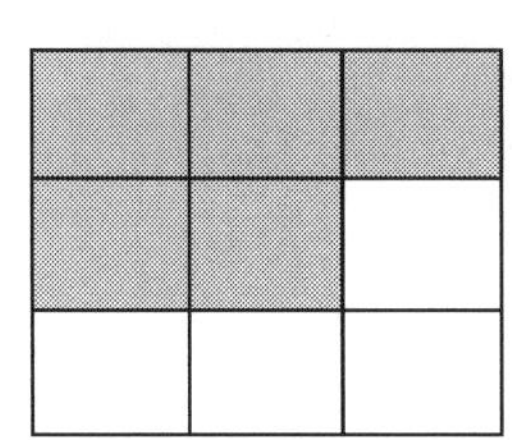

**A** Three ninths

**B** $\frac{5}{9}$

**C** Four fifths

**D** $\frac{5}{4}$

Common Core Standard 3.NF.1 – Numbers & Operations - Fractions

☐ **Mr. Chin has a produce stand. He has 5 apples, 7 oranges, and10 strawberries. What fraction of Mr. Chin's fruit are apples? Be sure to show your work.**

**A** 10/17

**B** 5/22

**C** 7/22

**D** 5/17

Common Core Standard 3.NF.1 – Numbers & Operations – Fractions

☐ **Which model shows the fraction $\frac{4}{9}$ below?**

**A**

**C**

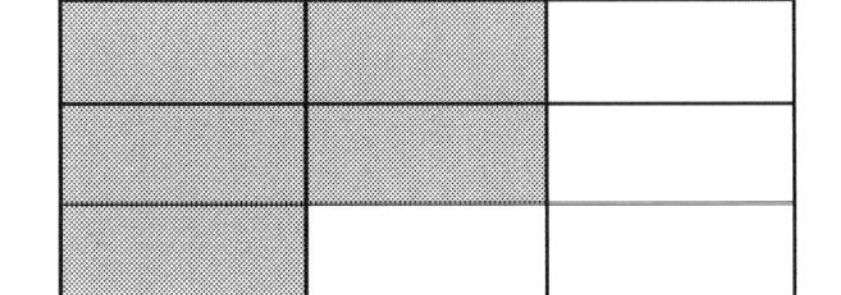

**B**

**D**

Name ____________________

**DIAGNOSTIC**

Common Core Standard 3.NF.2 – Numbers & Operations - Fractions

☐ **Which point on the number line best represents $6\frac{1}{4}$?**

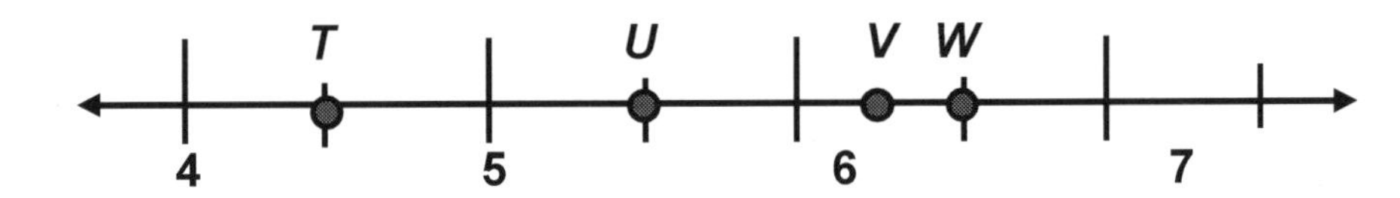


A T

B U

C W

D V

Common Core Standard 3.NF.2 – Numbers & Operations – Fractions

☐ **Point S best represents which number?**

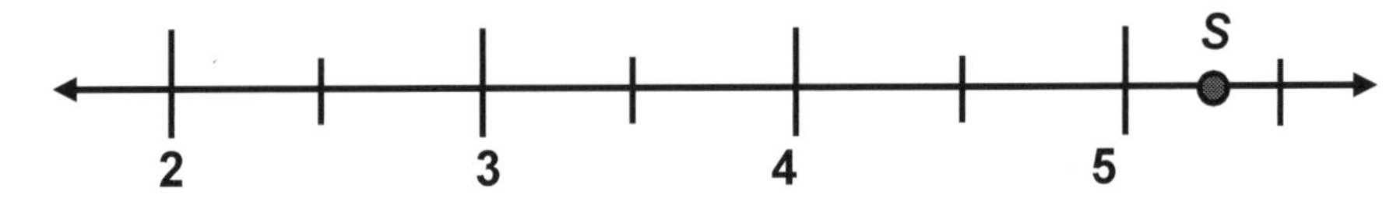


A $5\frac{1}{2}$

B $5\frac{1}{4}$

C $6\frac{1}{4}$

D $5\frac{3}{4}$

Common Core Standard 3.NF.2 – Numbers & Operations – Fractions

☐ **Which object on the number line is at a position greater than $\frac{6}{8}$?**

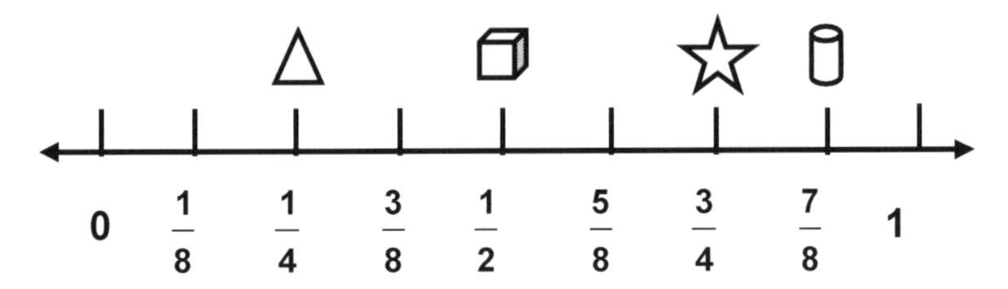


A Triangle

B Cylinder

C Star

D Cube

Name ____________________

DIAGNOSTIC

Common Core Standard 3.NF.2 – Numbers & Operations – Fractions

☐ **Which point on the number line best represents $8\frac{3}{4}$?**

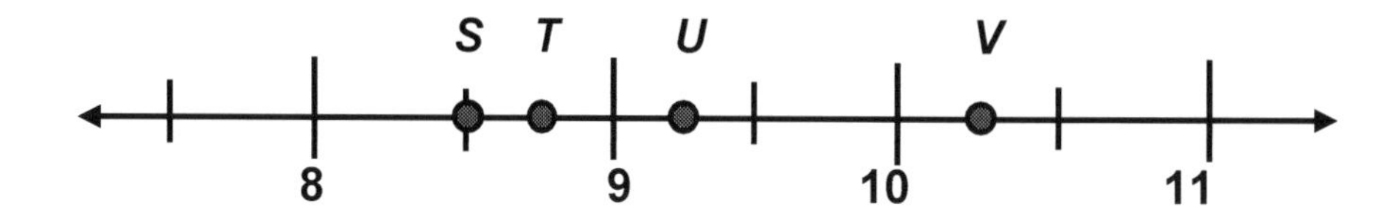


A V

B T

C S

D U

Common Core Standard 3.NF.2 – Numbers & Operations - Fractions

☐ **Point P best represents which number?**

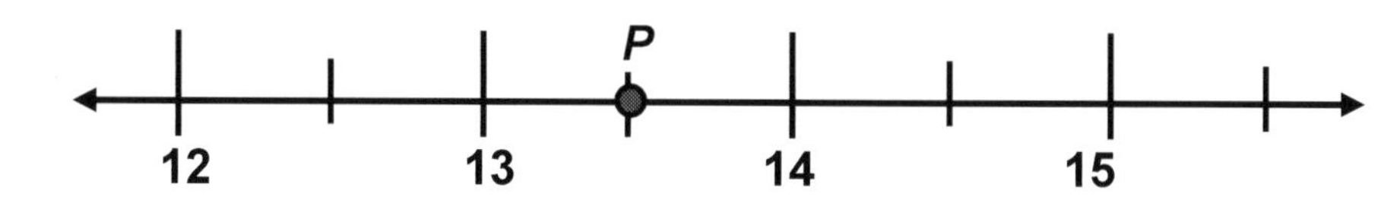


A $14\frac{3}{4}$

B $13\frac{3}{4}$

C $13\frac{1}{4}$

D $13\frac{1}{2}$

Common Core Standard 3.NF.2 – Numbers & Operations – Fractions

☐ **Which object on the number line is at a position greater than $2\frac{5}{6}$?**

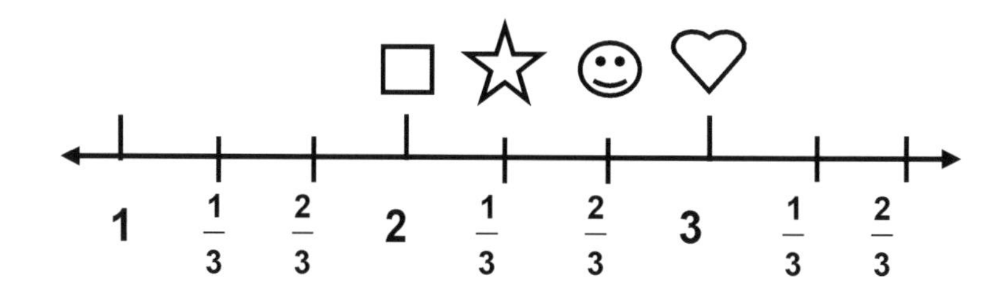


A Face

B Star

C Heart

D Cube

Name ___________________________

**PRACTICE**

Common Core Standard 3.NF.2 – Numbers & Operations - Fractions

☐ **Which point on the number line best represents $9\frac{1}{4}$?**

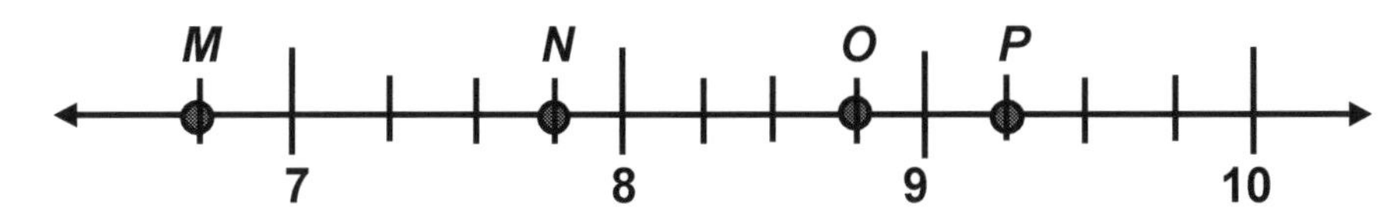


A *N*

B *O*

C *M*

D *P*

Common Core Standard 3.NF.2 – Numbers & Operations – Fractions

☐ **Point *Z* best represents which number?**

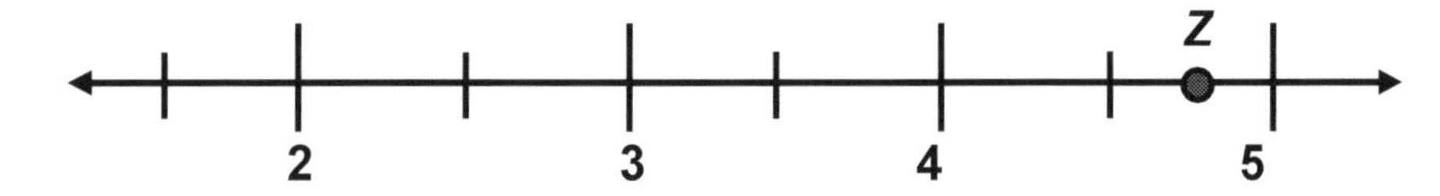


A $3\frac{1}{2}$

B $4\frac{3}{4}$

C $3\frac{1}{4}$

D $4\frac{1}{4}$

Common Core Standard 3.NF.2 – Numbers & Operations – Fractions

☐ **Which object on the number line is at position $5\frac{3}{4}$?**

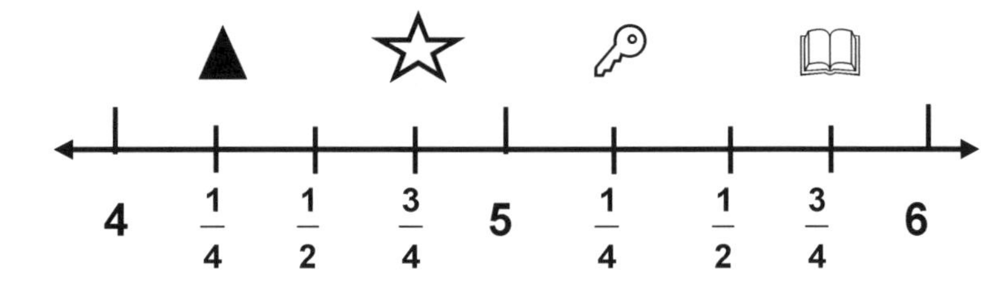


A Star

B Key

C Book

D Triangle

Name ____________________

**PRACTICE**

Common Core Standard 3.NF.2 – Numbers & Operations – Fractions

☐ **Which point on the number line best represents $5\frac{1}{2}$?**

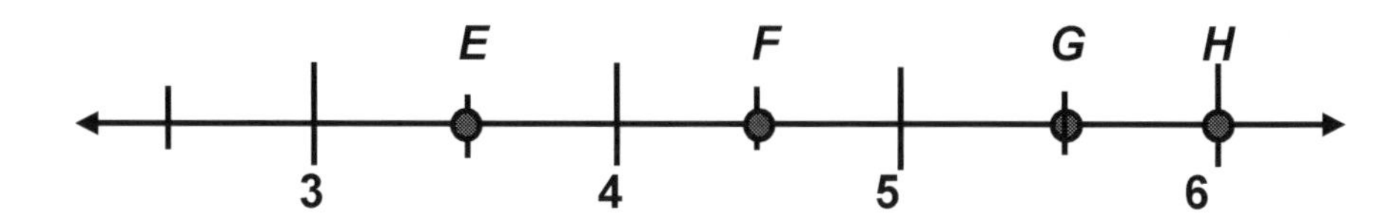


A *E*

B *H*

C *G*

D *F*

Common Core Standard 3.NF.2 – Numbers & Operations - Fractions

☐ **Point *X* best represents which number?**

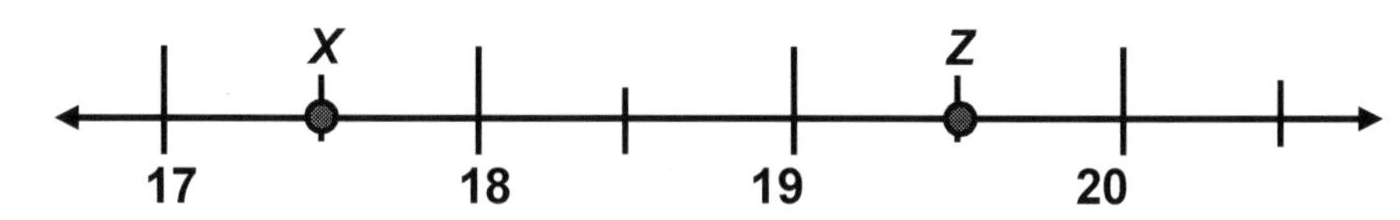


A $17\frac{3}{4}$

B $17\frac{1}{2}$

C $17\frac{1}{4}$

D $19\frac{1}{2}$

Common Core Standard 3.NF.2 – Numbers & Operations – Fractions

☐ **Which object on the number line is at position $5\frac{4}{8}$?**

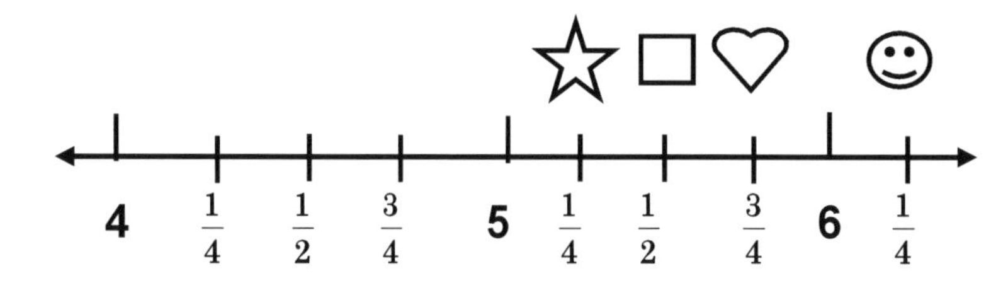


A Face

B Star

C Heart

D Box

Name ____________________

**PRACTICE**

Common Core Standard 3.NF.2 – Numbers & Operations - Fractions

☐ **Which point on the number line best represents $13\frac{1}{3}$?**

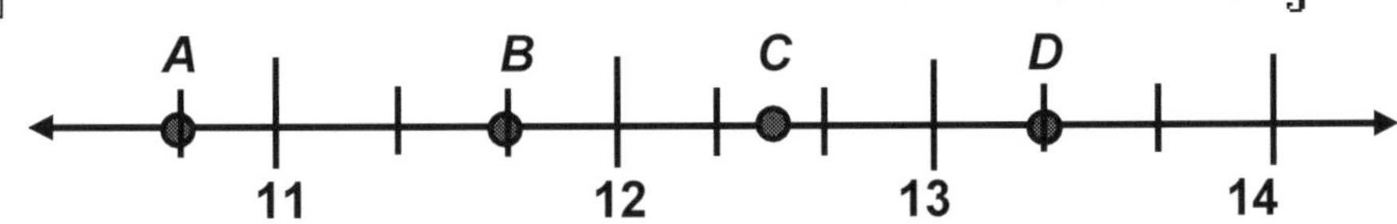


A    *C*

B    *A*

C    *B*

D    *D*

Common Core Standard 3.NF.2 – Numbers & Operations – Fractions

☐ **Point *Y* best represents which number?**

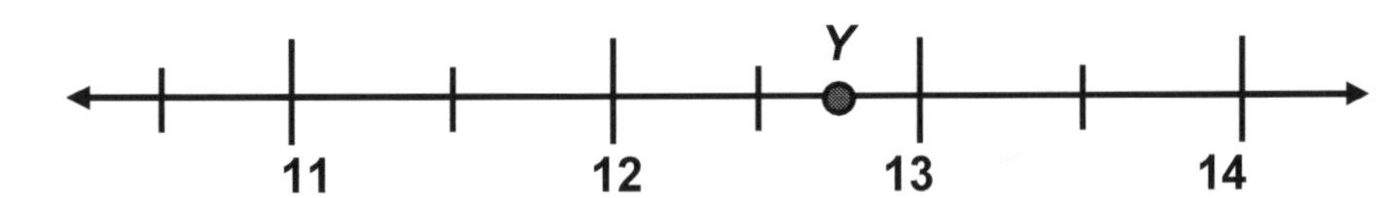


A    $12\frac{1}{2}$

B    $12\frac{3}{4}$

C    13

D    $13\frac{1}{4}$

Common Core Standard 3.NF.2 – Numbers & Operations – Fractions

☐ **Which object on the number line is at a position $1\frac{3}{4}$?**

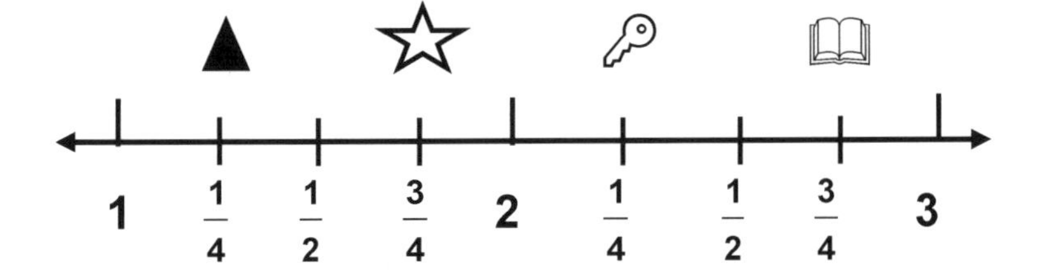


A    Star

B    Key

C    Book

D    Triangle

Name ____________________

**PRACTICE**

Common Core Standard 3.NF.2 – Numbers & Operations – Fractions

☐ **Which point on the number line best represents $5\frac{1}{4}$?**

A *E*

B *H*

C *G*

D *F*

Common Core Standard 3.NF.2 – Numbers & Operations - Fractions

☐ **Point *T* best represents which number?**

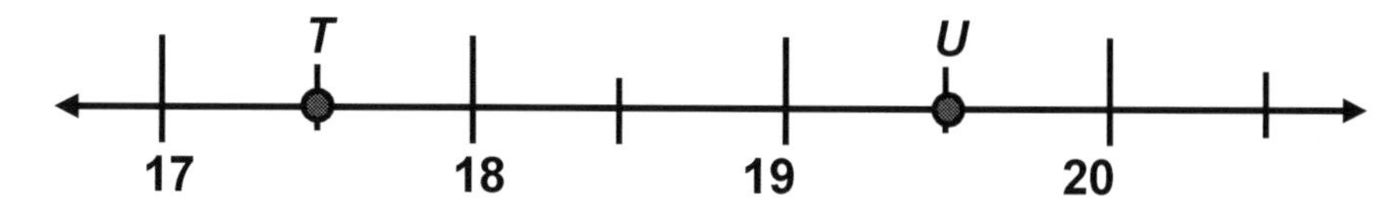


A $17\frac{3}{4}$

B $17\frac{1}{4}$

C $17\frac{1}{2}$

$19\frac{1}{2}$

Common Core Standard 3.NF.2 – Numbers & Operations – Fractions

☐ **Which object on the number line is at a position greater than $4\frac{6}{8}$?**

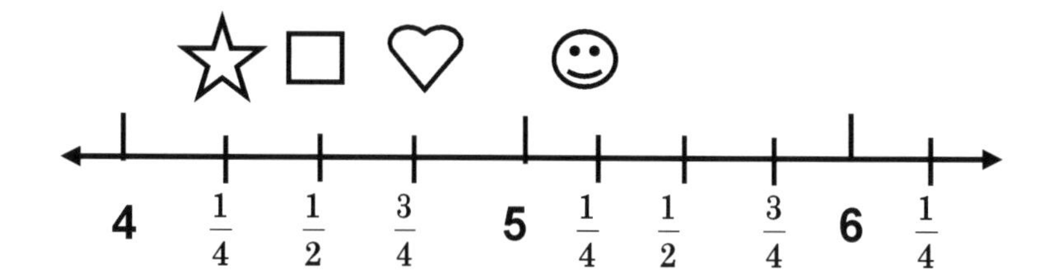


A Face

B Star

C Heart

D Cube

Name ____________________

**ASSESSMENT**

Common Core Standard 3.NF.2 – Numbers & Operations - Fractions

☐ **Which point on the number line best represents $\frac{3}{4}$?**

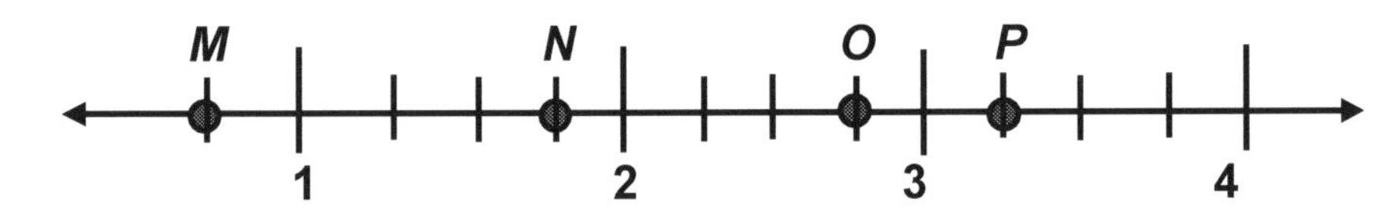


A *N*

B *O*

C *P*

D *M*

Common Core Standard 3.NF.2 – Numbers & Operations – Fractions

☐ **Point *E* best represents which number?**

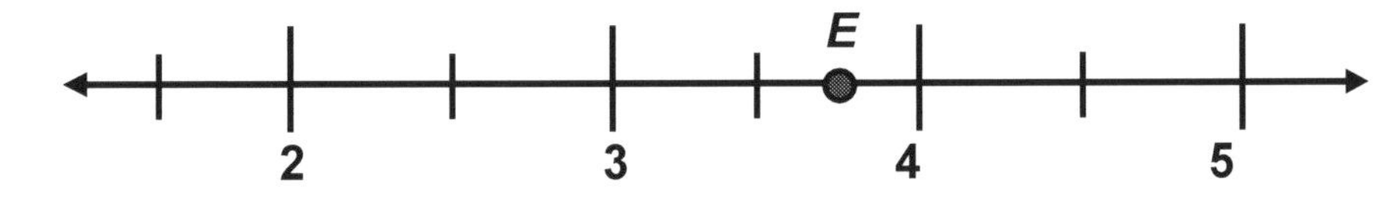


A $3\frac{1}{2}$

B $3\frac{3}{4}$

C $3\frac{1}{4}$

D $4\frac{1}{4}$

Common Core Standard 3.NF.2 – Numbers & Operations – Fractions

☐ **Which object on the number line is at a position less than $1\frac{2}{4}$?**

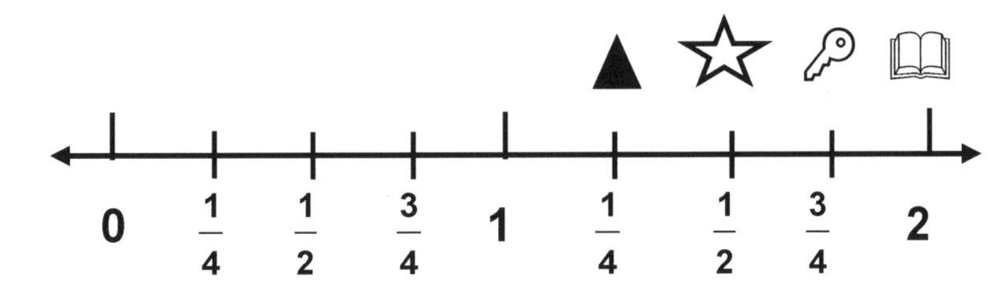


A Star

B Key

C Book

D Triangle

Name ____________________

**ASSESSMENT**

Common Core Standard 3.NF.2 – Numbers & Operations – Fractions

☐ **Which point on the number line best represents $3\frac{1}{2}$?**

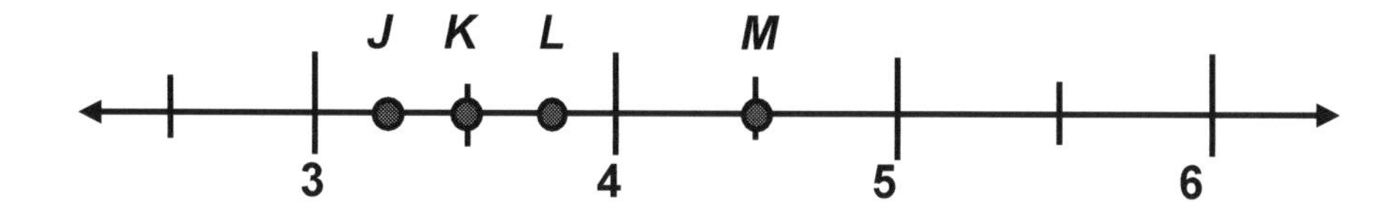


A *K*

B *L*

C *J*

D *M*

Common Core Standard 3.NF.2 – Numbers & Operations - Fractions

☐ **Point *F* best represents which number?**

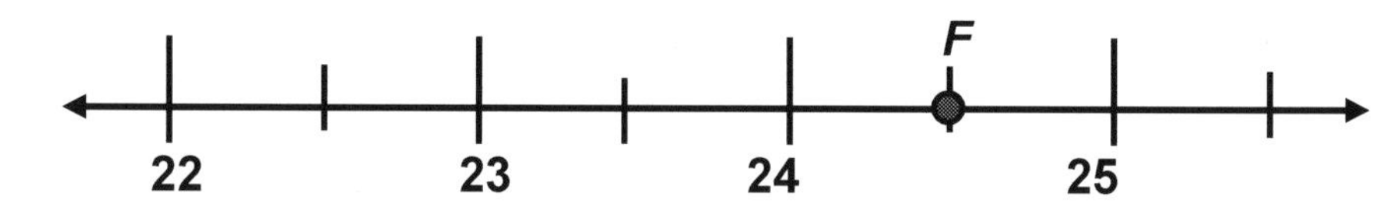


A $24\frac{3}{4}$

B $25\frac{1}{4}$

C $24\frac{1}{4}$

D $24\frac{1}{2}$

Common Core Standard 3.NF.2 – Numbers & Operations – Fractions

☐ **Which object on the number line is at a position greater than $2\frac{3}{6}$?**

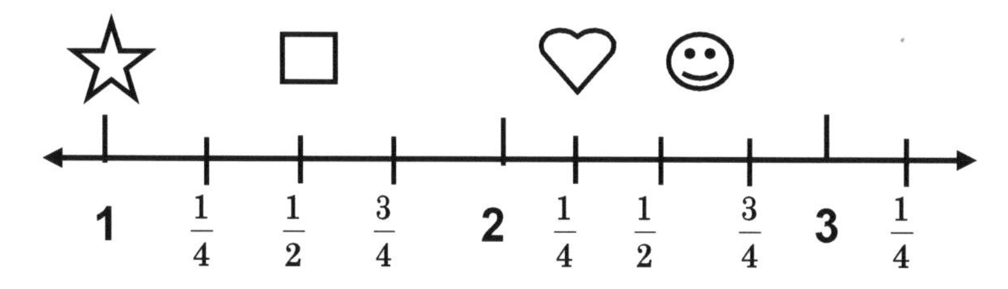


A Face

B Star

C Heart

D Cube

Name ______________________________

**DIAGNOSTIC**

Common Core Standard 3.NF.3 – Numbers & Operations – Fractions

☐ **Look at the shaded parts of the models. Which models show $\frac{2}{10} = \frac{1}{5}$?**

A 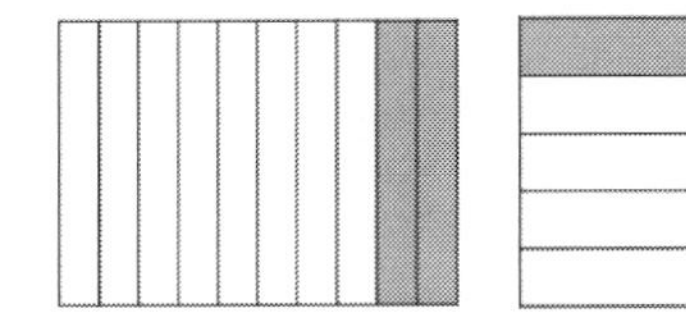

C 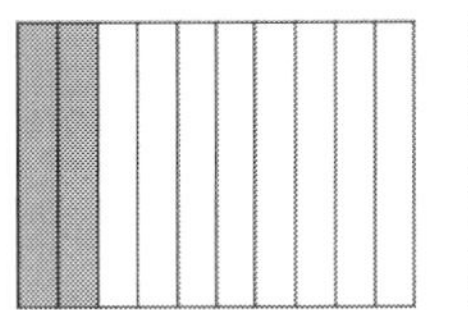 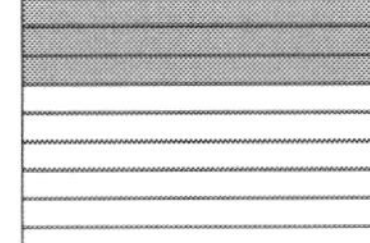

B 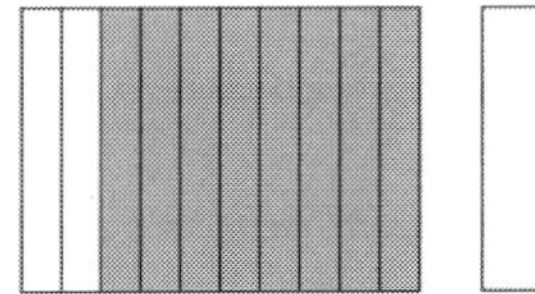 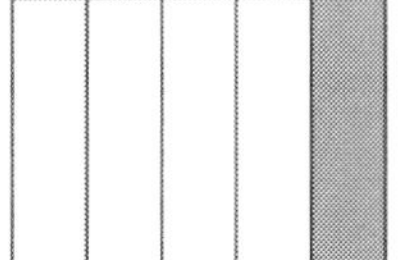

D 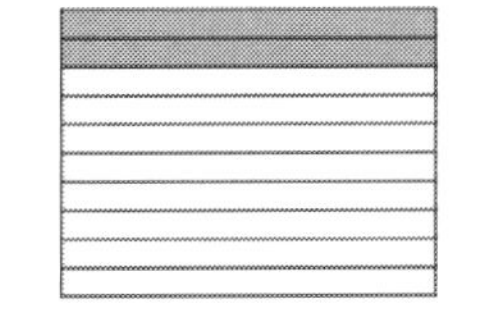 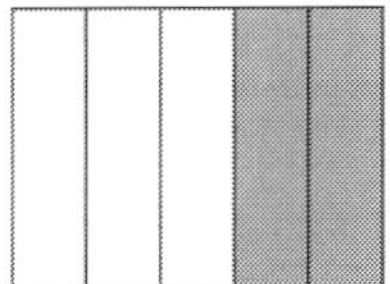

Common Core Standard 3.NF.3 – Numbers & Operations – Fractions

☐ **The 2 models are shaded to show that ______**

A $\frac{1}{2} < \frac{1}{5}$

B $\frac{3}{5} > \frac{1}{2}$

C $\frac{1}{2} = \frac{3}{5}$

D $\frac{2}{5} > \frac{1}{2}$

Common Core Standard 3.NF.3 – Numbers & Operations – Fractions

☐ **Which number fits the missing value for the fraction below?**

$$\frac{20}{8} = \frac{10}{\quad}$$

A 4

B 3

C 2

D 5

Name ______________________

**DIAGNOSTIC**

Common Core Standard 3.NF.3 – Numbers & Operations – Fractions

☐ 
**The 2 shapes are shaded to show that ______**

A $\frac{7}{8} > \frac{3}{4}$

B $\frac{1}{4} < \frac{1}{8}$

C $\frac{3}{4} = \frac{7}{8}$

D $\frac{1}{8} > \frac{1}{4}$

| $\frac{1}{8}$ | $\frac{1}{8}$ | $\frac{1}{8}$ | $\frac{1}{8}$ | $\frac{1}{8}$ | $\frac{1}{8}$ | $\frac{1}{8}$ | $\frac{1}{8}$ |
|---|---|---|---|---|---|---|---|

| $\frac{1}{4}$ | $\frac{1}{4}$ | $\frac{1}{4}$ | $\frac{1}{4}$ |
|---|---|---|---|

Common Core Standard 3.NF.3 – Numbers & Operations - Fractions

☐ **Which sign fits the missing value for the fraction below?**

$$\frac{20}{28} \square \frac{20}{27}$$

A >

B <

C =

D None of the above

Common Core Standard 3.NF.3 – Numbers & Operations – Fractions

☐ 
**Look at the shaded parts of the figures. Which figures show $\frac{3}{8} > \frac{1}{4}$?**

A 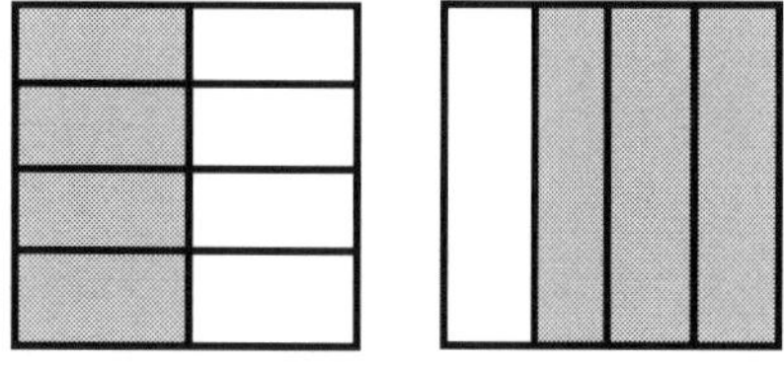

C 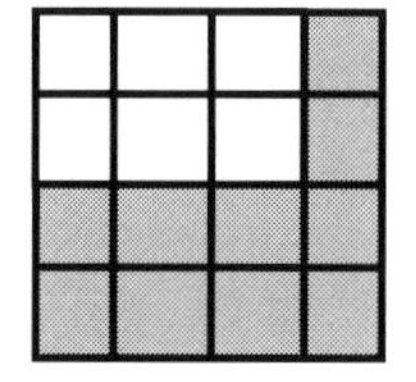 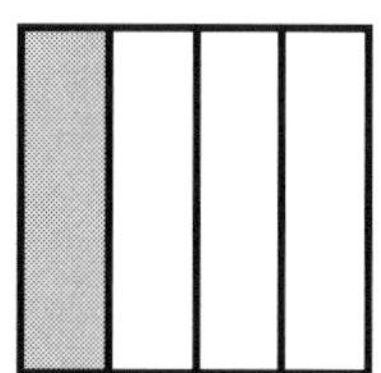

B 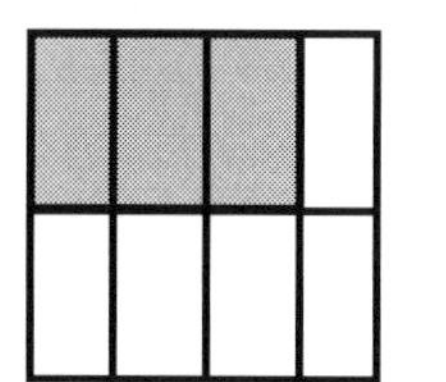 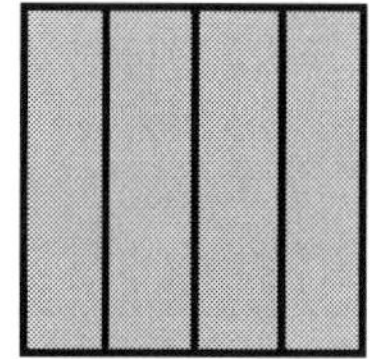

D 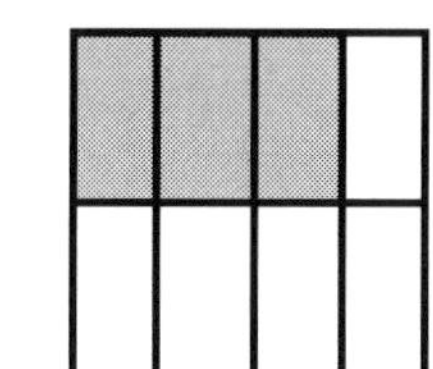 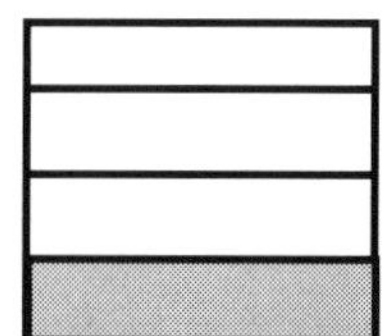

Name ____________________________

**PRACTICE**

Common Core Standard 3.NF.3 – Numbers & Operations – Fractions

☐ **Look at the shaded parts of the models. Which models show $\frac{3}{9} > \frac{1}{4}$ ?**

A 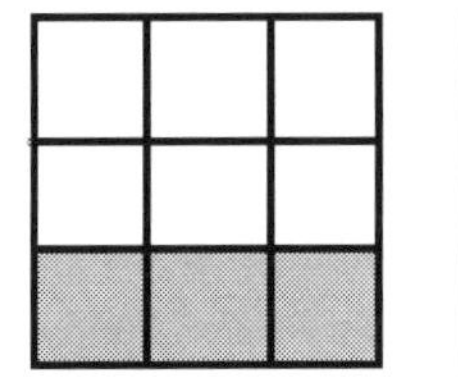 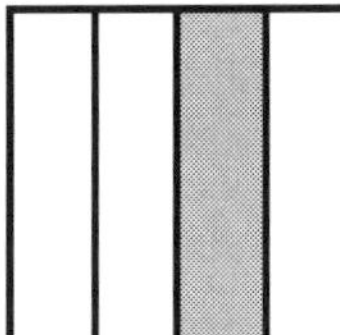

C 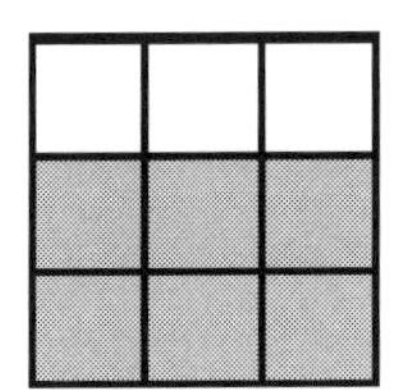 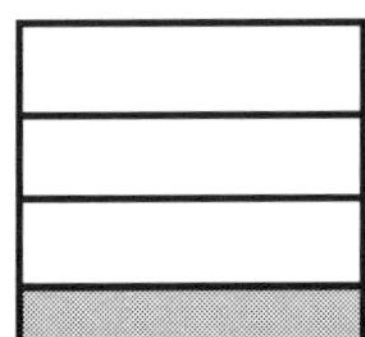

B 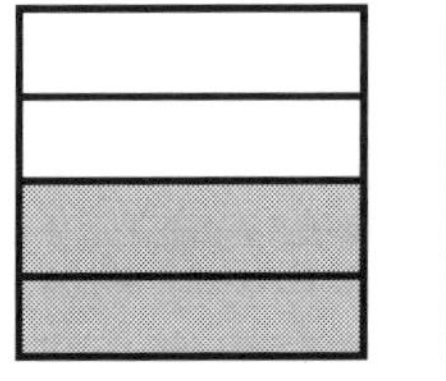 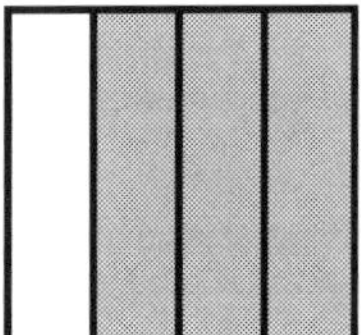

D 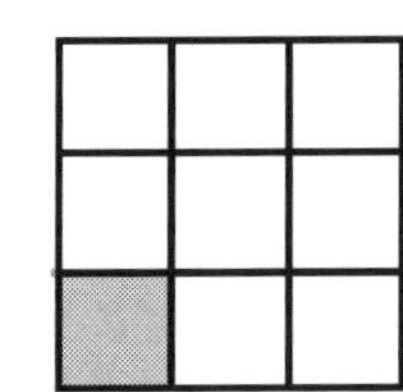 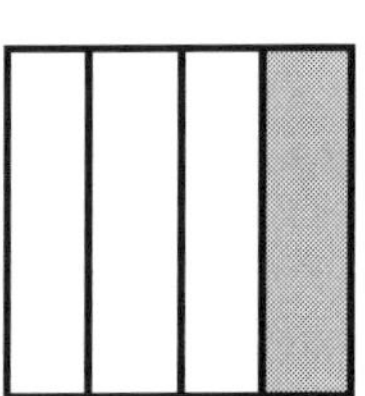

Common Core Standard 3.NF.3 – Numbers & Operations – Fractions

☐ **The models are shaded to show that _____**

A $\frac{2}{3} > \frac{3}{8}$

B $\frac{1}{3} = \frac{1}{8}$

C $\frac{3}{8} < \frac{1}{3}$

D $\frac{2}{3} > \frac{1}{8}$

$\frac{1}{3}$ $\frac{1}{3}$ $\frac{1}{3}$

$\frac{1}{8}$ $\frac{1}{8}$ $\frac{1}{8}$ $\frac{1}{8}$ $\frac{1}{8}$ $\frac{1}{8}$ $\frac{1}{8}$ $\frac{1}{8}$

Common Core Standard 3.NF.3 – Numbers & Operations – Fractions

☐ **Which number fits the missing value for the fraction below?**

$$\frac{56}{49} = \frac{8}{\phantom{0}}$$

A 6

B 5

C 9

D 7

Name ______________________________

**PRACTICE**

Common Core Standard 3.NF.3 – Numbers & Operations – Fractions

☐ **Look at the shaded parts of the figures. Which statement shows the fraction model?**

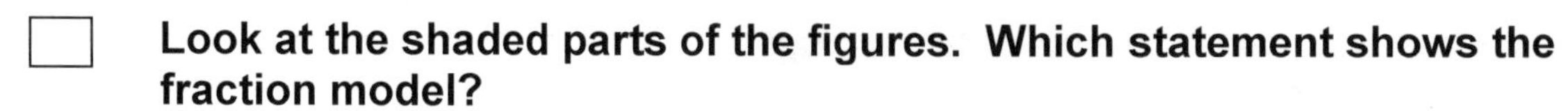

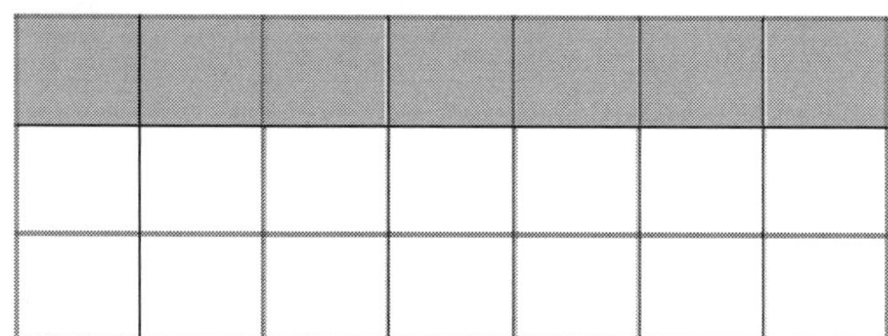

A $\frac{7}{21} > \frac{1}{3}$

B $\frac{1}{3} < \frac{7}{21}$

C $\frac{7}{21} = \frac{1}{3}$

D $\frac{21}{7} < \frac{3}{1}$

Common Core Standard 3.NF.3 – Numbers & Operations - Fractions

☐ **Which sign fits the missing value for the fraction below?**

$$\frac{2}{3} \square \frac{7}{21}$$

A >

B <

C =

D None of the above

Common Core Standard 3.NF.3 – Numbers & Operations – Fractions

☐ **The 2 shapes are shaded to show that ______**

A $\frac{1}{7} > \frac{1}{4}$

B $\frac{6}{7} < \frac{3}{4}$

C $\frac{3}{4} = \frac{6}{7}$

D $\frac{6}{7} > \frac{3}{4}$

| $\frac{1}{7}$ | $\frac{1}{7}$ | $\frac{1}{7}$ | $\frac{1}{7}$ | $\frac{1}{7}$ | $\frac{1}{7}$ | $\frac{1}{7}$ |
|---|---|---|---|---|---|---|

| $\frac{1}{4}$ | $\frac{1}{4}$ | $\frac{1}{4}$ | $\frac{1}{4}$ |
|---|---|---|---|

Name ______________________

**PRACTICE**

Common Core Standard 3.NF.3 – Numbers & Operations – Fractions

☐ **Look at the shaded parts of the models. Which models show $\frac{3}{4} > \frac{3}{5}$?**

**A** 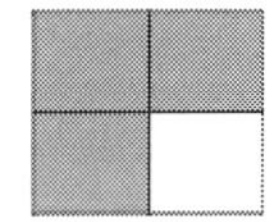

**C** 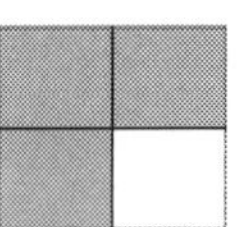 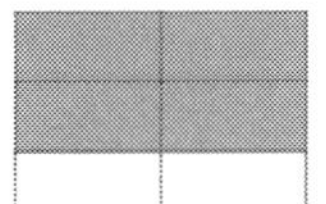

**B** 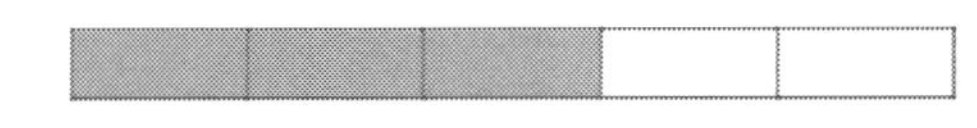 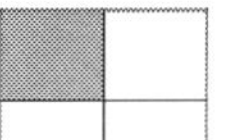

**D**   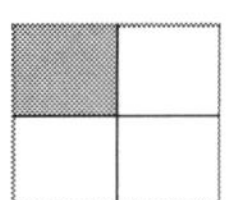

Common Core Standard 3.NF.3 – Numbers & Operations – Fractions

☐ **The models are shaded to show that _____**

A $\frac{1}{8} < \frac{2}{4}$

B $\frac{4}{8} = \frac{2}{4}$

C $\frac{4}{8} > \frac{2}{4}$

D $\frac{2}{4} > \frac{4}{8}$

| $\frac{1}{8}$ | $\frac{1}{8}$ | $\frac{1}{8}$ | $\frac{1}{8}$ |
|---|---|---|---|
| $\frac{1}{8}$ | $\frac{1}{8}$ | $\frac{1}{8}$ | $\frac{1}{8}$ |

| $\frac{1}{4}$ | $\frac{1}{4}$ | $\frac{1}{4}$ | $\frac{1}{4}$ |
|---|---|---|---|

Common Core Standard 3.NF.3 – Numbers & Operations – Fractions

☐ **Which number fits the missing value for the fraction below?**

$$\frac{40}{64} = \frac{5}{\_\_}$$

A 5

B 7

C 9

D 8

Name ___________________________

**PRACTICE**

Common Core Standard 3.NF.3 – Numbers & Operations – Fractions

☐ **Look at the shaded parts of the figures. Which statement shows the fraction model?**

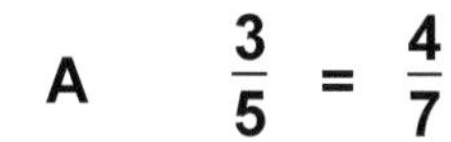

**A** $\frac{3}{5} = \frac{4}{7}$

**B** $\frac{3}{5} > \frac{4}{7}$

**C** $\frac{3}{7} > \frac{2}{5}$

**D** $\frac{3}{5} < \frac{4}{7}$

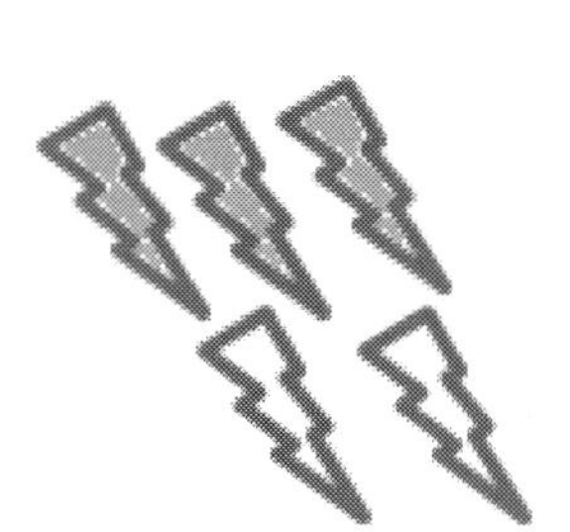

Common Core Standard 3.NF.3 – Numbers & Operations - Fractions

☐ **Which sign fits the missing value for the fraction below?**

$$\frac{8}{16} \square \frac{4}{12}$$

**A** >

**B** <

**C** =

**D** None of the above

Common Core Standard 3.NF.3 – Numbers & Operations – Fractions

☐ **The 2 shapes are shaded to show that ______**

**A** $\frac{4}{6} > \frac{4}{6}$

**B** $\frac{4}{6} < \frac{4}{6}$

**C** $\frac{4}{6} = \frac{4}{6}$

**D** $\frac{2}{6} > \frac{4}{6}$

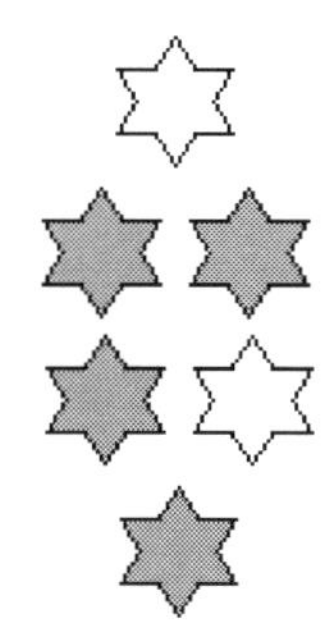

Name ______________________

**ASSESSMENT**

Common Core Standard 3.NF.3 – Numbers & Operations – Fractions

☐ **Look at the shaded parts of the models. Which models show $\frac{1}{4} < \frac{3}{9}$?**

**A** 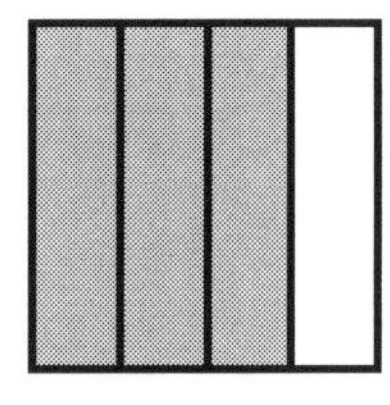 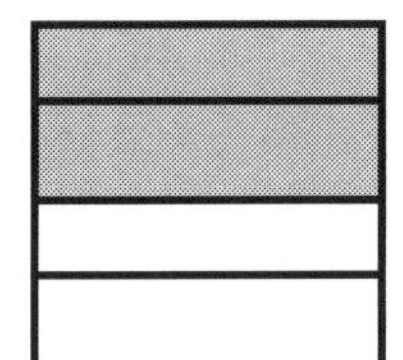

**C** 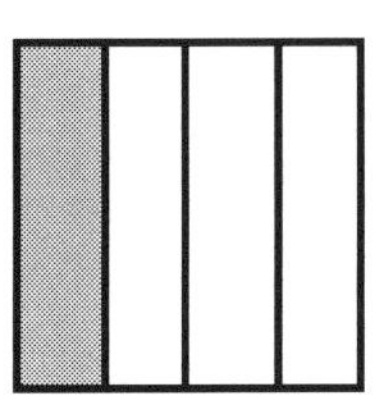 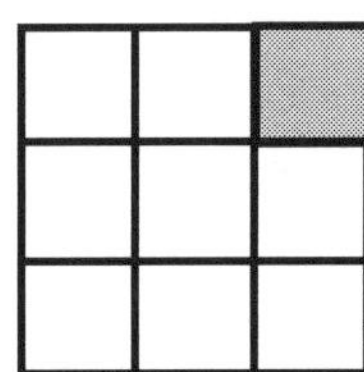

**B** 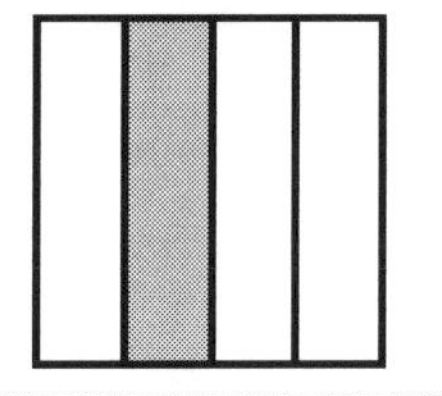 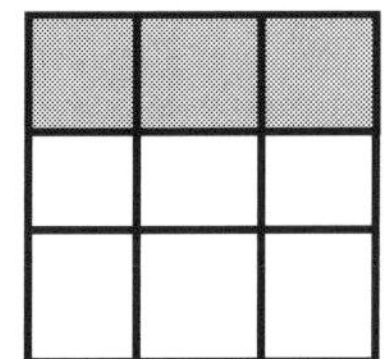

**D** 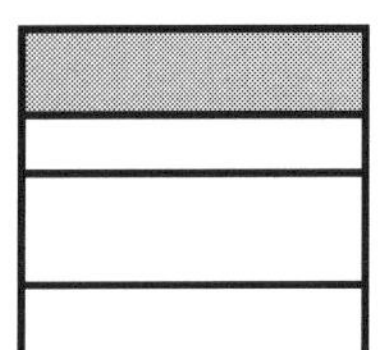 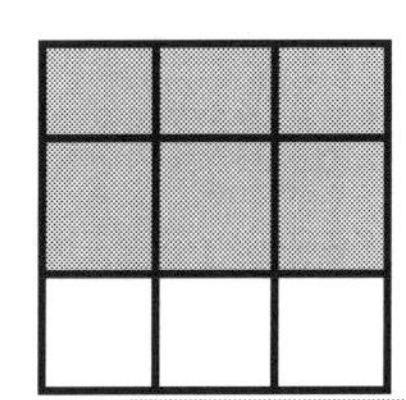

Common Core Standard 3.NF.3 – Numbers & Operations – Fractions

☐ **The models are shaded to show that _____**

A $\frac{2}{3} < \frac{1}{6}$

B $\frac{1}{3} = \frac{1}{6}$

C $\frac{5}{6} > \frac{2}{3}$

D $\frac{2}{3} > \frac{5}{6}$

$\frac{1}{3}$ $\frac{1}{3}$ $\frac{1}{3}$

$\frac{1}{6}$ $\frac{1}{6}$ $\frac{1}{6}$ $\frac{1}{6}$ $\frac{1}{6}$ $\frac{1}{6}$

Common Core Standard 3.NF.3 – Numbers & Operations – Fractions

☐ **Which number fits the missing value for the fraction below?**

$$\frac{36}{54} = \frac{\quad}{6}$$

A 6

B 3

C 2

D 4

Name ____________________________

ASSESSMENT

Common Core Standard 3.NF.3 – Numbers & Operations – Fractions

☐ **Look at the shaded parts of the figures. Which statement shows the fraction model?**

A $\frac{9}{12} = \frac{1}{9}$

B $\frac{9}{18} > \frac{1}{2}$

C $\frac{9}{18} = \frac{1}{2}$

D $\frac{9}{18} < \frac{1}{4}$

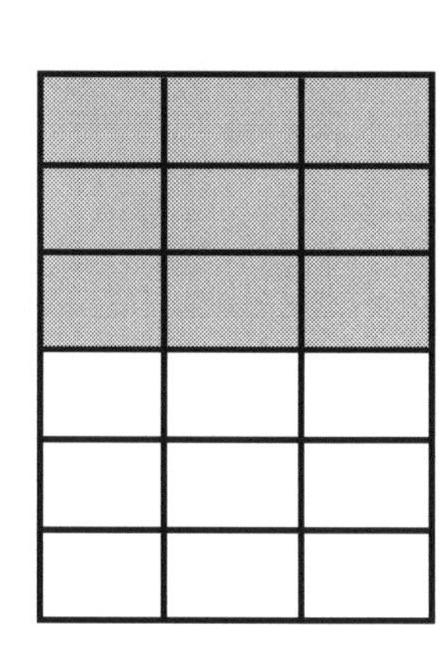

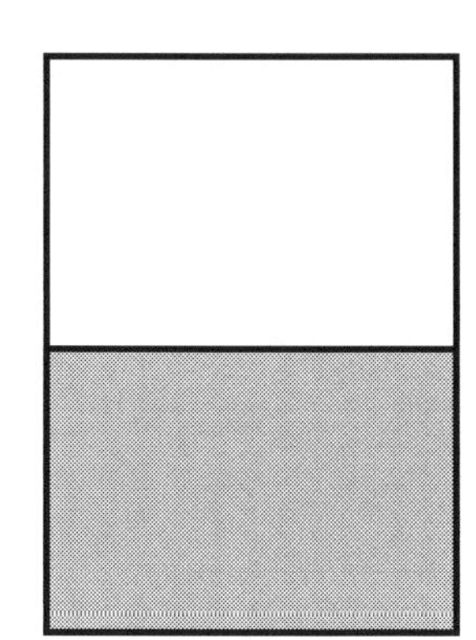

Common Core Standard 3.NF.3 – Numbers & Operations - Fractions

☐ **Which sign fits the missing value for the fraction below?**

$$\frac{3}{4} \square \frac{5}{10}$$

A >

B <

C =

D None of the above

Common Core Standard 3.NF.3 – Numbers & Operations – Fractions

☐ **The 2 shapes are shaded to show that ______**

A $\frac{7}{8} > \frac{3}{4}$

B $\frac{1}{4} < \frac{1}{8}$

C $\frac{3}{4} = \frac{7}{8}$

D $\frac{1}{8} > \frac{1}{4}$

| $\frac{1}{8}$ | $\frac{1}{8}$ | $\frac{1}{8}$ | $\frac{1}{8}$ | $\frac{1}{8}$ | $\frac{1}{8}$ | $\frac{1}{8}$ | $\frac{1}{8}$ |
|---|---|---|---|---|---|---|---|

| $\frac{1}{4}$ | $\frac{1}{4}$ | $\frac{1}{4}$ | $\frac{1}{4}$ |
|---|---|---|---|

Name ____________________

**DIAGNOSTIC**

Common Core Standard 3.MD.1 – Measurement & Data

☐ **Which clock shows 2 hours before 8 o'clock?**

   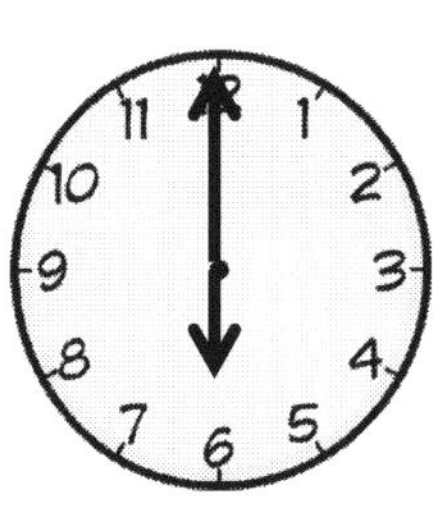

**A** **B** **C** **D**

Common Core Standard 3.MD.1 – Measurement & Data

☐ **Which clock shows the time 6:45?**

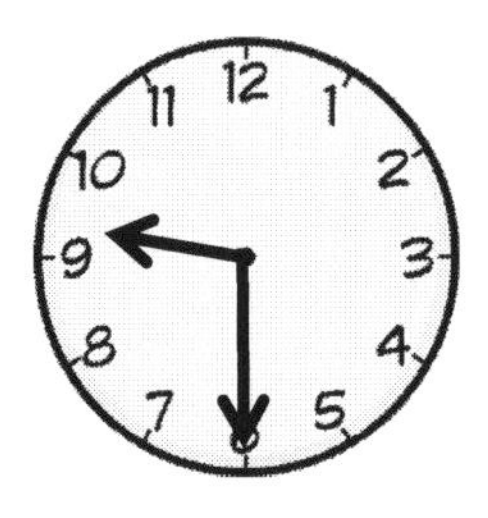  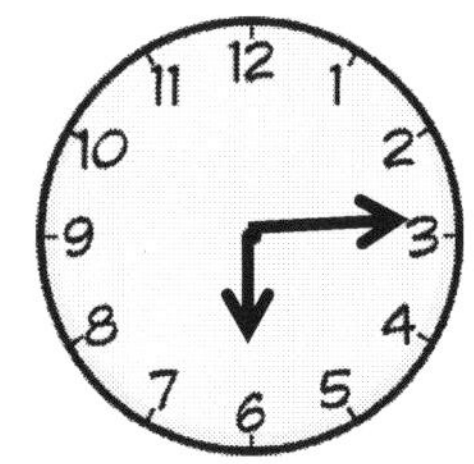 

**A** **B** **C** **D**

Common Core Standard 3.MD.1 – Measurement & Data

☐ **Pedro's favorite TV show begins in 15 minutes. It is now 8:45. Which clock shows the time that Pedro's TV show will begin?**

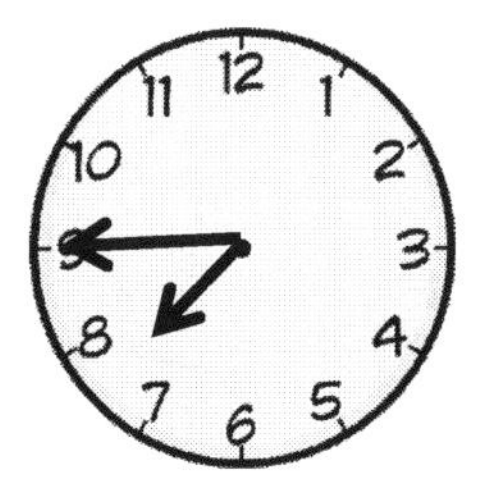   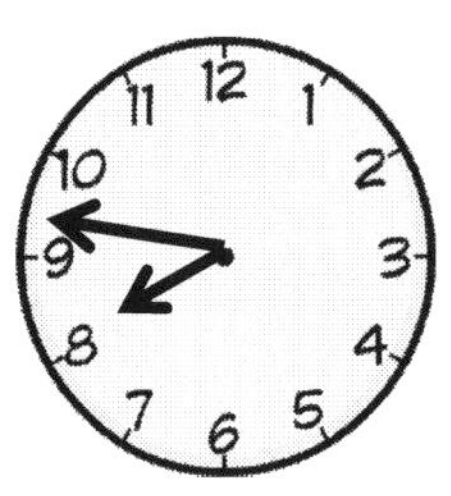

**A** **B** **C** **D**

Name ____________________

**DIAGNOSTIC**

Common Core Standard 3.MD.1 – Measurement & Data

☐ **Look at the clock. Which clock below shows the same time?**

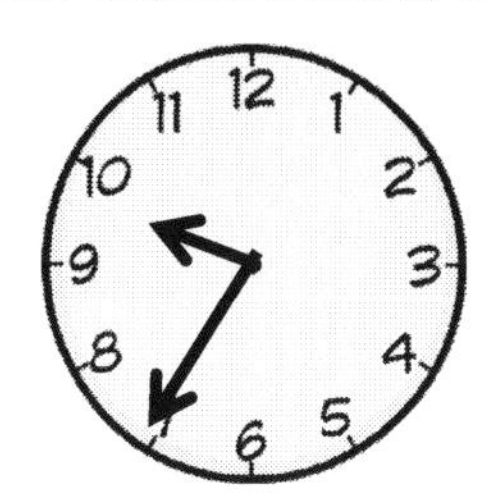

| 7:10 | 9:35 | 10:07 | 7:50 |
|---|---|---|---|
| A | B | C | D |

Common Core Standard 3.MD.1 – Measurement & Data

☐ **What time is shown on the clock?**

**A** 2:01

**B** 1:10

**C** 2:05

**D** 2:10

Common Core Standard 3.MD.1 – Measurement & Data

☐ **Which clock shows a time *between* 4:00 and 5:00?**

A

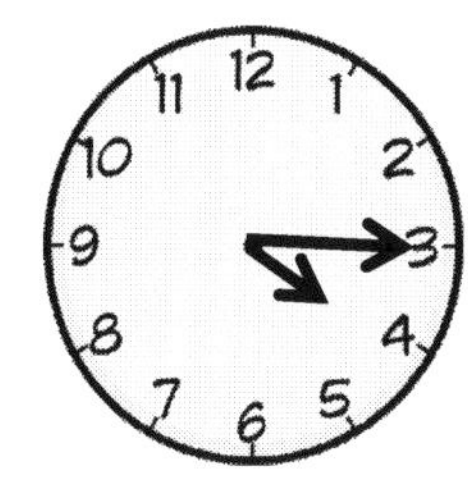

B

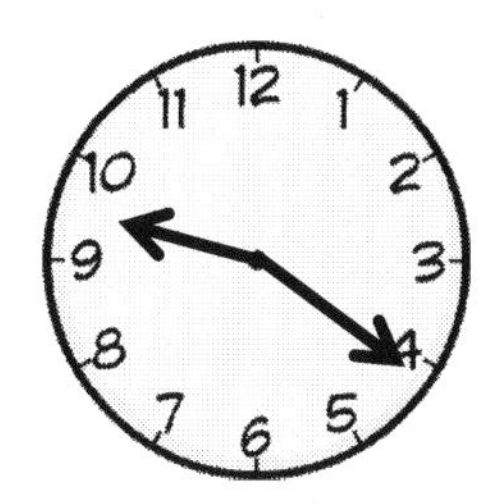

C

D

Name ________________________

**PRACTICE**

Common Core Standard 3.MD.1 – Measurement & Data

☐ **Which clock shows three and one-half hours past 4:30?**

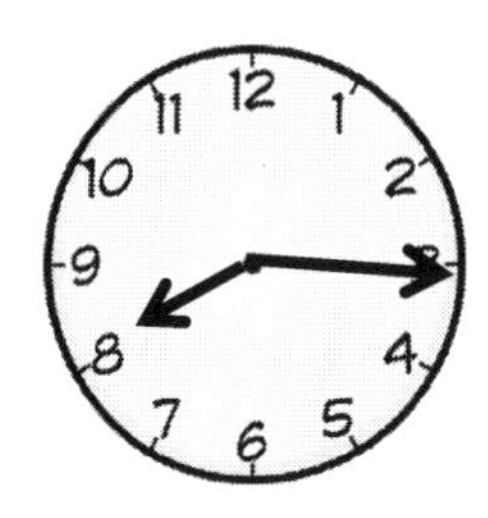

A B C D

Common Core Standard 3.MD.1 – Measurement & Data

☐ **Ricardo's best friend is coming for a visit in 20 minutes. It is now 1:45. Which clock shows the time Ricardo's friend will arrive at his house?**

A B C D

Common Core Standard 3.MD.1 – Measurement & Data

☐ **Look at the clock. Which clock below shows the same time?**

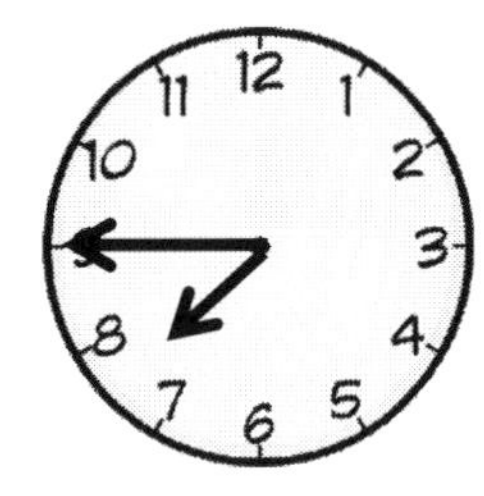

| 7:45 | 8:09 | 7:15 | 6:45 |
|---|---|---|---|
| A | B | C | D |

Name ______________________

**PRACTICE**

Common Core Standard 3.MD.1 – Measurement & Data

☐ **What time is shown on the clock?**

**A** **5:06**

**B** **6:30**

**C** **5:60**

**D** **5:30**

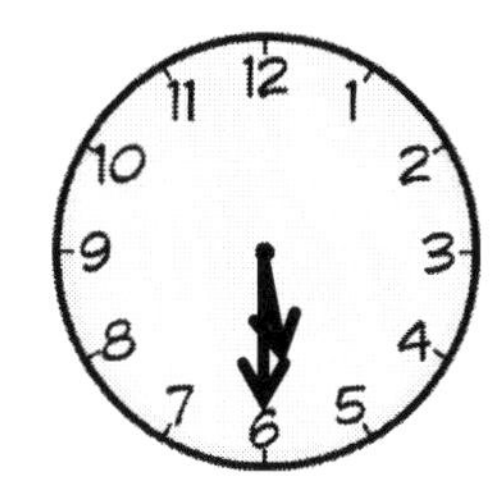

Common Core Standard 3.MD.1 – Measurement & Data

☐ **Which clock shows a time *between* 3:20 and 4:20?**

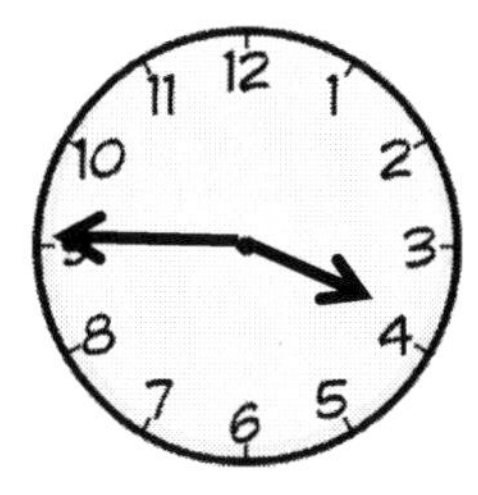

**A** **B** **C** **D**

Common Core Standard 3.MD.1 – Measurement & Data

☐ **Which clock shows four hours and fifteen minutes past 9:45?**

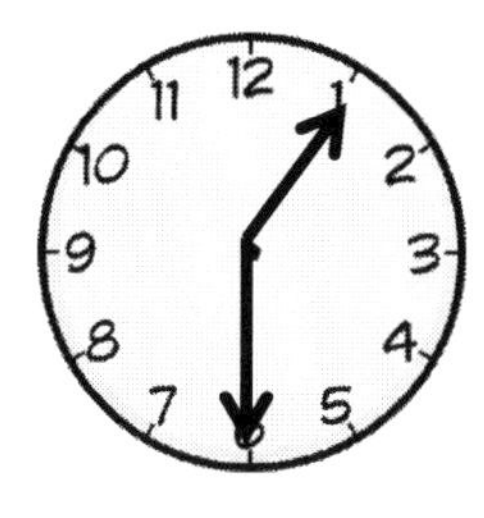

**A** **B** **C** **D**

Name ________________________

**PRACTICE**

Common Core Standard 3.MD.1 – Measurement & Data

☐ **What time is shown on the clock?**

**A** Half past eleven o'clock

**B** Quarter until eleven 'clock

**C** Quarter after eleven 'clock

**D** Quarter until ten o'clock

Common Core Standard 3.MD.1 – Measurement & Data

☐ **A professional swimmer held her breath for two minutes. How many seconds did she hold her breath?**

**A** 60 seconds

**B** 60 minutes

**C** 120 minutes

**D** 120 seconds

Common Core Standard 3.MD.1 – Measurement & Data

☐ **Which clock shows forty-five minutes until five o'clock?**

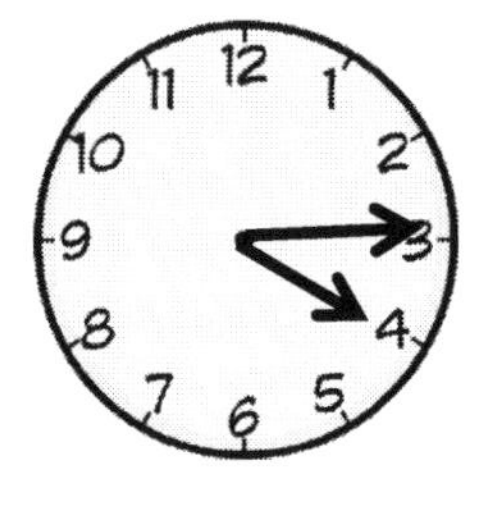

**A**

**B**

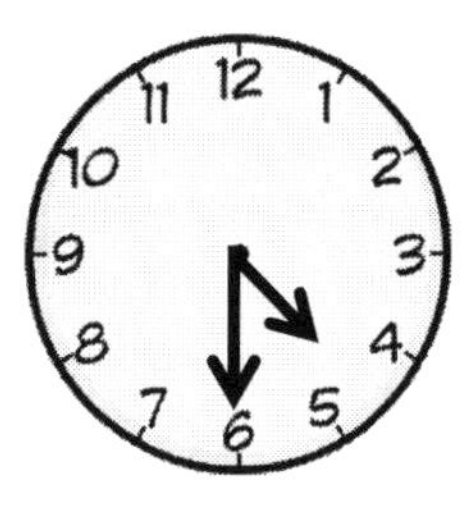

**C**

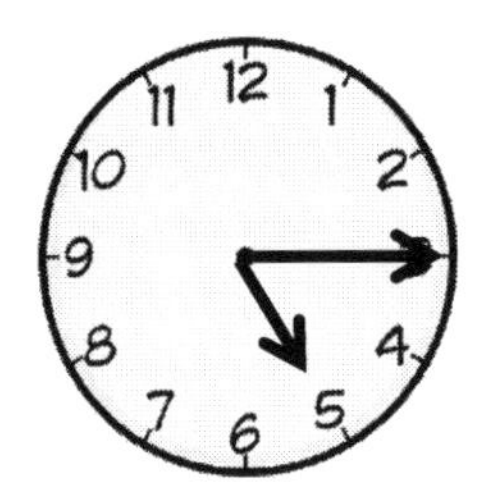

**D**

Name ____________________

PRACTICE

Common Core Standard 3.MD.1 – Measurement & Data

☐ Which clock shows the same time as the watch?

| 3:09 | 9:03 | 9:15 | 3:45 |
|---|---|---|---|
| A | B | C | D |

Common Core Standard 3.MD.1 – Measurement & Data

☐ Mr. Butler worked 8 hours on Monday. How many minutes has he worked on Monday?

A 80 minutes

B 480 minutes

C 400 minutes

D 96 minutes

Common Core Standard 3.MD.1 – Measurement & Data

☐ Bethany and her family left at 11:45 AM for their vacation. It took them 6 hours to reach their destination. What time did they arrive?

A 5:45 AM

B 6:45 PM

C 4:45 PM

D 5:45 PM

Name ______________________

**ASSESSMENT**

Common Core Standard 3.MD.1 – Measurement & Data

☐ **Which clock shows 15 minutes past 8:00?**

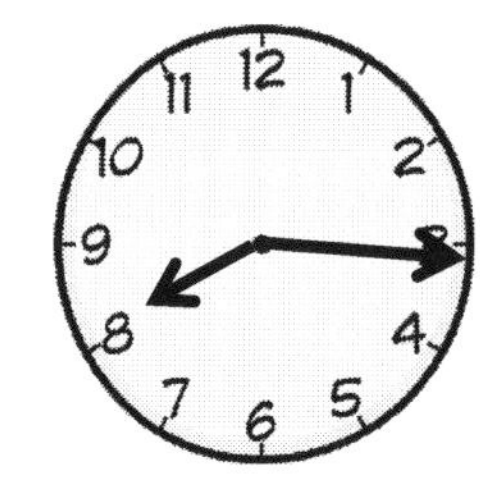

**A** **B** **C** **D**

Common Core Standard 3.MD.1 – Measurement & Data

☐ **What time is shown on the clock?**

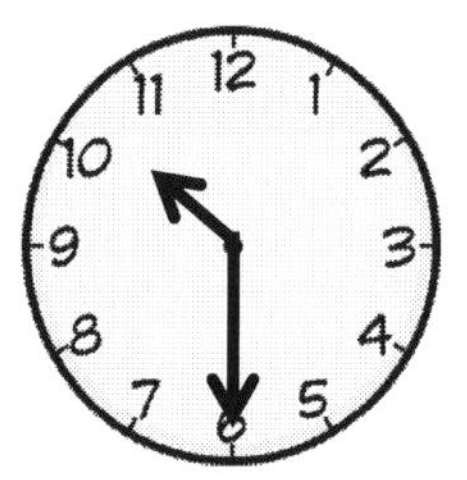

**A** **Quarter past ten o'clock**

**B** **Ten o'clock**

**C** **Quarter until ten o'clock**

**D** **Half past ten o'clock**

Common Core Standard 3.MD.1 – Measurement & Data

☐ **Jason rode his bicycle for one hour. How many *minutes* did he ride his bicycle?**

**A** **60 seconds**

**B** **60 minutes**

**C** **30 minutes**

**D** **12 minutes**

Name ________________________

**ASSESSMENT**

Common Core Standard 3.MD.1 – Measurement & Data

☐ **How many minutes are there in 48 hours?**

**A** **2860 minutes**

**B** **1152 minutes**

**C** **2880 minutes**

**D** **576 minutes**

Common Core Standard 3.MD.1 – Measurement & Data

☐ **Which clock shows thirty-five minutes until eight o'clock?**

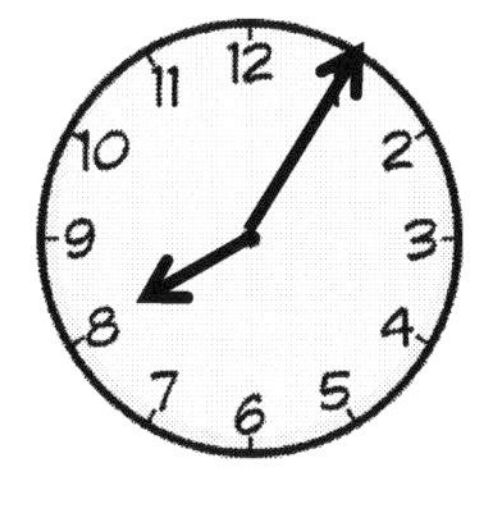

**A**

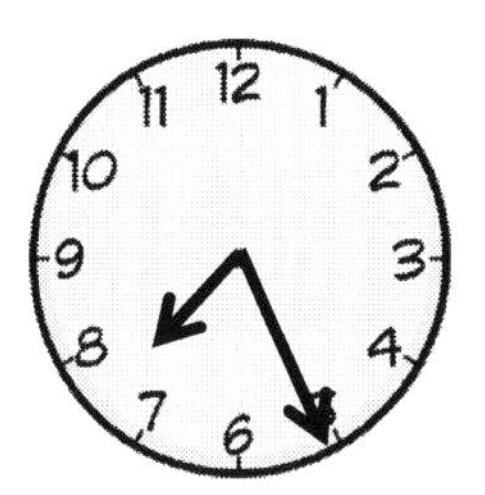

**B**

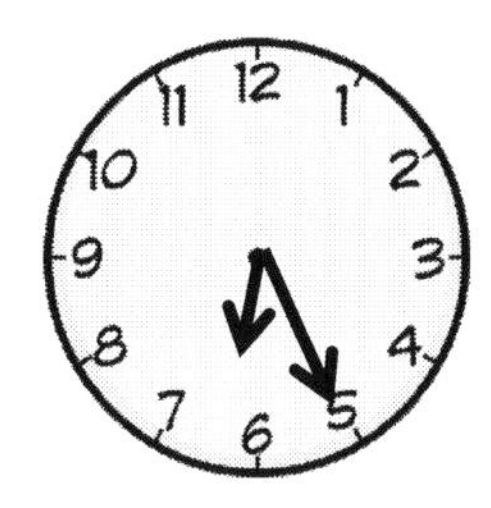

**C**

**D**

Common Core Standard 3.MD.1 – Measurement & Data

☐ **Which clock shows the same time as the watch?**

| 2:30 | 3:35 | 7:10 | 2:35 |
|---|---|---|---|
| **A** | **B** | **C** | **D** |

Name ________________________

**DIAGNOSTIC**

Common Core Standard 3.MD.2 – Measurement & Data

☐ **Which of the following objects would most likely weigh 4 pounds altogether?**

A an apple and a banana

B a puppy and a kitten

C a car and a kite

D a rabbit and a bicycle

Common Core Standard 3.MD.2 – Measurement & Data

☐ **Which container could hold only *up to* 8 ounces of water?**

A Container C

B Container B

C Container D

D Container A

A C B D

Common Core Standard 3.MD.2 – Measurement & Data

☐ **Which objects are most likely to have a mass of 6 kilograms?**

A adult man and a cat

B rabbit and a cat

C ant and a grasshopper

D teenager and a dog

Name ________________________

DIAGNOSTIC

Common Core Standard 3.MD.2 – Measurement & Data

☐ **Mrs. Womack bought a bottle of water to carry with her when she exercises. Which of the following could completely fill the bottle of water shown below?**

**A** 2 gallons

**B** 2 ounces

**C** 2 milliliters

**D** 2 liters

Common Core Standard 3.MD.2 – Measurement & Data

☐ **Which unit of measurement would most likely be used to measure the weight of an engine on a train?**

**A** Ounces

**B** Feet

**C** Grams

**D** Tons

Common Core Standard 3.MD.2 – Measurement & Data

☐ **Which container could *not* hold 16 ounces of liquid shown below?**

**A** Container D

**B** Container C

**C** Container A

**D** Container B

A

C

B

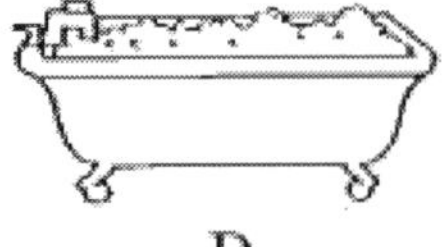

D

Name ________________________

**PRACTICE**

Common Core Standard 3.MD.2 – Measurement & Data

☐ **Which is the best estimate of the weight of the second box shown below?**

**A** 7 ounces

**B** 8 ounces

**C** 9 ounces

**D** 6 ounces

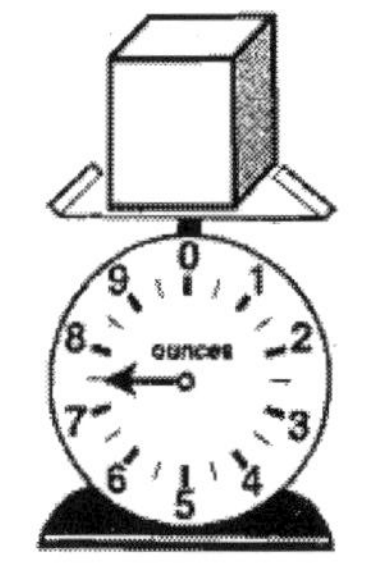
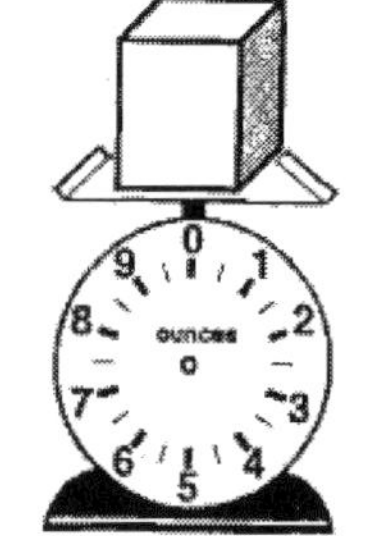
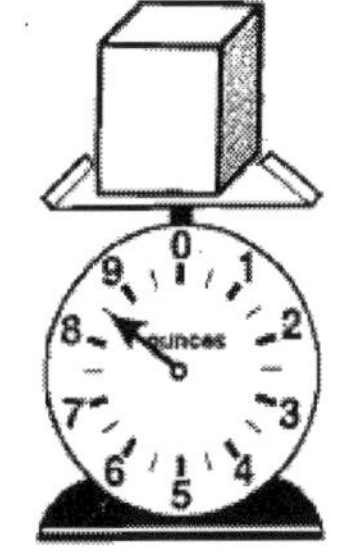
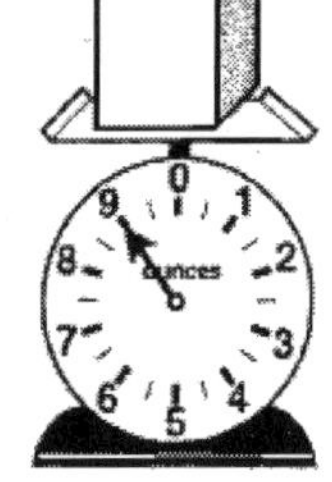

Common Core Standard 3.MD.2 – Measurement & Data

☐ **Which is the best estimate of the weight of a cat?**

**A** 35 pounds

**B** 15 ounces

**C** 6 grams

**D** 3 kilograms

Common Core Standard 3.MD.2 – Measurement & Data

☐ **Which is the best estimate of the weight of a pear?**

**A** 7 pounds

**B** 7 kilograms

**C** 7 ounces

**D** 7 milligrams

Name ___________________________

**PRACTICE**

Common Core Standard 3.MD.2 – Measurement & Data

☐ **Which is the best estimate of the weight of bananas shown below?**

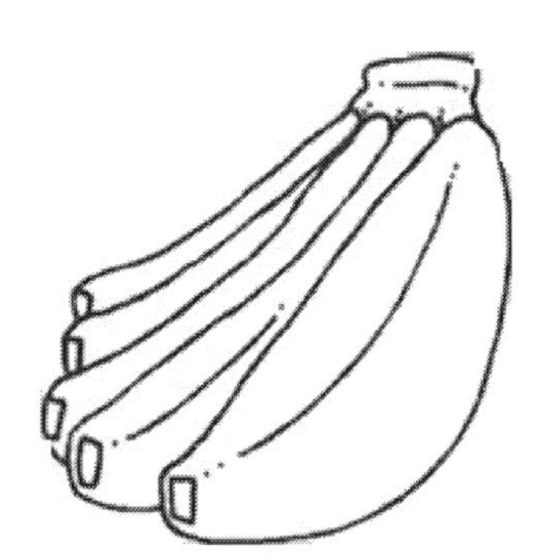

**A** 30 grams

**B** 5 kilograms

**C** 20 ounces

**D** 3 pints

Common Core Standard 3.MD.2 – Measurement & Data

☐ **Which object is most likely could hold 8 ounces?**

**A** Coffee Cup

**B** Milk Jug

**C** Bathtub

**D** Swimming Pool

Common Core Standard 3.MD.2 – Measurement & Data

☐ **Which is the best estimate of the weight of the elephant shown below?**

**A** 300 grams

**B** 4 tons

**C** 500 ounces

**D** 100 pounds

Name ______________________

PRACTICE

Common Core Standard 3.MD.2 – Measurement & Data

☐ **Which is the best estimate of the weight of an egg below?**

A 2 kilograms

B 15 grams

C 2 ounces

D 1 pound

Common Core Standard 3.MD.2 – Measurement & Data

☐ **Which is the best estimate of the weight of a car?**

A 1.5 tons

B 100 ounces

C 500 pounds

D 20 gallons

Common Core Standard 3.MD.2 – Measurement & Data

☐ **Which is the best estimate of the weight of a whale?**

A 90 pounds

B 90 kilograms

C 90 ounces

D 90 milligrams

Name ____________________

PRACTICE

Common Core Standard 3.MD.2 – Measurement & Data

☐ **If Jeff has a 48 pound bag of peaches and he puts each individual peach in 6 bags equally. What is the weight of each bag of peaches?**

A 42 pounds

B 8 kilograms

C 6 pounds

D 8 pounds

Common Core Standard 3.MD.2 – Measurement & Data

☐ **Which object is most likely could hold 1 gallon?**

A Soft Drink

B Milk Jug

C Bathtub

D Swimming Pool

Common Core Standard 3.MD.2 – Measurement & Data

☐ **Which is the best estimate of the weight of the pencil below?**

A 6 ounces

B 6 grams

C 1 kilogram

D 1/2 pound

Name ______________________

ASSESSMENT

Common Core Standard 3.MD.2 – Measurement & Data

☐ Which object is most likely to have a mass of 3 kilograms?

A Deck of cards

B Mattress

C Stamp

D Bag of sugar

Common Core Standard 3.MD.2 – Measurement & Data

☐ Mr. Douglas filled a pail with water. How much water could he have put in the pail shown below?

A 50 liters

B 500 liters

C 5 liters

D 5000 liters

Common Core Standard 3.MD.2 – Measurement & Data

☐ Which of the following objects would most likely be on the scale if the weight of the object is 2 ounces?

A Bag of oranges

B Gallon jug of milk

C Jelly sandwich

D Car

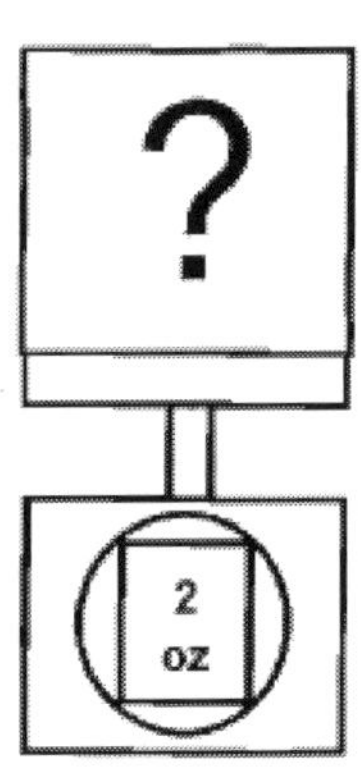

Name ______________________

ASSESSMENT

Common Core Standard 3.MD.2 – Measurement & Data

☐ **When filled with liquid, which object is most likely to have a capacity of 64 ounces?**

A Swimming pool

B Backpack

C Coffee pot

D Pond

Common Core Standard 3.MD.2 – Measurement & Data

☐ **Which object is most likely to have a mass of 15 grams?**

A Envelope

B Bicycle

C Tomato

D Book

Common Core Standard 3.MD.2 – Measurement & Data

☐ **Which container could hold 3500 mL of lemonade from below?**

A Container C

B Container D

C Container B

D Container A

A

C

B

D

Name ________________________

**DIAGNOSTIC**

Common Core Standard 3.MD.3 – Measurement & Data

☐ 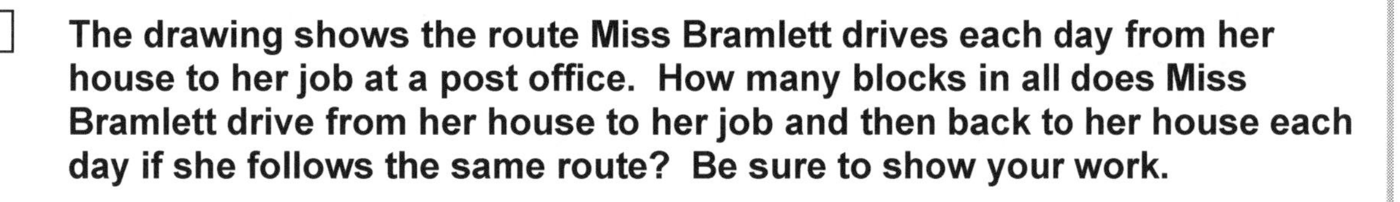

**The drawing shows the route Miss Bramlett drives each day from her house to her job at a post office. How many blocks in all does Miss Bramlett drive from her house to her job and then back to her house each day if she follows the same route? Be sure to show your work.**

**A 10 blocks**

**B 9 blocks**

**C 20 blocks**

**D 18 blocks**

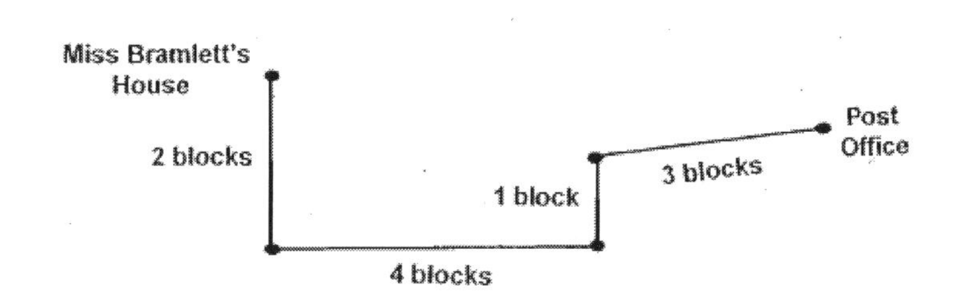


Common Core Standard 3.MD.3 – Measurement & Data

☐ **The drawing shows the number of timbers Mr. Baker used to border a vegetable garden and a flower garden. How many timbers in all did Mr. Baker use in both gardens? Be sure to show your work.**

**A 6 timbers**

**B 12 timbers**

**C 22 timbers**

**D 28 timbers**

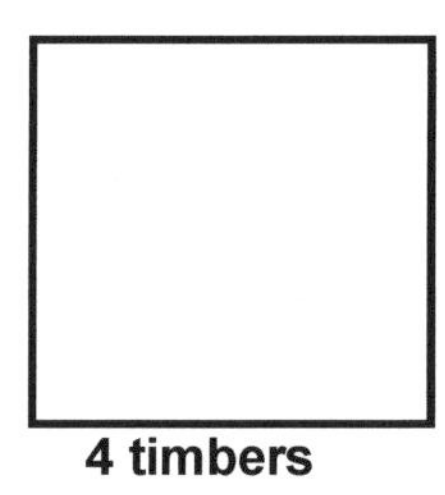

4 timbers

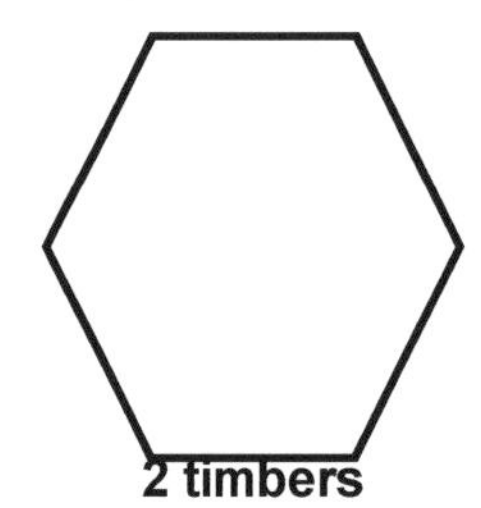

2 timbers

Common Core Standard 3.MD.3 – Measurement & Data

☐ **Cindy and her father like to hike. The drawing shows the trail they took on their hike last weekend. If they followed the same trail, how many miles in all did Cindy and her father hike from Lawson Park to Lookout Hill and then back to Lawson Park? Be sure to show your work.**

**A 11 mi.**

**B 22 mi.**

**C 20 mi.**

**D 12 mi.**

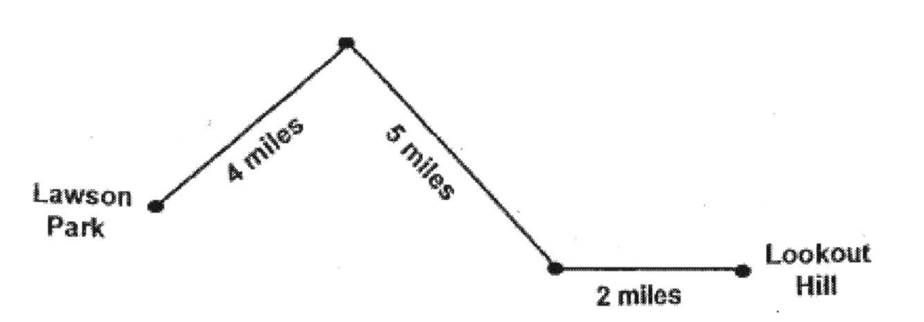

Name ____________________________

**DIAGNOSTIC**

Common Core Standard 3.MD.3 – Measurement & Data

☐ **A group of students made a tally chart of the number of cars parked in a school parking lot on 4 days.**

| | |
|---|---|
| **Monday** | 𝍸 𝍸 |
| **Tuesday** | 𝍸 𝍸 \|\| |
| **Wednesday** | 𝍸 \|\|\| |
| **Thursday** | 𝍸 𝍸 |

**Each tally mark means 2 cars.**

**Which graph matches the facts given in the chart?**

**A**

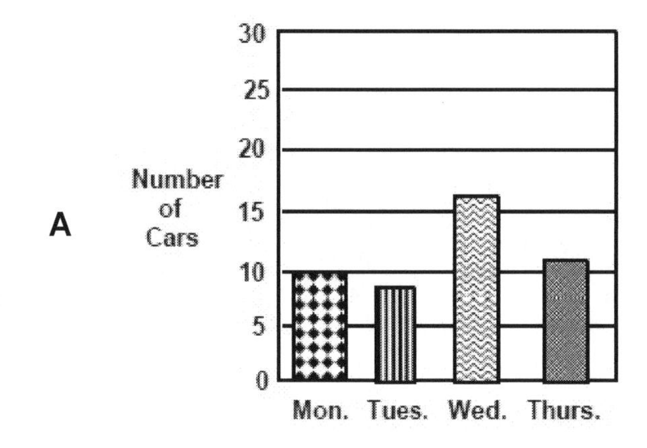


**C**

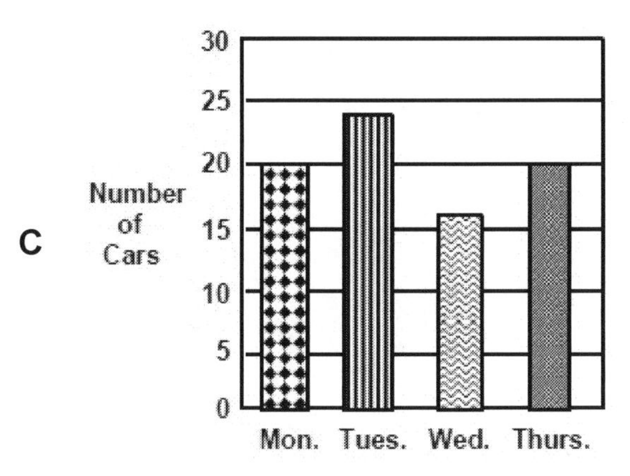


**B**

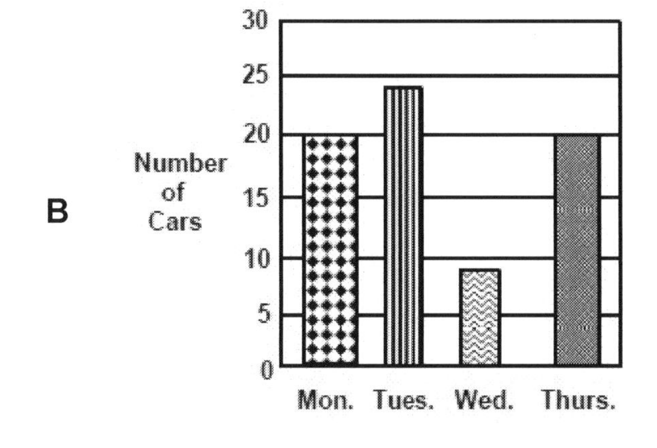


**D**

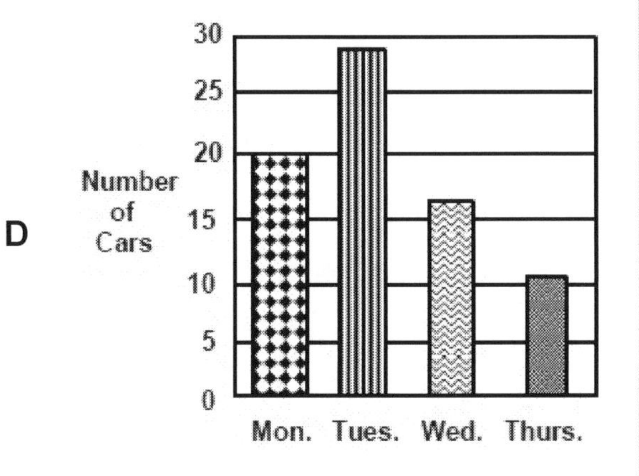

Name ____________________________

**PRACTICE**

Common Core Standard 3.MD.3 – Measurement & Data

☐ **Megan read 10 pages on Monday. According to the time line, on which day did she read the greatest number of pages?**

**A** Wednesday

**B** Thursday

**C** Monday

**D** Tuesday

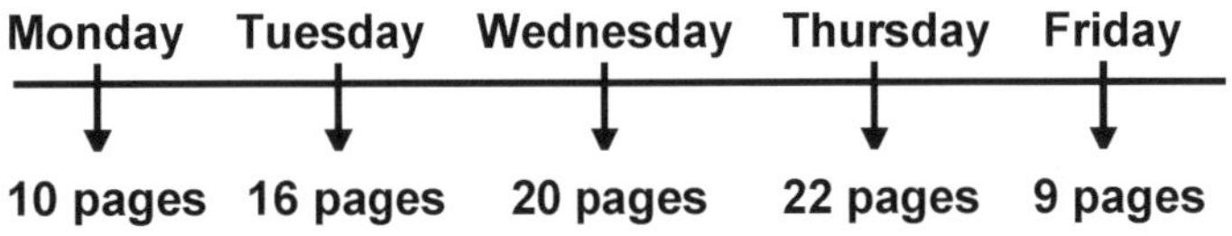

| Monday | Tuesday | Wednesday | Thursday | Friday |
|---|---|---|---|---|
| 10 pages | 16 pages | 20 pages | 22 pages | 9 pages |

Common Core Standard 3.MD.3 – Measurement & Data

☐ **Mr. Tucker asked his students to choose their favorite vegetable from a list of 4 vegetables. Carrots and peas received 2 votes each, corn received 14 votes, and beans received 4 votes. Which graph shows this information?**

**A**

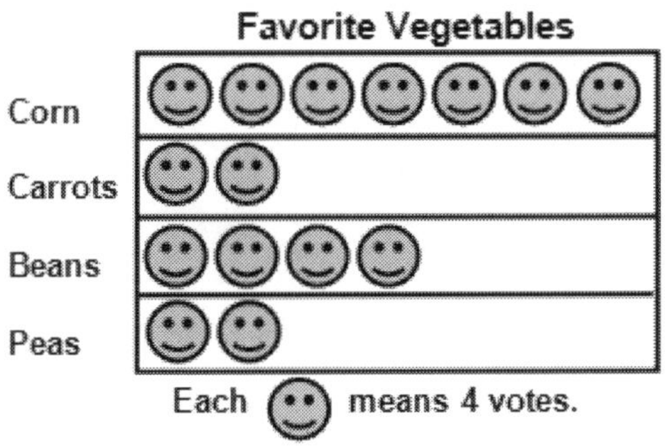

Favorite Vegetables

Corn

Carrots

Beans

Peas

Each ☺ means 4 votes.

**C**

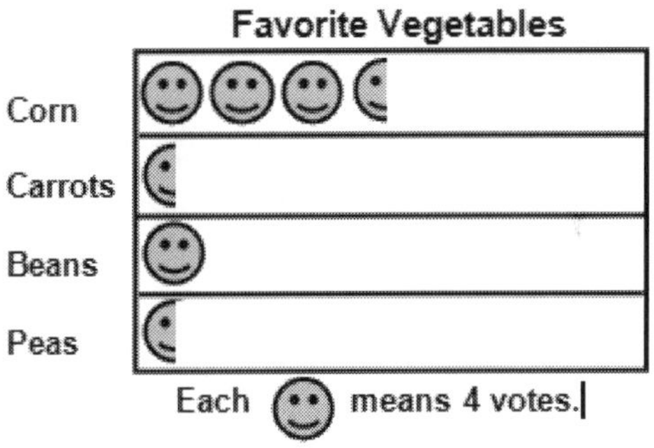

Favorite Vegetables

Corn

Carrots

Beans

Peas

Each ☺ means 4 votes.

**B**

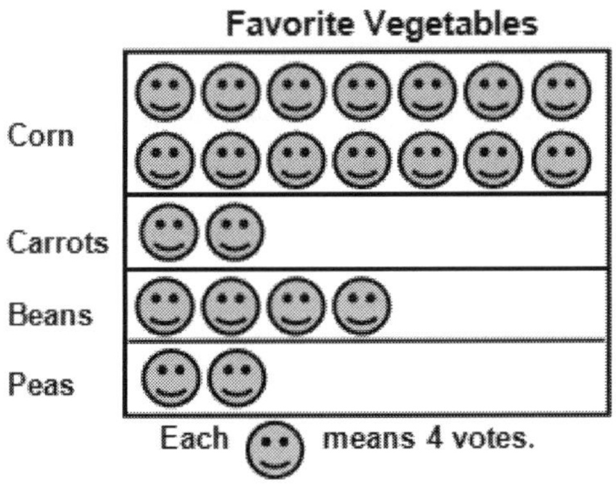

Favorite Vegetables

Corn

Carrots

Beans

Peas

Each ☺ means 4 votes.

**D**

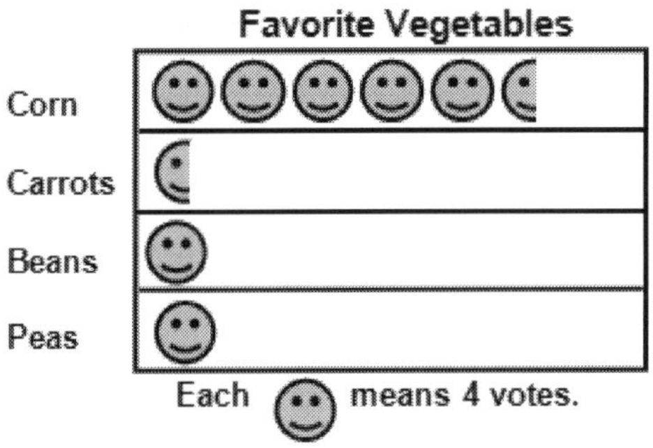

Favorite Vegetables

Corn

Carrots

Beans

Peas

Each ☺ means 4 votes.

Name ____________________

**PRACTICE**

Common Core Standard 3.MD.3 – Measurement & Data

☐ **The chart shows the number of computers in Forrest School.**

| FORREST SCHOOL COMPUTERS | |
|---|---|
| **Location** | **Number of Computers** |
| Library | 10 |
| Computer Lab | 20 |
| Office | 7 |

**Which graph matches the facts given in the chart?**

**A**

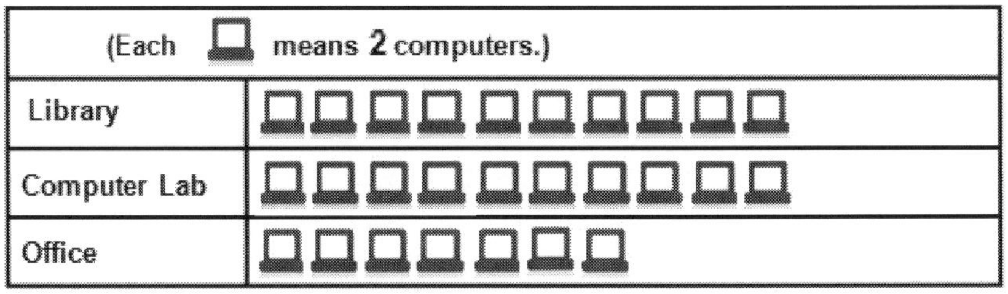

| (Each [computer] means 2 computers.) | |
|---|---|
| Library | |
| Computer Lab | |
| Office | |

**B**

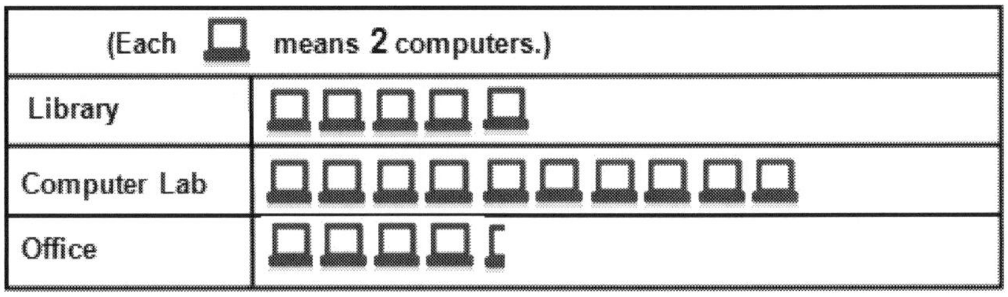

| (Each [computer] means 2 computers.) | |
|---|---|
| Library | |
| Computer Lab | |
| Office | |

**C**

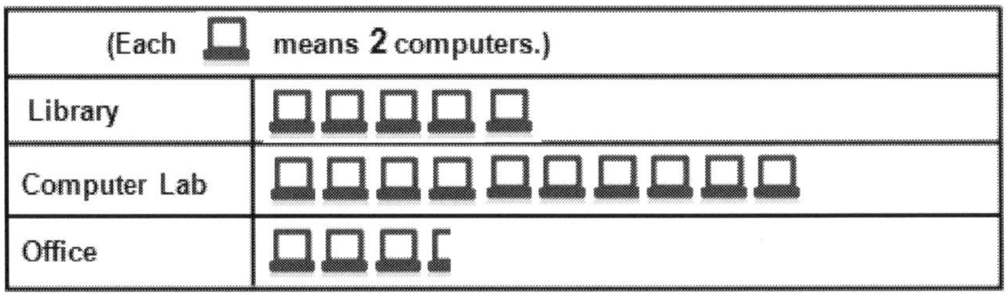

| (Each [computer] means 2 computers.) | |
|---|---|
| Library | |
| Computer Lab | |
| Office | |

**D**

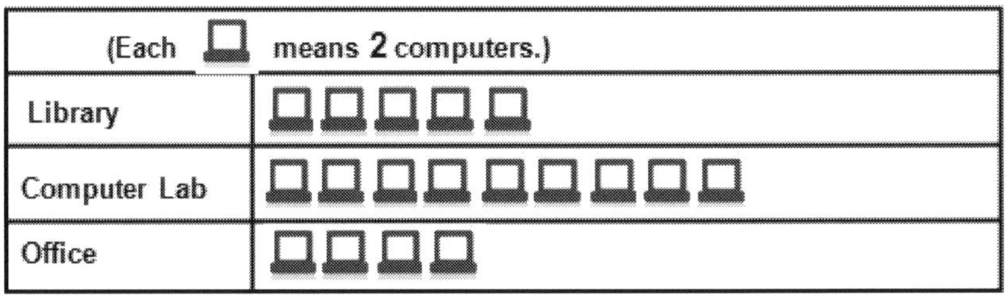

| (Each [computer] means 2 computers.) | |
|---|---|
| Library | |
| Computer Lab | |
| Office | |

Name ________________________

**PRACTICE**

Common Core Standard 3.MD.3 – Measurement & Data

☐ **The chart shows how the students in Brad's class get to school. Which information is needed to complete the chart?**

| Bus | | Walk | Bicycle |
|---|---|---|---|
| Gerald<br>Pete<br>Carlos<br>Carol | Tommy<br>Sara<br>Brad<br>Sharon | Sean<br>Lee<br>Amy<br>Gail<br>Abby | Phil<br>Jose<br>James<br>Mike |

**A** The total number of students in the class

**B** The day the chart was made

**C** The number of students who ride in a car

**D** The name of a way some students get to school

Common Core Standard 3.MD.3 – Measurement & Data

☐ **What would be a good title for this graph?**

**A** Phil's Age

**B** Phil's Height Each Year

**C** Height in Inches

**D** Age 8, 9, 10

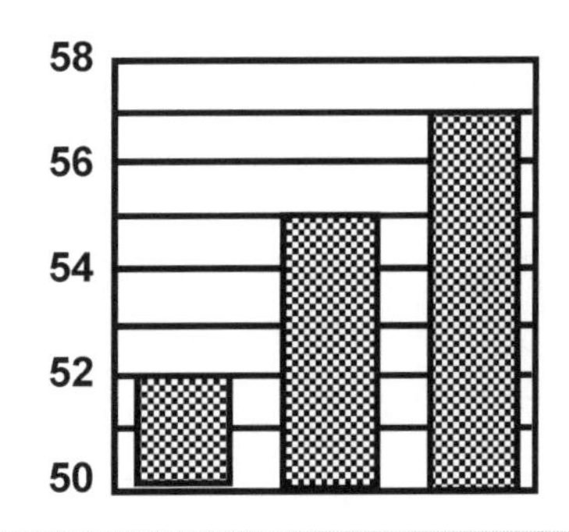


Common Core Standard 3.MD.3 – Measurement & Data

☐ **Anna made a graph. How did she collect the information found in it?**

**A** She filled in one square for each book she read.

**B** She added all the pages she read that week.

**C** She recorded the number of pages she read each day.

**D** She read 5 pages in a book every day.

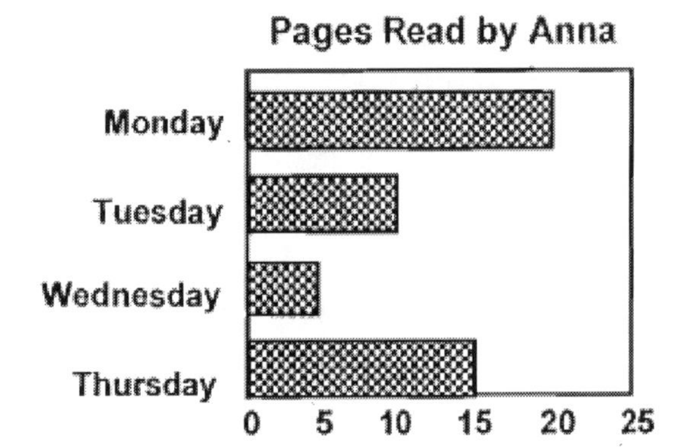

Name ____________________

**PRACTICE**

Common Core Standard 3.MD.3 – Measurement & Data

☐ **The third grade classes at Bingham Elementary voted for their favorite subject in school. The chart shows how the students voted.**

| Science | 𝍸 \| |
|---|---|
| Reading | 𝍸 |
| Math | 𝍸 \|\|\| |
| Language | \|\| |

Each tally mark means 10 votes.

**Which graph matches the tally chart?**

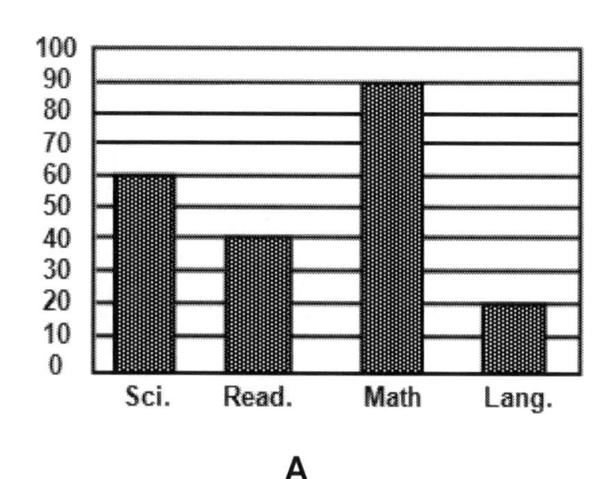


A

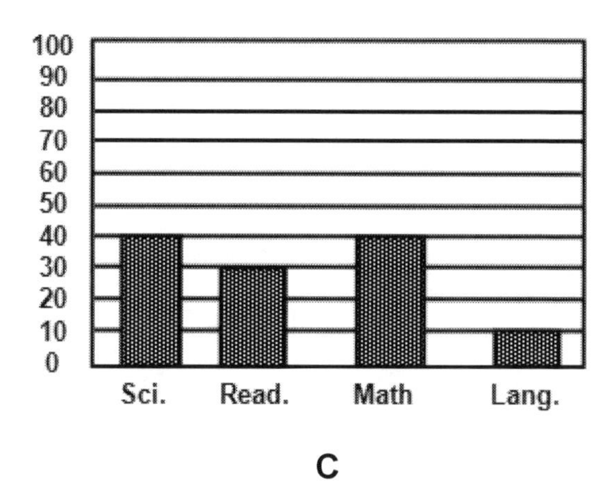


C

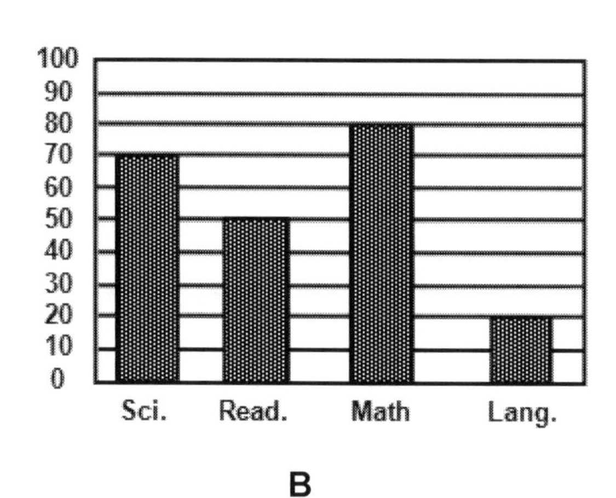


B

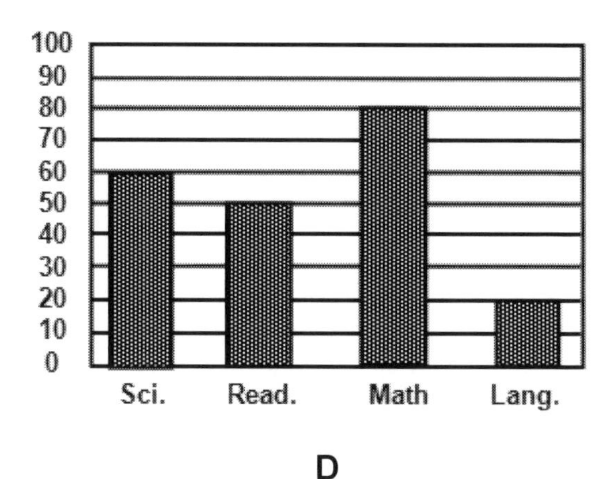


D

Name ___________________________

PRACTICE

Common Core Standard 3.MD.3 – Measurement & Data

☐ The graph shows the number of each kind of book that Miki read last month.

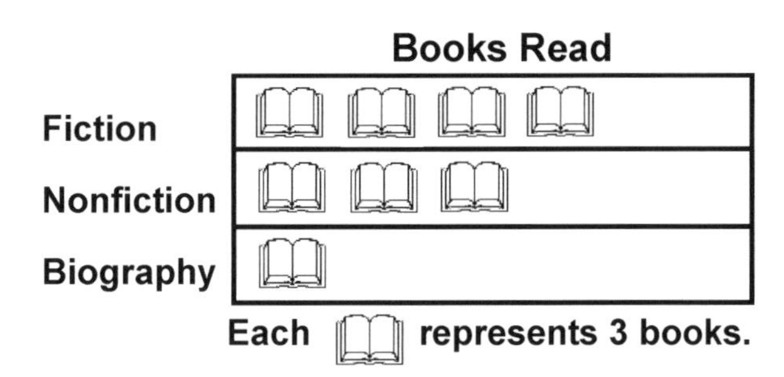


Which table matches the information on the graph?

A

Books Read

| Fiction | 4 |
|---|---|
| Nonfiction | 3 |
| Biography | 1 |

C

Books Read

| Fiction | 12 |
|---|---|
| Nonfiction | 9 |
| Biography | 3 |

B

Books Read

| Fiction | 12 |
|---|---|
| Nonfiction | 9 |
| Biography | 1 |

D

Books Read

| Fiction | 4 |
|---|---|
| Nonfiction | 3 |
| Biography | 3 |

Name ___________________________

**PRACTICE**

Common Core Standard 3.MD.3 – Measurement & Data

☐ **Sarah and Miranda recorded their piano practice time for one week. Each girl made a tally mark for every 20 minutes of practice.**

**Piano Practice**

| | |
|---|---|
| **Sarah** | ||| |
| **Miranda** | |||| |

**Each tally mark means 20 minutes.**

**Which graph matches the tally chart?**

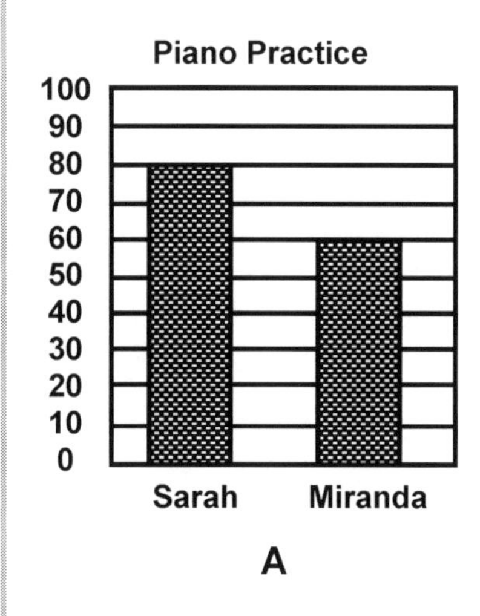


**A**

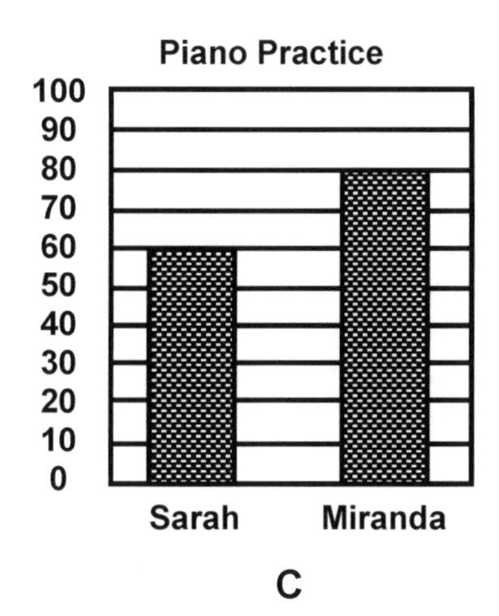


**C**

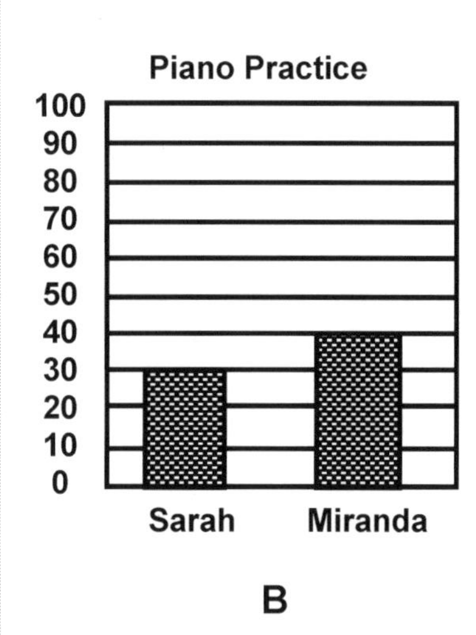


**B**

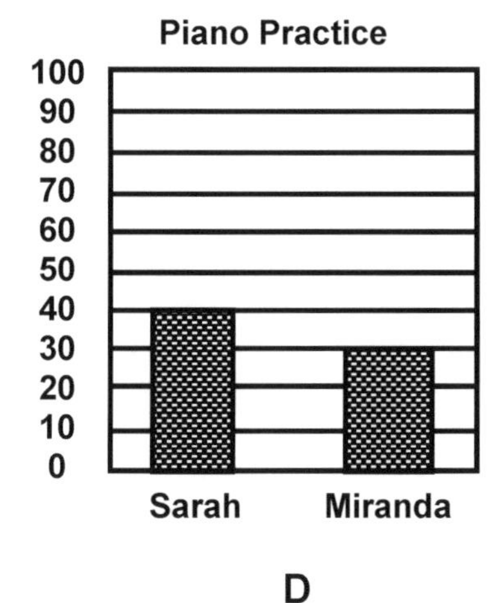


**D**

Name ______________________

**ASSESSMENT**

Common Core Standard 3.MD.3 – Measurement & Data

☐ **The graph shows the kinds of trees in Forest Park. Which information is needed to complete the graph?**

**A** The total number of trees in the park

**B** The number of trees counted

**C** A name of a kind of tree in the park

**D** The names of bushes in the park

Trees in Forest Park

| | |
|---|---|
| Oak | 🌳🌳🌳🌳🌳🌳🌳🌳🌳🌳 |
| Pine | 🌳🌳🌳🌳🌳🌳🌳🌳🌳🌳🌳🌳🌳 |
| Maple | 🌳🌳 |
| | 🌳🌳🌳 |
| Pecan | 🌳🌳🌳🌳🌳 |

🌳 = 3

Common Core Standard 3.MD.3 – Measurement & Data

☐ **The time line shows the amounts of money Walt spent on Saturday. How much did he spend on a book?**

**A** $7.00

**B** $2.00

**C** $5.00

**D** $10.00

Dollar Amounts

1 2 3 4 5 6 7 8 9 10

Soda (2), Ball (4), CD (5), T-Shirt (7), Book (10)

Common Core Standard 3.MD.3 – Measurement & Data

☐ **Amber is making a graph to show the number of books in each room. Which information was *not* needed to make the graph below?**

**A** The names of the books

**B** The value of each book picture

**C** The number of books for each room

**D** The number of books for Room A

| | |
|---|---|
| Room A | ▯▯▯▯▯▯ |
| Room B | ▯▯▯▯▯ |
| Room C | ▯▯▯▯▯▯▯ |
| Room D | ▯▯▯▯▯▯▯ |

Each ▯ = 5 books

Name ____________________

**ASSESSMENT**

Common Core Standard 3.MD.3 – Measurement & Data

☐ **Ms. Stone's class voted on their favorite kind of dog. The chart shows the number of students in Ms. Stone's class who voted for each kind of dog.**

| Kind of Dog | Mutts | Collies | Shepherds | Poodles |
|---|---|---|---|---|
| Number of Students | 9 | 2 | 6 | 4 |

**Which graph below matches the facts given in the chart?**

A

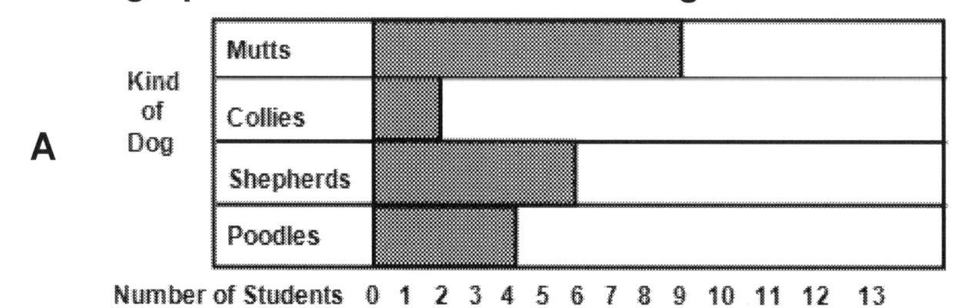


B

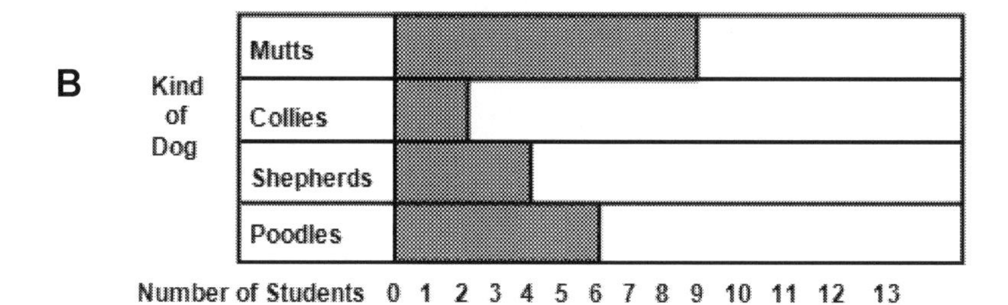


C

Kind of Dog

Mutts

Collies

Shepherds

Poodles

Number of Students 0 1 2 3 4 5 6 7 8 9 10 11 12 13

D

Kind of Dog

Mutts

Collies

Shepherds

Poodles

Number of Students 0 1 2 3 4 5 6 7 8 9 10 11 12 13

Name ______________________

**DIAGNOSTIC**

Common Core Standard 3.MD.4 – Measurement & Data

☐ **Look at the nail. How many inches long is it?**

A 1 inch

B 3 inches

C 4 inches

D 2 inches

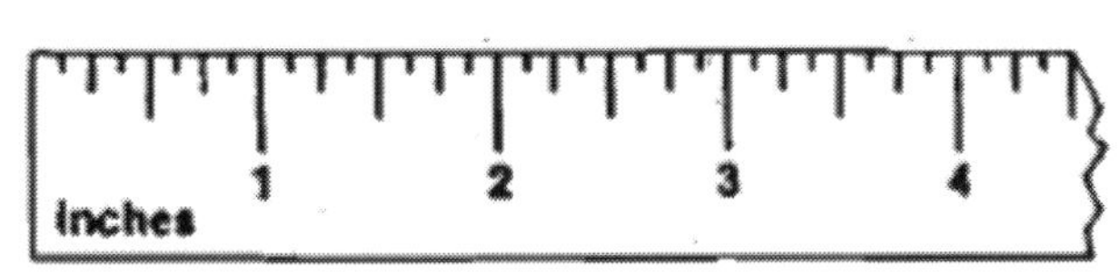

Common Core Standard 3.MD.4 – Measurement & Data

☐ **If you measure the length of the carrot using peanuts, how many peanuts long is the carrot?**

A 3

B 6

C 5

D 4

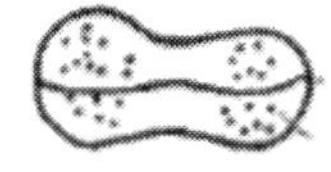

Common Core Standard 3.MD.4 – Measurement & Data

☐ **Look at the candle. How many inches tall is it?**

A 2 inches

B 4 inches

C 5 inches

D 3 inches

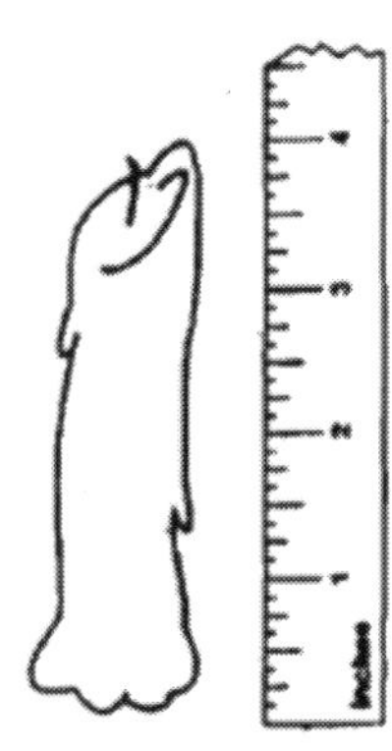

Name ___________________________

**DIAGNOSTIC**

Common Core Standard 3.MD.4 – Measurement & Data

☐ **Which paper clip measures 1 inch in length?**

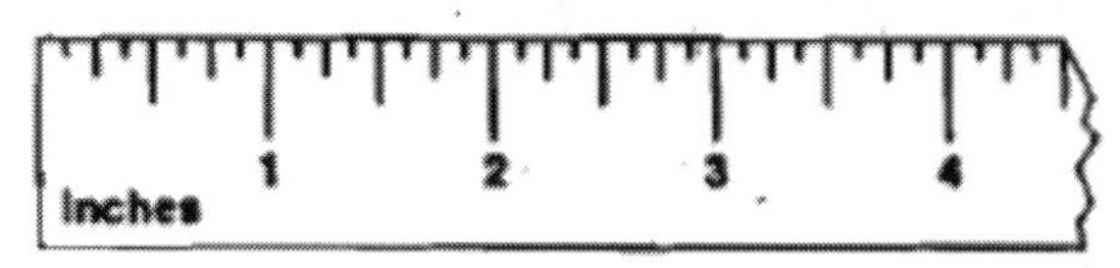


A

B

C

D

Common Core Standard 3.MD.4 – Measurement & Data

☐ **Look at the leaf. How many inches long are the leaf and its stem?**

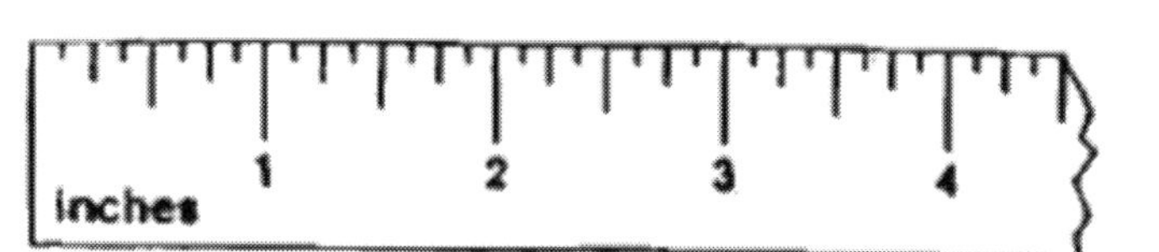

A **3 inches**

B **4 inches**

C **1 inch**

D **2 inches**

Common Core Standard 3.MD.4 – Measurement & Data

☐ **If you measure the length of the comb using paper clips, how many paper clips long is the comb?**

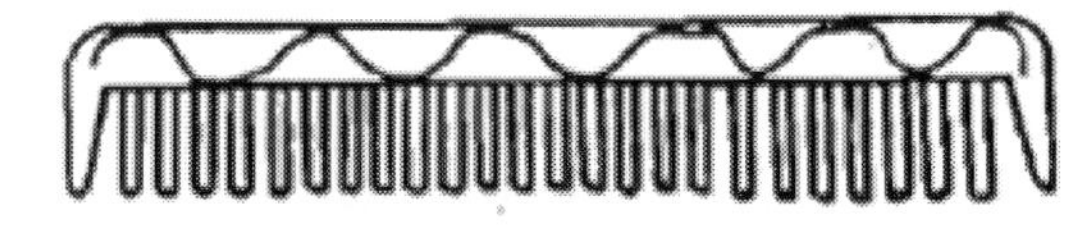

A **2**

B **3**

C **4**

D **5**

Name ________________________

**PRACTICE**

Common Core Standard 3.MD.4 – Measurement & Data

☐ 
**How many yards does a football field measure, from goal line to goal line?**

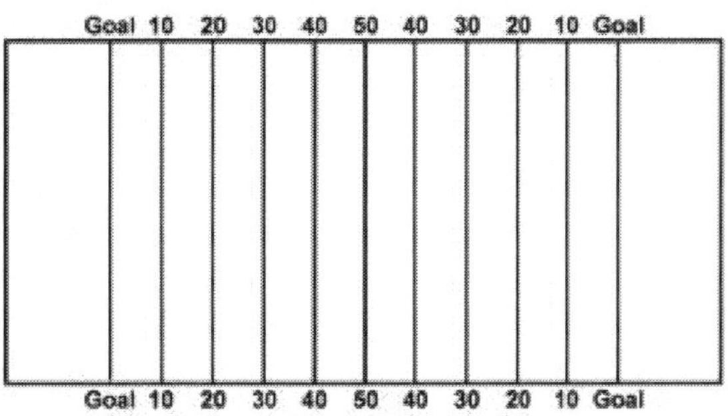


**A** 100 feet

**B** 50 yards

**C** 100 yards

**D** 200 yards

Common Core Standard 3.MD.4 – Measurement & Data

☐ 
**Look at the ruler below, approximately how many inches does 5 centimeters equal?**

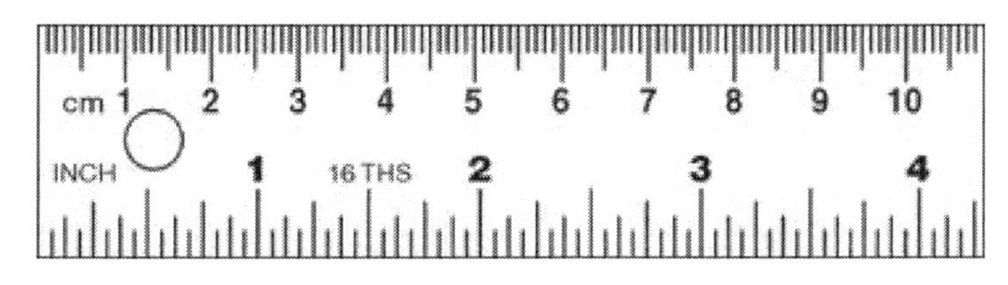


**A** 3 inches

**B** 5 inches

**C** 2 inches

**D** 1 inch

Common Core Standard 3.MD.4 – Measurement & Data

☐ **DeShawn wants to measure his little brother's foot. If he uses a 12 inch ruler, approximately what is the length of his little brother's foot?**

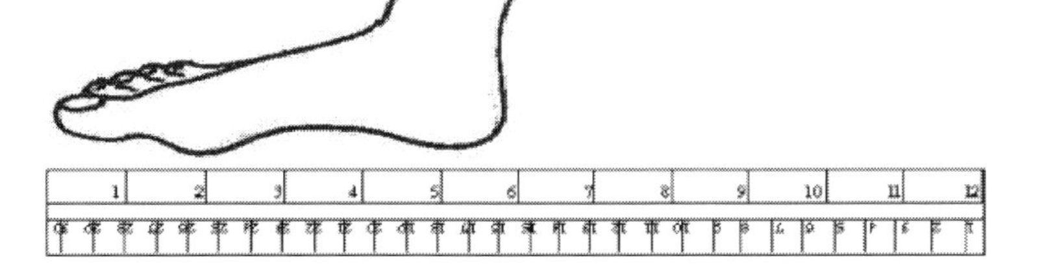


**A** 5 inches

**B** 7 inches

**C** 4 inches

**D** 6 inches

Name ____________________________

**PRACTICE**

Common Core Standard 3.MD.4 – Measurement & Data

☐ **Look at the picture below. What would be approximate length of the nail in centimeters?**

**A** **6 centimeters**

**B** **7 centimeters**

**C** **7 inches**

**D** **6 inches**

Common Core Standard 3.MD.4 – Measurement & Data

☐ **Look at the spoon. How many inches long is it?**

**A** **5 inches**

**B** **4 inches**

**C** **3 inches**

**D** **2inches**

Common Core Standard 3.MD.4 – Measurement & Data

☐ **Look at the boom box. How many inches tall is it?**

**A** **1 inch**

**B** **2 inches**

**C** **4 inches**

**D** **3 inches**

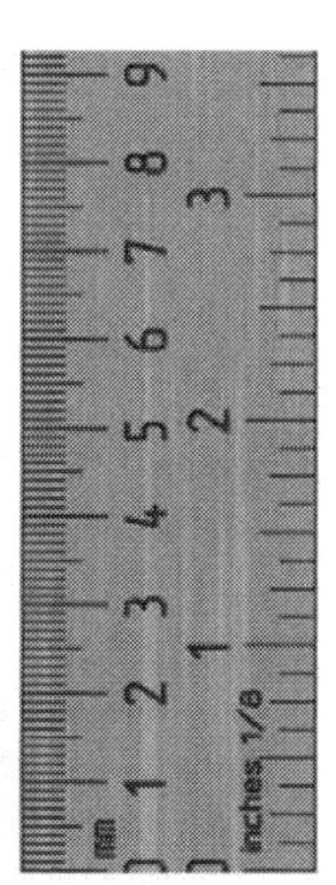

PRACTICE

Name ______________________

Common Core Standard 3.MD.4 – Measurement & Data

☐ **How long is the base of Michele's birthday present using the inch ruler below?**

**A** **7 inches**

**B** **6 inches**

**C** **7 feet**

**D** **8 inches**

Common Core Standard 3.MD.4 – Measurement & Data

☐ **If a yard equals 3 feet and Sam's back yard was measured at 9 yards, how many feet is Sam's back yard?**

**A** **27 feet**

**B** **12 feet**

**C** **3 yards**

**D** **12 yards**

Common Core Standard 3.MD.4 – Measurement & Data

☐ **Look at the picture below. What would be approximate length of the needle in centimeters?**

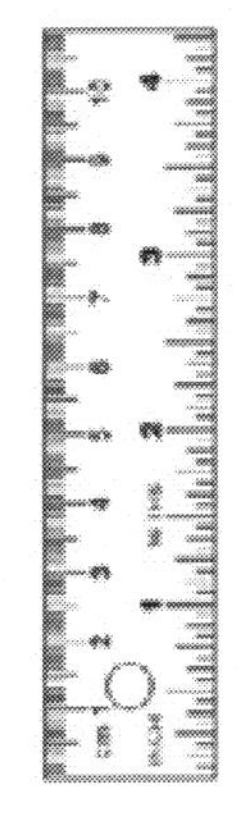

**A** **7 centimeters**

**B** **8 centimeters**

**C** **8 inches**

**D** **9 centimeters**

Name ___________________________

**PRACTICE**

Common Core Standard 3.MD.4 – Measurement & Data

☐ **Katie's mother wants to buy Katie a new bed for her room. Katie's room has only 72 inches of space left. If the bed is 5 feet long, how much room will Katie have left in her room?**

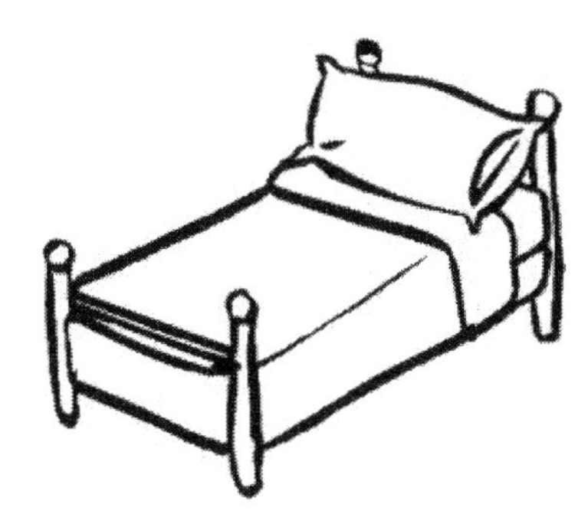

**A 77 inches**

**B 67 inches**

**C 12 inches**

**D 10 inches**

Common Core Standard 3.MD.4 – Measurement & Data

☐ **What is the approximate length of the cell phone pictured below in inches?**

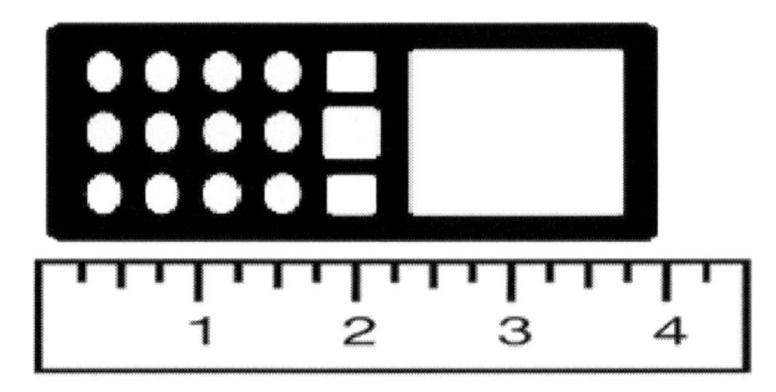


**A 5 inches**

**B 4 inches**

**C 3 inches**

**D 2inches**

Common Core Standard 3.MD.4 – Measurement & Data

☐ **If you measure the length of the bar below using pumpkins, how many pumpkins long is the bar?**

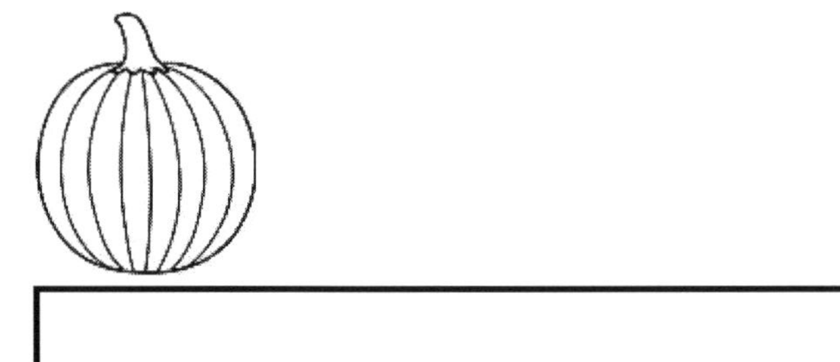

**A 2**

**B 3**

**C 4**

**D 5**

Name 

ASSESSMENT

Common Core Standard 3.MD.4 – Measurement & Data

☐ **Look at the soda can. How many inches tall is it?**

A 2 inches

B 4 inches

C 3 inches

D 5 inches

Common Core Standard 3.MD.4 – Measurement & Data

☐ **Which pencil measures 2 inches in length?**

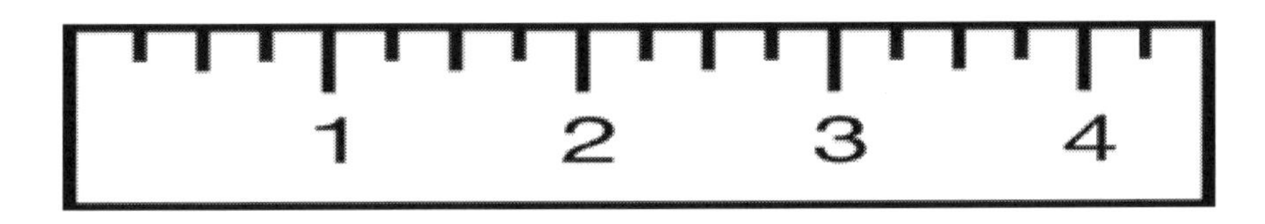


A

B

C

D

Common Core Standard 3.MD.4 – Measurement & Data

☐ **If you measure the length of the tube of toothpaste using a paper clip, approximately how many paper clips long is the tube of toothpaste?**

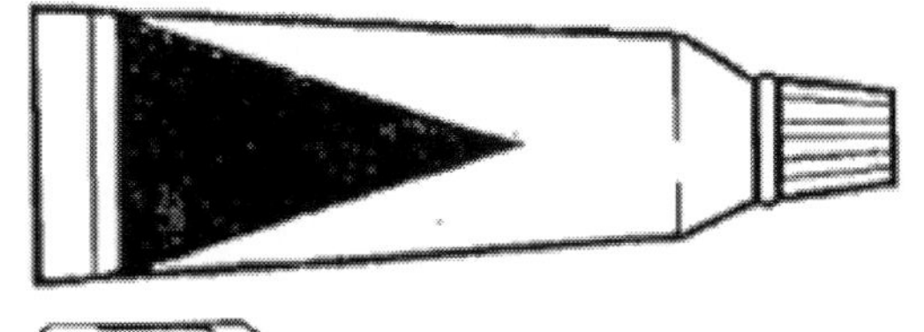

A 2

B 3

C 4

D 5

Name ____________________

**ASSESSMENT**

Common Core Standard 3.MD.4 – Measurement & Data

☐ **Look at the truck below. What would be approximate length of the truck if the box below is 5 feet long?**

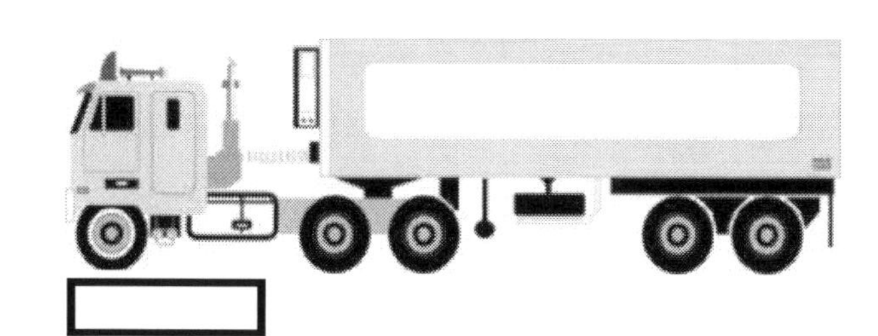

| | |
|---|---|
| A | 20 inches |
| B | 20 feet |
| C | 20 yards |
| D | 20 centimeters |

Common Core Standard 3.MD.4 – Measurement & Data

☐ **Which line below measures approximately 3 1/2 inches in length?**

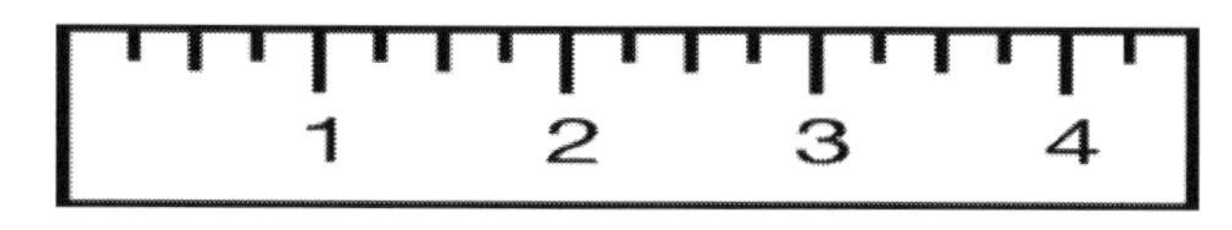

| | |
|---|---|
| A | *C* |
| B | *B* |
| C | *D* |
| D | *A* |

Common Core Standard 3.MD.4 – Measurement & Data

☐ **If you measure the height of button using the ruler next to it, approximately how tall is the button in centimeters?**

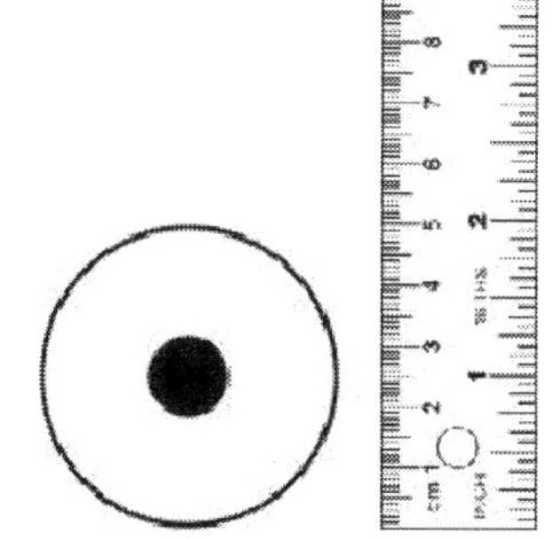

| | |
|---|---|
| A | 4 centimeters |
| B | 3 centimeters |
| C | 6 centimeters |
| D | 5 centimeters |

Name ________________________

**DIAGNOSTIC**

Common Core Standard 3.MD.5 – Measurement & Data

☐ **A wading pool at a city park measures 9 feet by 12 feet. What is the area of the pool? Each square stands for 1 square foot. Be sure to show your work.**

**A** 21 square feet

**B** 107 square feet

**C** 108 square feet

**D** 99 square feet

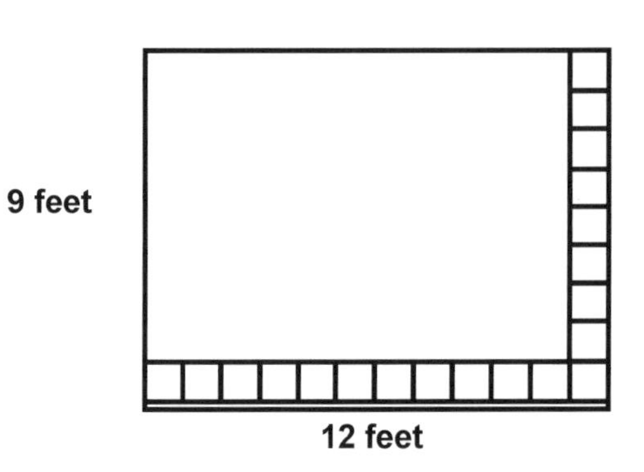


Common Core Standard 3.MD.5 – Measurement & Data

☐ **Find the area of the figure. Be sure to show your work.**

**A** 14 square inches

**B** 5 square inches

**C** 12 square inches

**D** 8 square inches

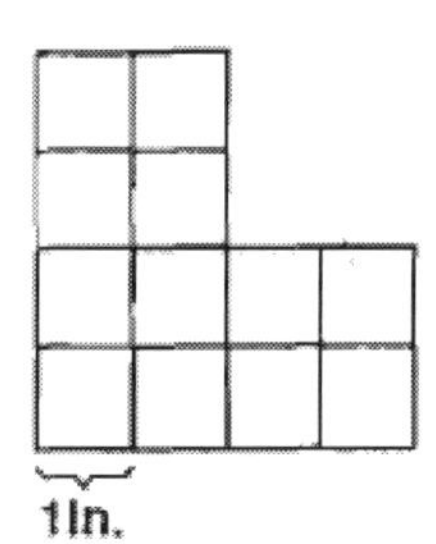


Common Core Standard 3.MD.5 – Measurement & Data

☐ **This square measures $8\frac{1}{2}$ centimeters on each side. What is the area of the shaded part? Be sure to show your work.**

**A** 81 square centimeters

**B** 46 square centimeters

**C** 48 square centimeters

**D** 45 square centimeters

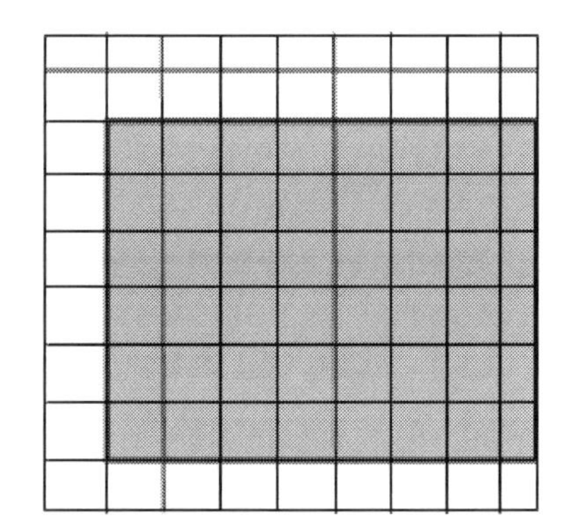

Name ________________________

**DIAGNOSTIC**

Common Core Standard 3.MD.5 – Measurement & Data

☐ **Which shows the *smallest* shaded area?**

A

B

C

D

Common Core Standard 3.MD.5 – Measurement & Data

☐ **A rug in Jacob's bedroom measures 5 feet by 8 feet. What is the area of the rug? Be sure to show your work.**

**A** **12 square feet**

**B** **40 square feet**

**C** **13 square feet**

**D** **45 square feet**

5 feet

8 feet

Common Core Standard 3.MD.5 – Measurement & Data

☐ **Find the area of the shaded part of the figure. Be sure to show your work.**

**A** **20 square centimeters**

**B** **27 square centimeters**

**C** **54 square centimeters**

**D** **28 square centimeters**

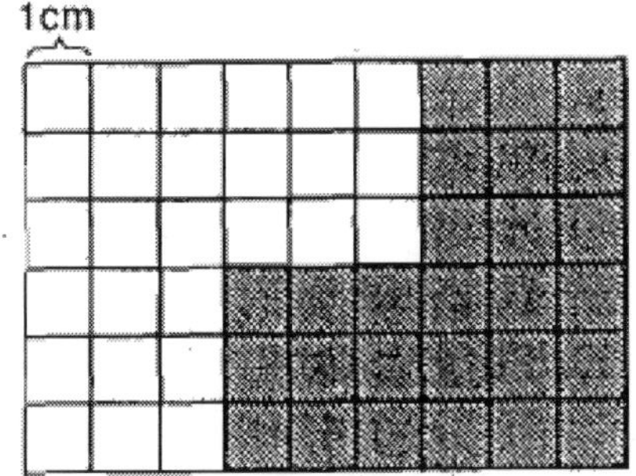

Name ______________________

**PRACTICE**

Common Core Standard 3.MD.5 – Measurement & Data

☐ **Find the area of the figure below in square inches. Be sure to show your work.**

**A** 20 square inches

**B** 24 square feet

**C** 24 square meters

**D** 24 square inches

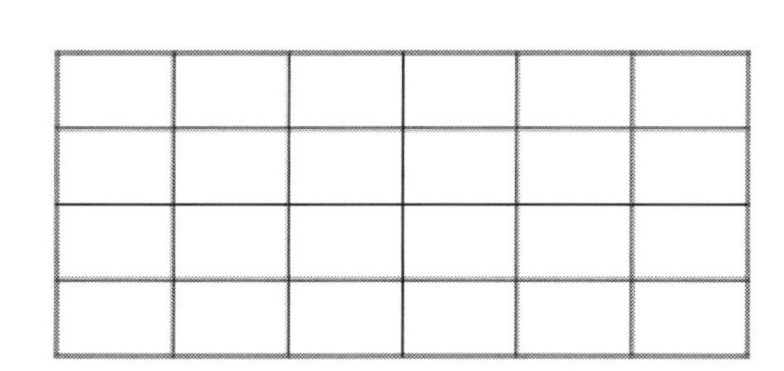

Common Core Standard 3.MD.5 – Measurement & Data

☐ **Which shows the *largest* shaded area?**

**A**

**C**

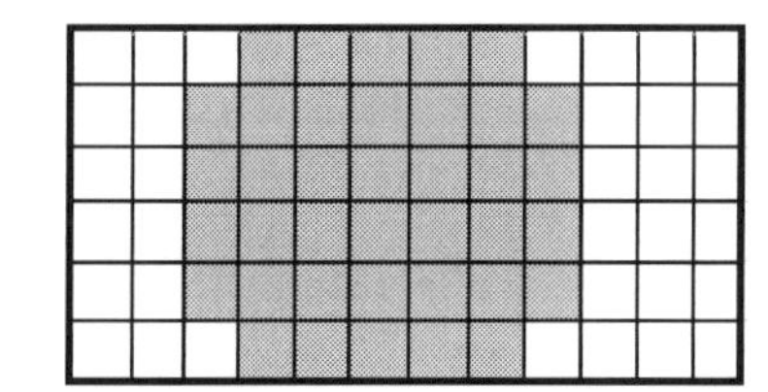

**B**

**D**

Common Core Standard 3.MD.5 – Measurement & Data

☐ **Which of the figures below are shaded to show 8 square units?**

**A**

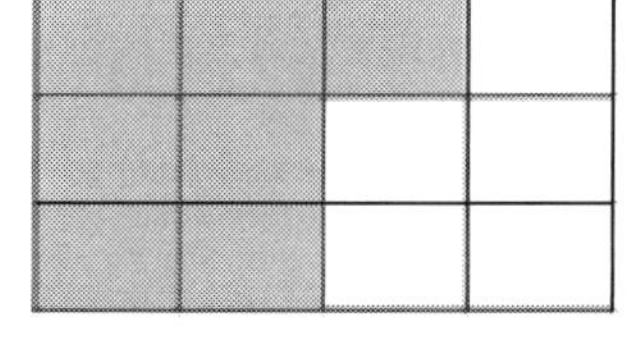

**C**

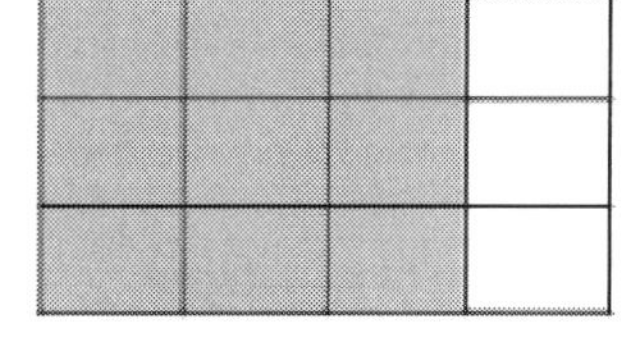

**B**

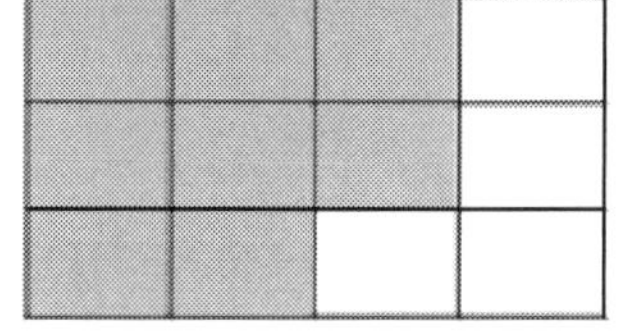

**D**

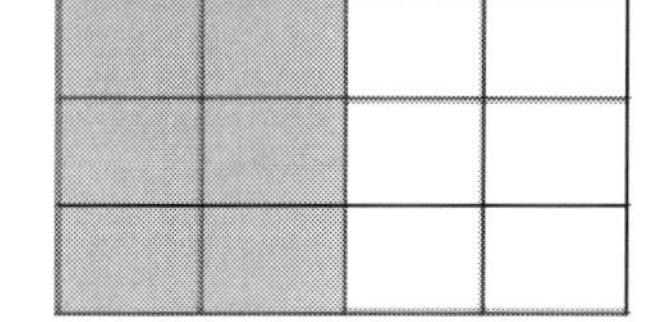

Name ________________________

**PRACTICE**

Common Core Standard 3.MD.5 – Measurement & Data

☐ **How many square units would a 7 column, 8 row figure be made up of? Be sure to show your work.**

| | | | |
|---|---|---|---|
| **A** | **42 square units** | **C** | **64 square units** |
| **B** | **56 square units** | **D** | **49 square units** |

Common Core Standard 3.MD.5 – Measurement & Data

☐ **How many square centimeters does Swahiti's stamp have? Be sure to show your work.**

**A** **63 square centimeters**

**B** **15 square centimeters**

**C** **48 square centimeters**

**D** **54 square centimeters**

Common Core Standard 3.MD.5 – Measurement & Data

☐ **Find the area of the figure below if each block is 1 sq. ft? Be sure to show your work.**

**A** **30 square feet**

**B** **20 square feet**

**C** **31 square feet**

**D** **12 square feet**

Name ___________________________

PRACTICE

Common Core Standard 3.MD.5 – Measurement & Data

☐ **Find the area of the figure below in square inches. Be sure to show your work.**

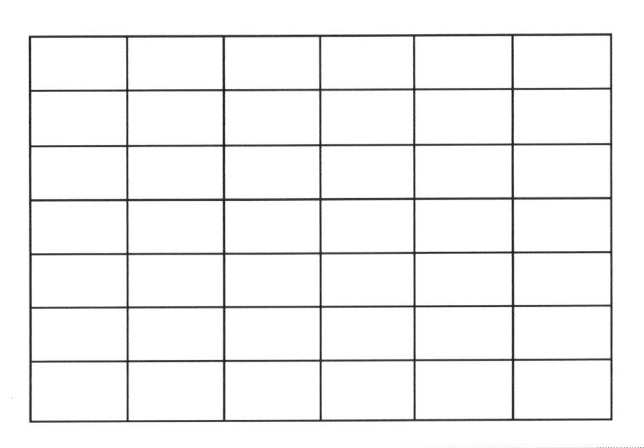

A 40 square inches

B 36 square inches

C 42 square inches

D 35 square inches

Common Core Standard 3.MD.5 – Measurement & Data

☐ **Which shows the *largest* shaded area?**

A 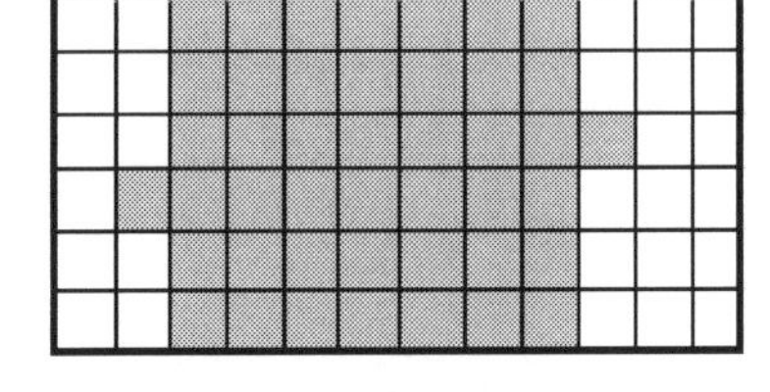

C 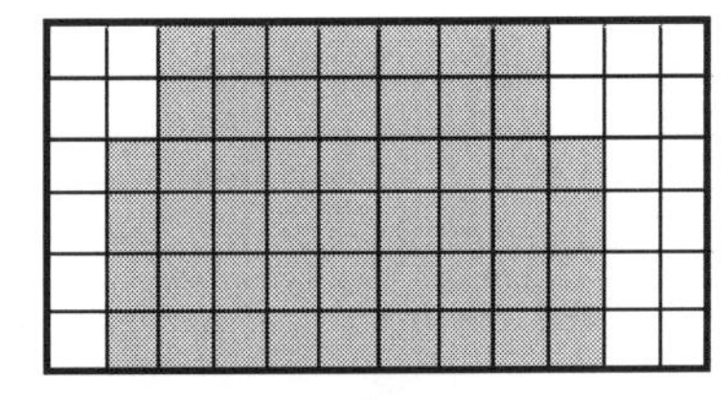

B 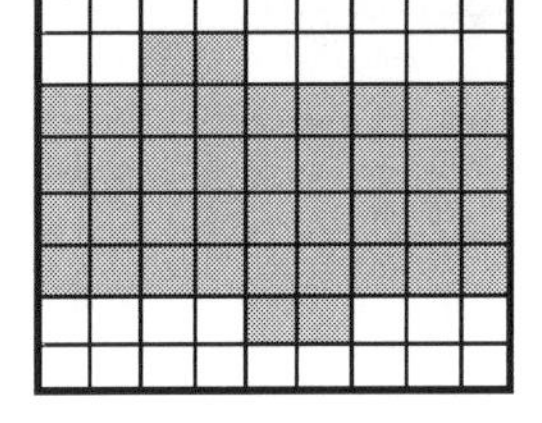

D 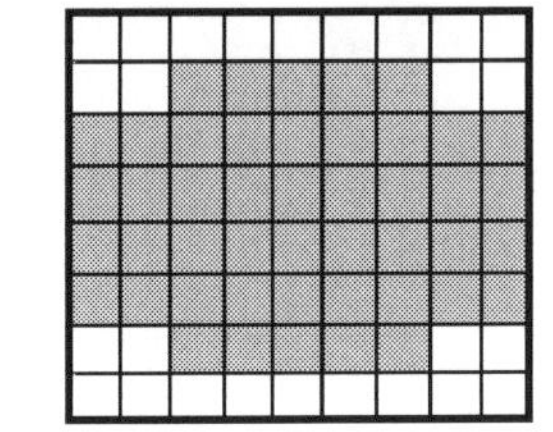

Common Core Standard 3.MD.5 – Measurement & Data

☐ **Which of the figures below are shaded to show 7 square units?**

A 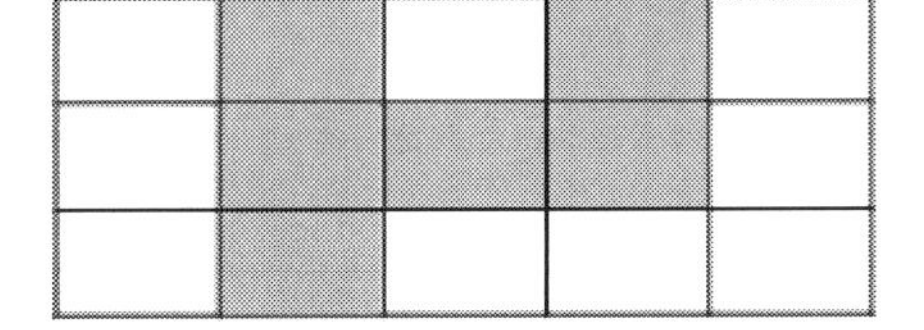

C 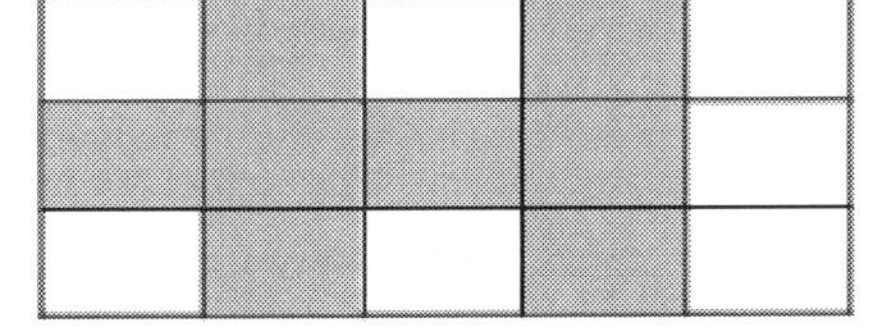

B 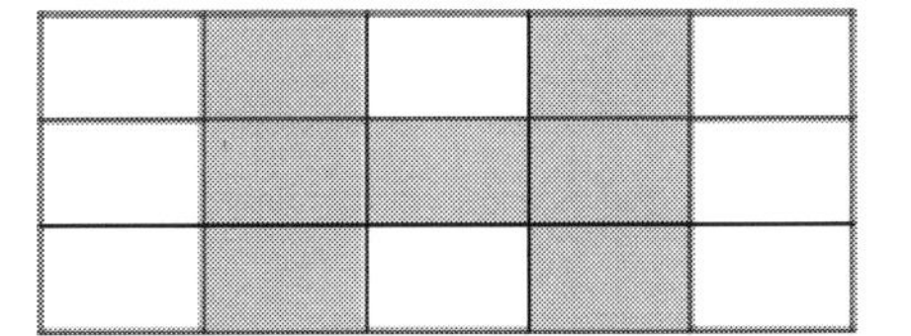

D 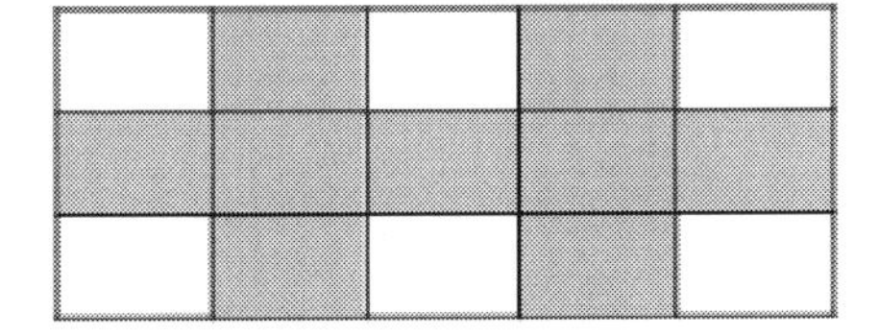

Name ______________________

**PRACTICE**

Common Core Standard 3.MD.5 – Measurement & Data

☐ **How many square units would a 3 column, 11 row figure be made up of? Be sure to show your work.**

**A** **36 square units**

**B** **30 square units**

**C** **14 square units**

**D** **33 square units**

Common Core Standard 3.MD.5 – Measurement & Data

☐ **How many square centimeters are in the shaded area below? Be sure to show your work.**

**A** **17 square centimeters**

**B** **18 square centimeters**

**C** **19 square centimeters**

**D** **10 square centimeters**

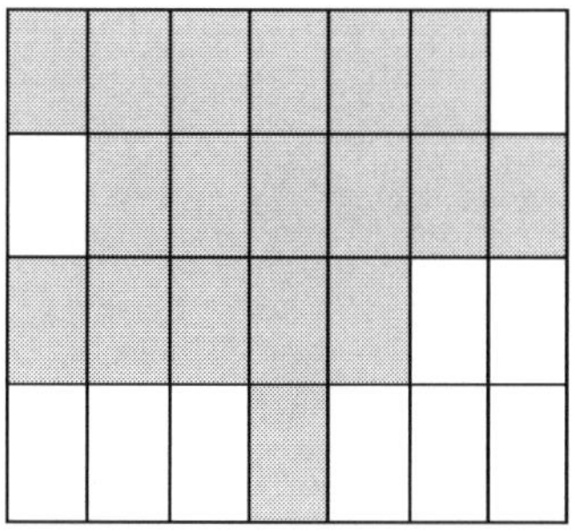

Common Core Standard 3.MD.5 – Measurement & Data

☐ **How many square meters are in the shaded area below? Be sure to show your work.**

**A** **35 square feet**

**B** **38 square feet**

**C** **36 square feet**

**D** **37 square feet**

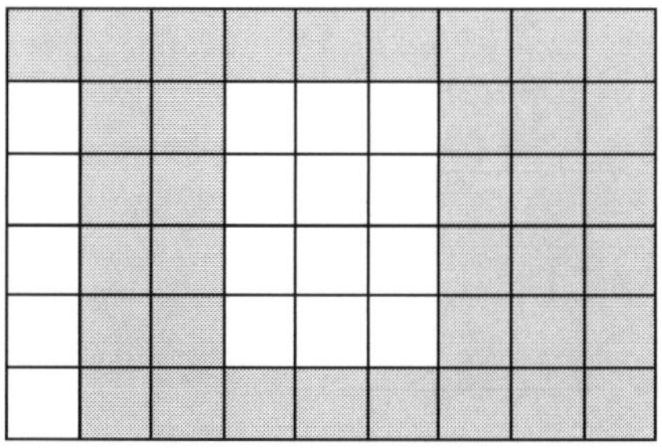

Name ________________________

**ASSESSMENT**

Common Core Standard 3.MD.5 – Measurement & Data

☐ **Find the area of the figure. Be sure to show your work.**

A 5 square meters

B 8 square meters

C 3 square meters

D 9 square meters

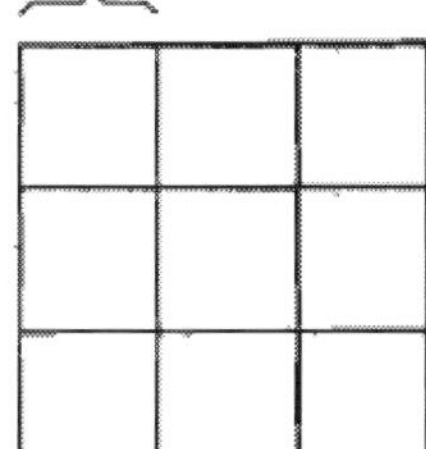


Common Core Standard 3.MD.5 – Measurement & Data

☐ **Which shows the *largest* shaded area?**

A 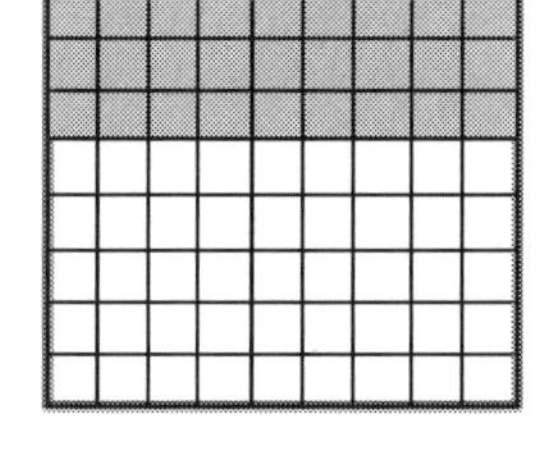

C 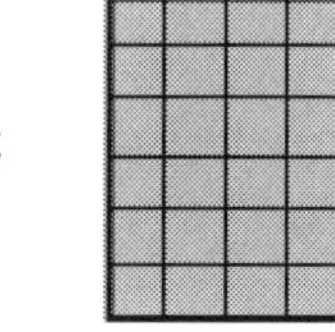

B 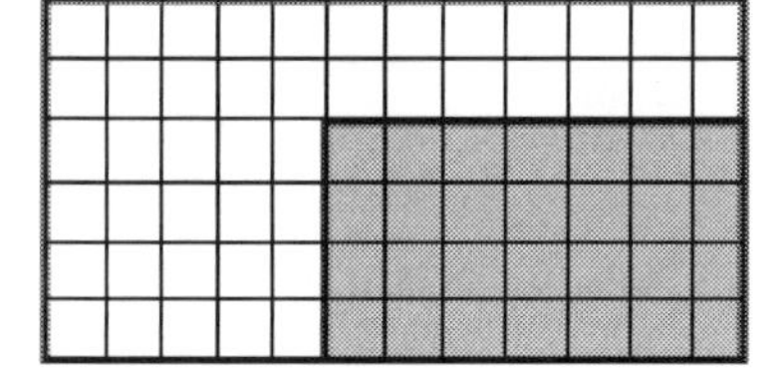

D 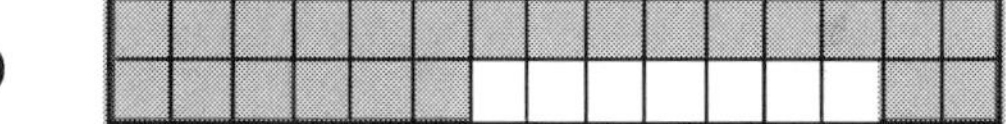

Common Core Standard 3.MD.5 – Measurement & Data

☐ **Which of the figures below are shaded to show 7 square units?**

A 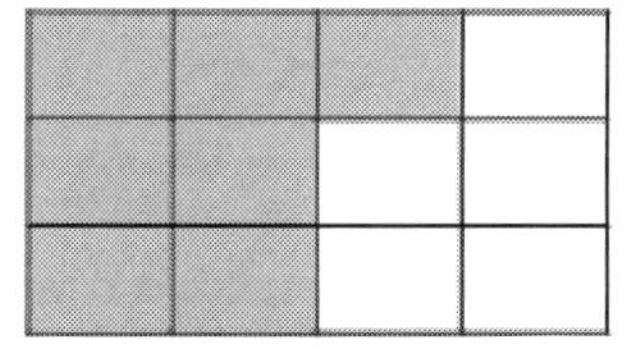

C 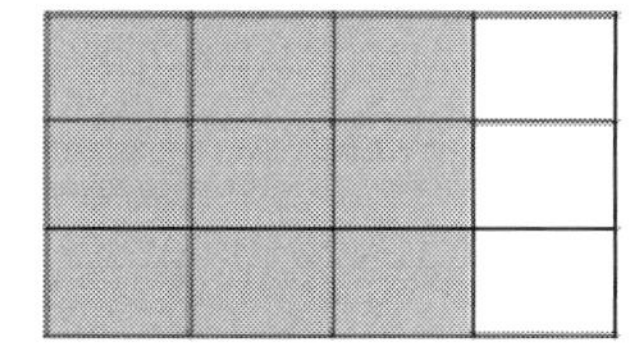

B 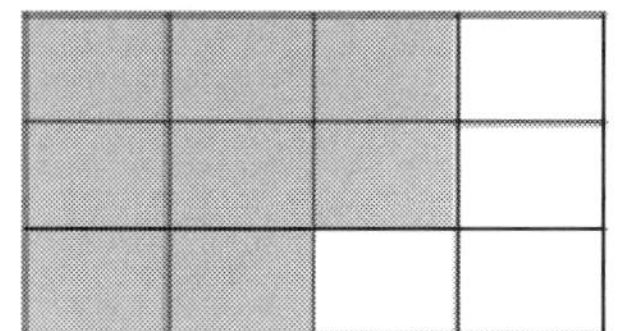

D 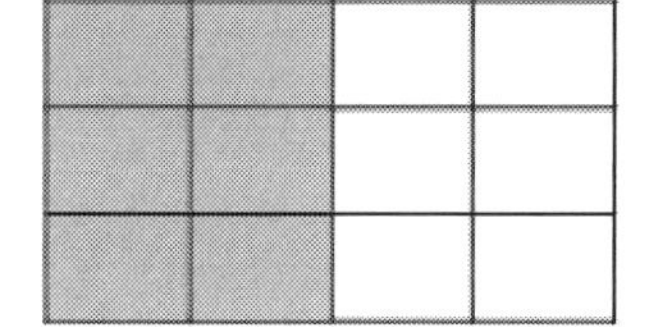

Name ________________________

**ASSESSMENT**

Common Core Standard 3.MD.5 – Measurement & Data

☐ **Which shows the *smallest* shaded area?**

A

C

B

D

Common Core Standard 3.MD.5 – Measurement & Data

☐ **Erica's swimming pool bedroom measures 10 feet by 9 feet. What is the area of her swimming pool? Be sure to show your work.**

A 99 square feet

B 90 square feet

C 81 square feet

D 72 square feet

Common Core Standard 3.MD.5 – Measurement & Data

☐ **Find the area of the figure below if each block is 1 sq. ft.**

A 20 square feet

B 12 square feet

C 13 square feet

D 10 square feet

Name ______________________

**DIAGNOSTIC**

Common Core Standard 3.MD.6 – Measurement & Data

☐ **What is the area of the shaded region?**

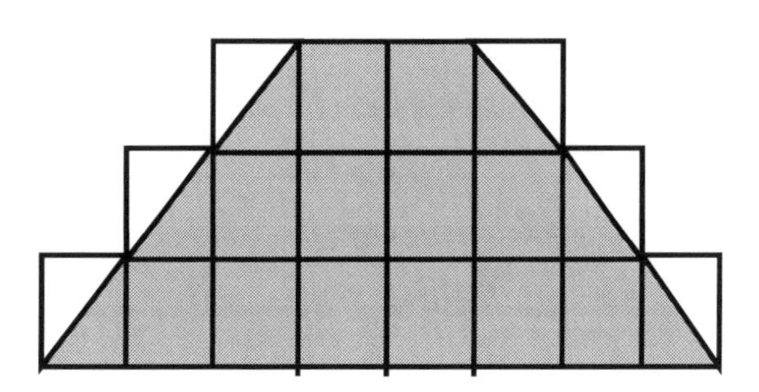

A 15 square meters

B 18 square meters

C 14 square meters

D 12 square meters

Common Core Standard 3.MD.6 – Measurement & Data

☐ **What is the area of *one* of the four triangles in the square?**

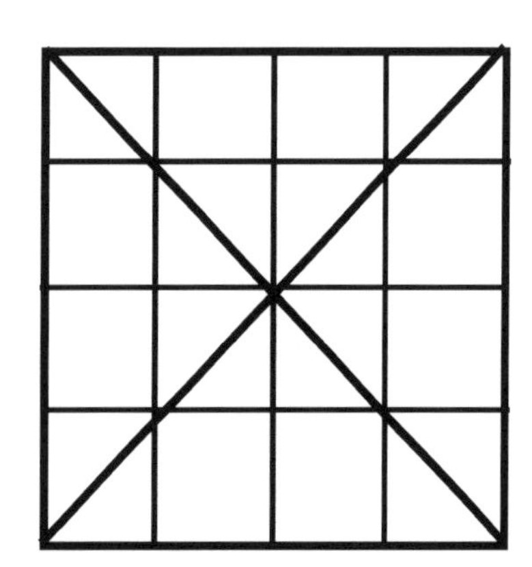

A 16 square units

B 6 square units

C 4 square units

D 3 square units

Common Core Standard 3.MD.6 – Measurement & Data

☐ **Which of the figures below represents 24 square inches?**

A 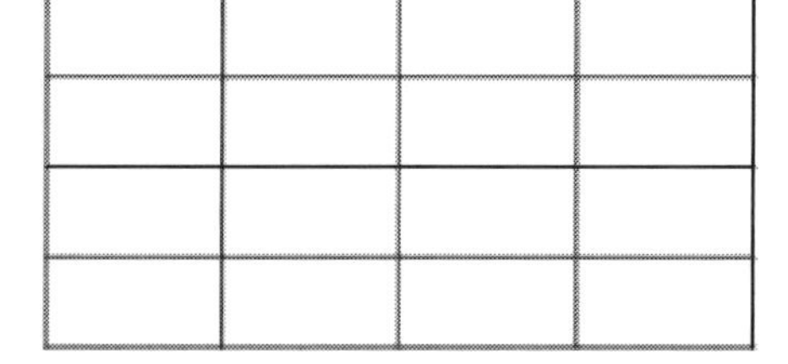

C 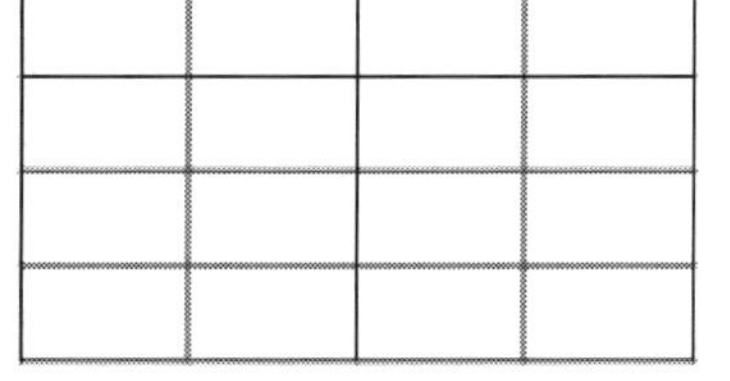

B 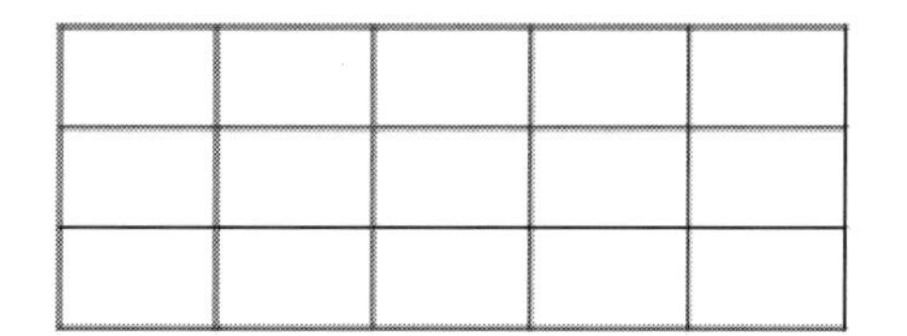

D 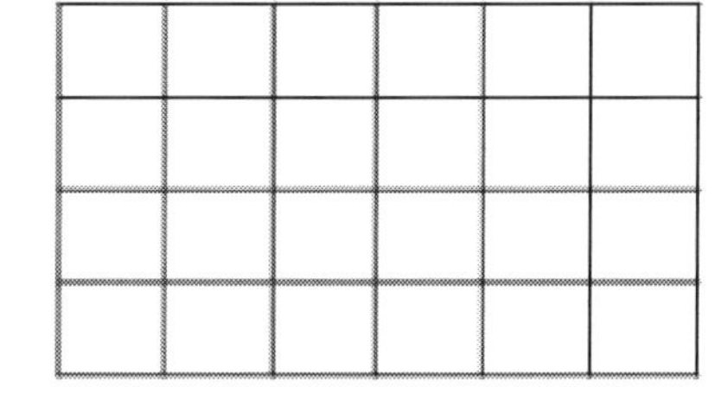

Name ____________________

**DIAGNOSTIC**

Common Core Standard 3.MD.6 – Measurement & Data

☐ **What is the area of the shaded design? Be sure to show your work.**

**A** **17 square units**

**B** **20 square units**

**C** **9 square units**

**D** **16 square units**

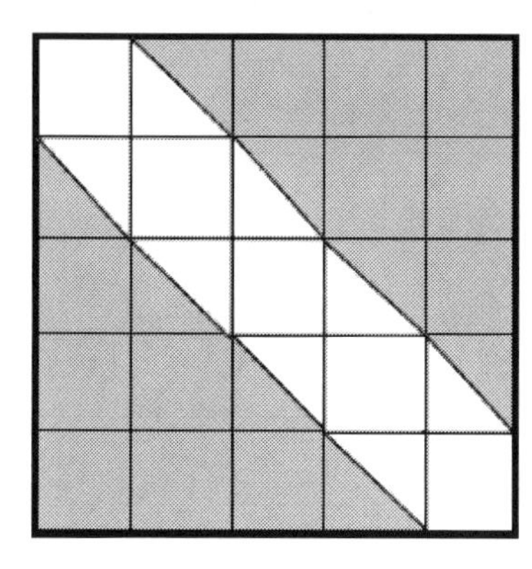

Common Core Standard 3.MD.6 – Measurement & Data

☐ **What is the area of triangle ABC? Be sure to show your work.**

**A** **12 square units**

**B** **15 square units**

**C** **$11\frac{1}{2}$ square units**

**D** **$12\frac{1}{2}$ square units**

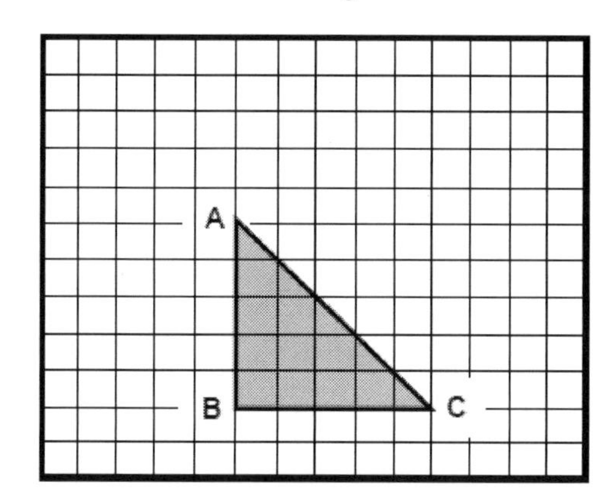


Common Core Standard 3.MD.6 – Measurement & Data

☐ **What is the area of *one* of the three small shapes inside the polygon? Be sure to show your work.**

**A** **21 square units**

**B** **22 square units**

**C** **$21\frac{1}{2}$ square units**

**D** **$20\frac{1}{2}$ square units**

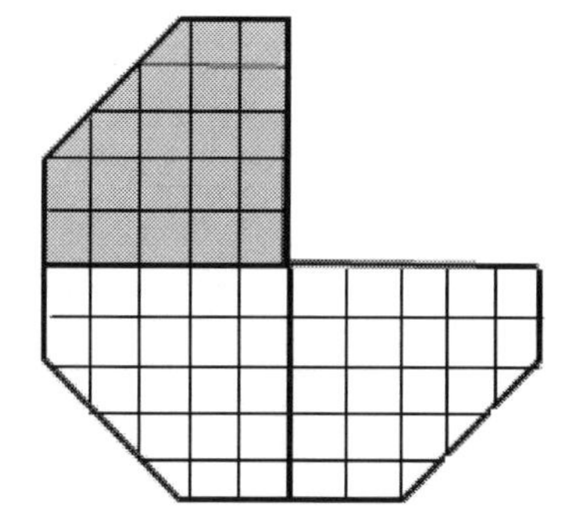

Name ________________________

**PRACTICE**

Common Core Standard 3.MD.6 – Measurement & Data

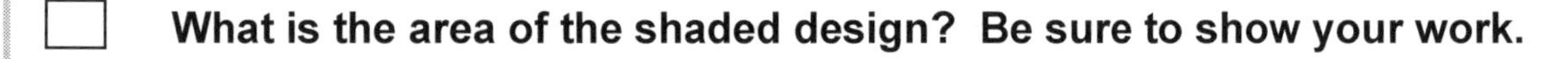

☐ **What is the area of the shaded design? Be sure to show your work.**

**A** **53 square feet**

**B** **52 square feet**

**C** **51 square feet**

**D** **57 square feet**

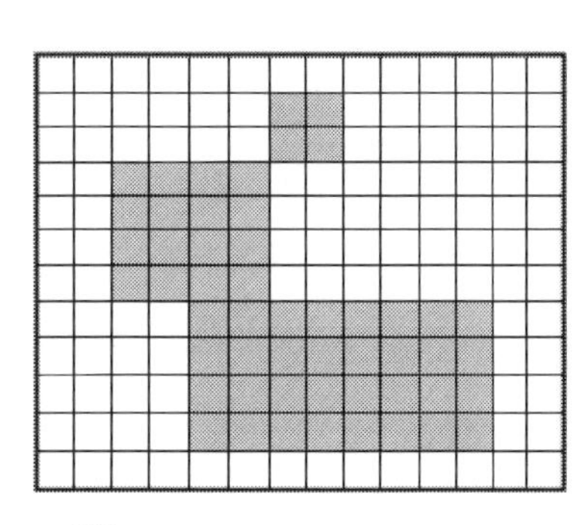

( ▢ = 1 square foot)

Common Core Standard 3.MD.6 – Measurement & Data

☐ **Which of the following has the same area as the figure in the box?**

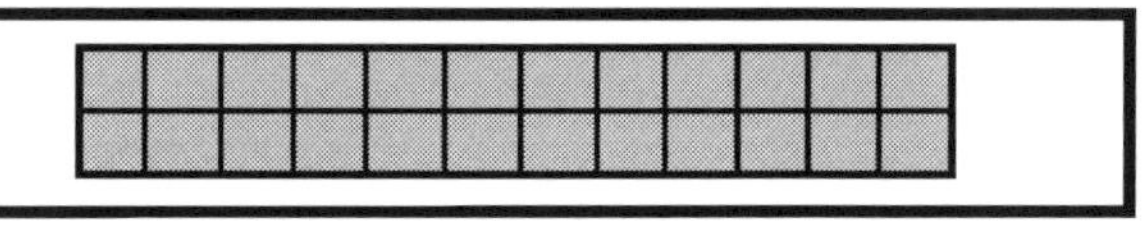

**A**

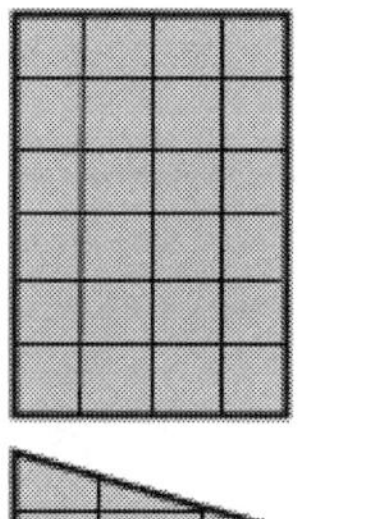

**C**

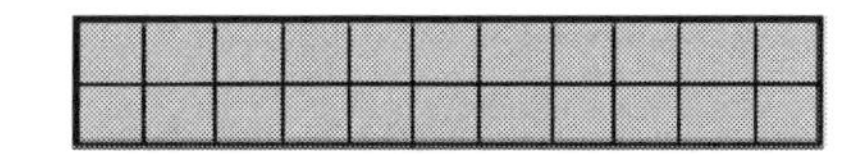

**B**

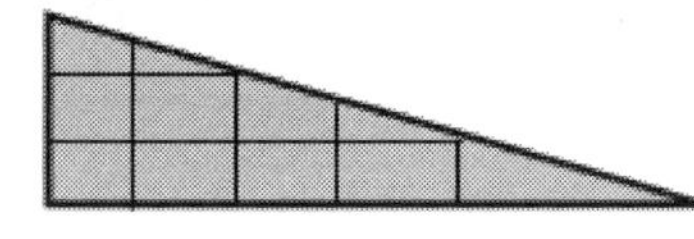

**D**

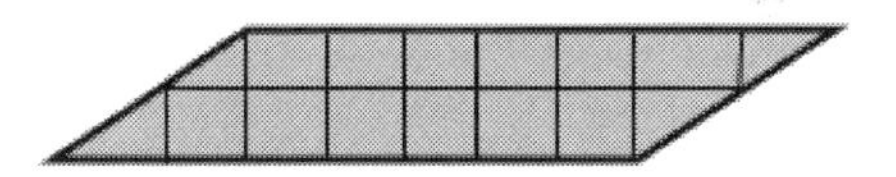

Common Core Standard 3.MD.6 – Measurement & Data

☐ **What is the area of the shaded figure? Be sure to show your work.**

**A** **16 square inches**

**B** **17 square inches**

**C** **18 square inches**

**D** **19 square inches**

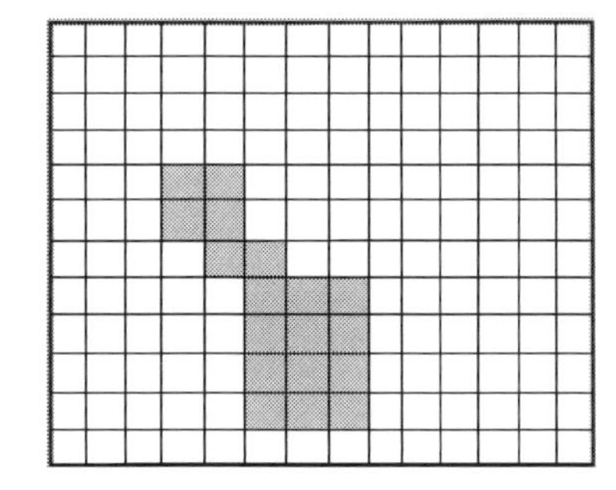

( ▢ = 1 square inch)

Name ______________________

**PRACTICE**

Common Core Standard 3.MD.6 – Measurement & Data

☐ **What is the area of the square that is NOT shaded? Be sure to show your work.**

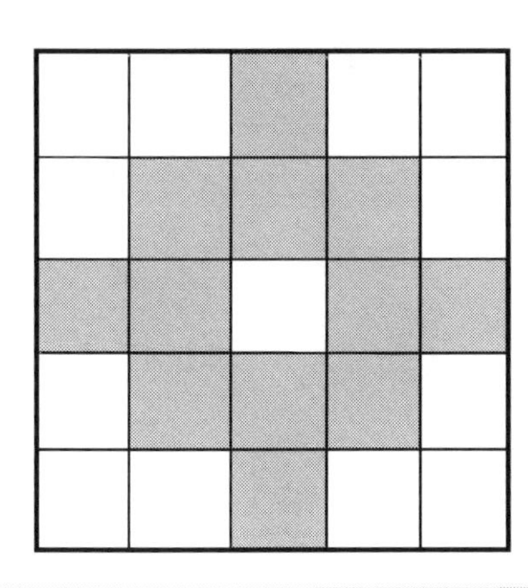

A 15 square units

B 14 square units

C 13 square units

D 16 square units

Common Core Standard 3.MD.6 – Measurement & Data

☐ **What is the area of arrow pictured below? Be sure to show your work.**

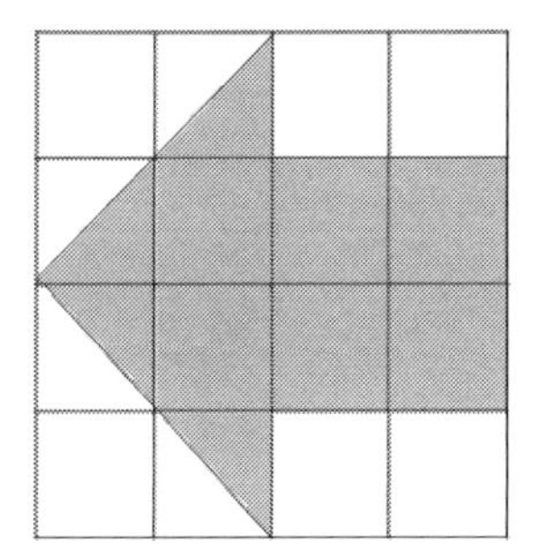

A 5 square units

B 6 square units

C 8 square units

D 7 square units

Common Core Standard 3.MD.6 – Measurement & Data

☐ **What is the area that is shaded? Be sure to show your work.**

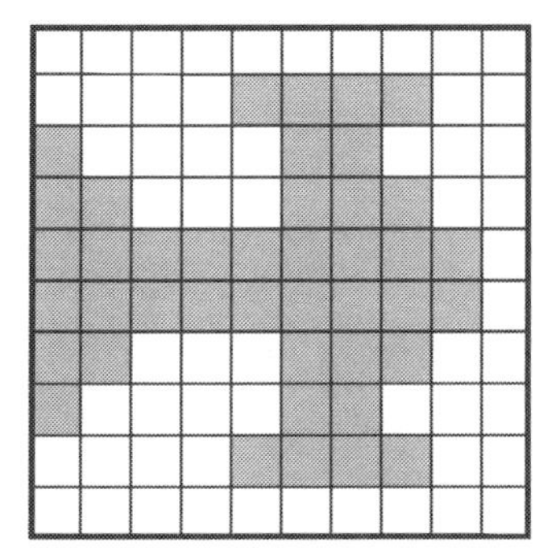

A 42 square units

B 45 square units

C 44 square units

D 43 square units

Name ______________________

PRACTICE

Common Core Standard 3.MD.6 – Measurement & Data

☐ **What is the area of the shaded design in square meters? Be sure to show your work.**

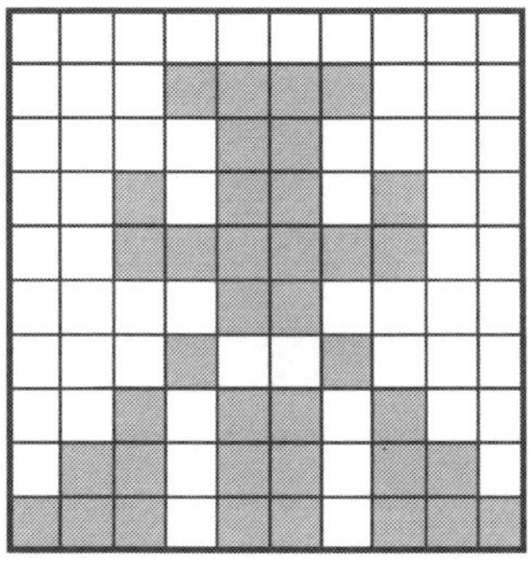

**A** 38 square centimeters

**B** 38 square inches

**C** 38 square feet

**D** 38 square meters

( ☐ = 1 square meter)

Common Core Standard 3.MD.6 – Measurement & Data

☐ **Look at the figure below, find the area of *only* the shaded part of the figure. Which answer best matches the figure's shaded area?**

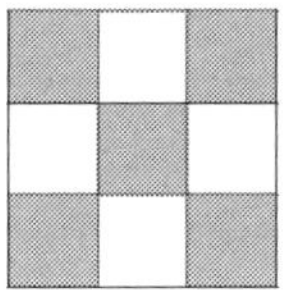

**A**

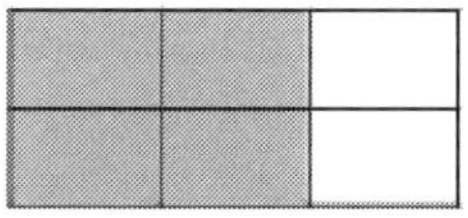

**B**

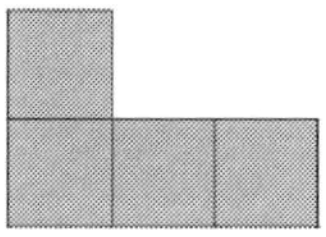

**C**

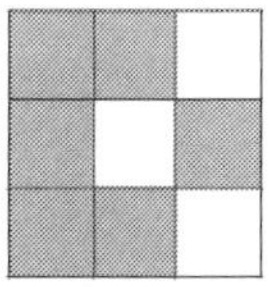

**D**

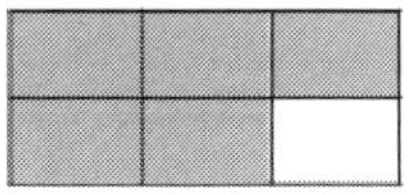

Common Core Standard 3.MD.6 – Measurement & Data

☐ **What is the area of the figure below? Be sure to show your work.**

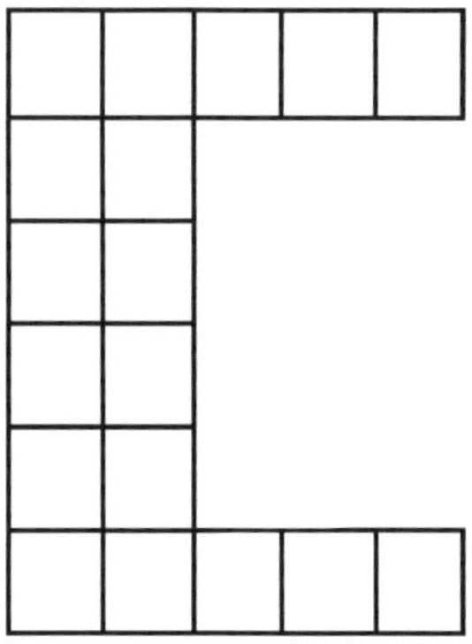

**A** 16 square inches

**B** 17 square inches

**C** 18 square inches

**D** 19 square inches

Name ___________________________

**PRACTICE**

Common Core Standard 3.MD.6 – Measurement & Data

☐ **What is the area of the square that is NOT shaded? Be sure to show your work.**

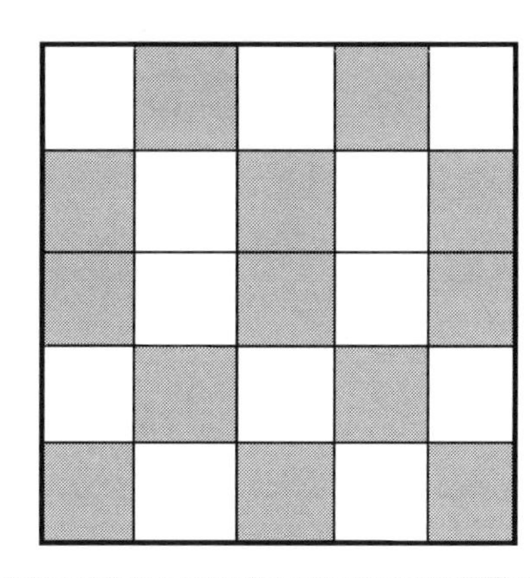

A 15 square units

B 12 square units

C 13 square units

D 16 square units

Common Core Standard 3.MD.6 – Measurement & Data

☐ **What is the shaded area of pictured below? Be sure to show your work.**

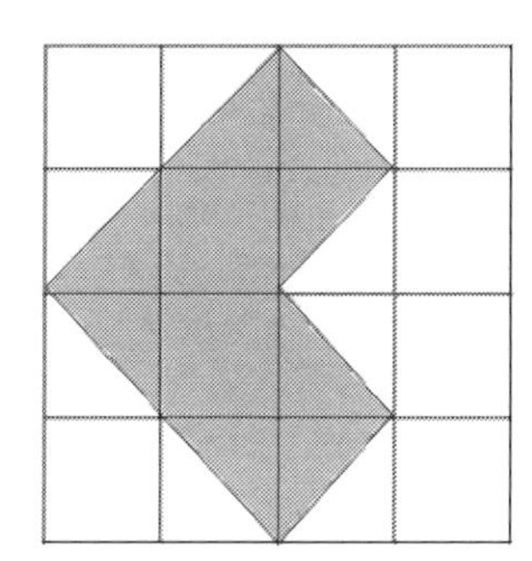

A 5 square units

B 6 square units

C 8 square units

D 7 square units

Common Core Standard 3.MD.6 – Measurement & Data

☐ **What is the area that is shaded? Be sure to show your work**

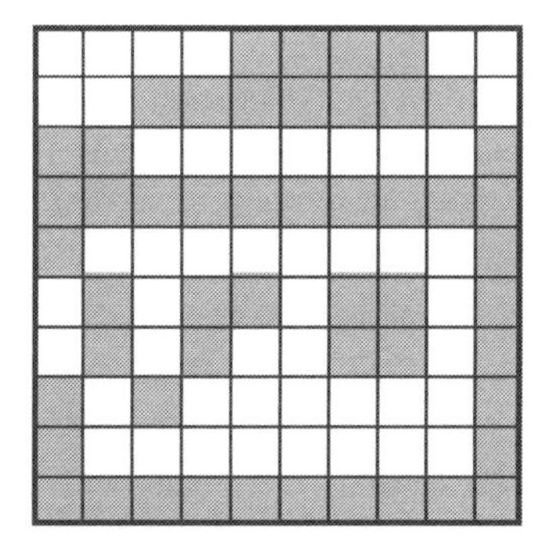

A 52 square units

B 55 square units

C 54 square units

D 53 square units

Name ____________________________

**ASSESSMENT**

Common Core Standard 3.MD.6 – Measurement & Data

☐ **What is the area of *half* of the four small triangles in the square? Be sure to show your work**

**A** **8 square units**

**B** **16 square units**

**C** **10 square units**

**D** **4 square units**

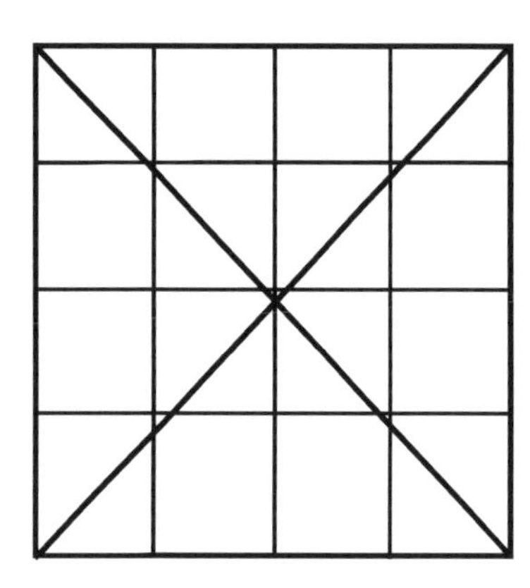

Common Core Standard 3.MD.6 – Measurement & Data

☐ **What is the area of the shaded part of the rectangle? Be sure to show your work.**

**A** **18 square units**

**B** **27 square units**

**C** **45 square units**

**D** **20 square units**

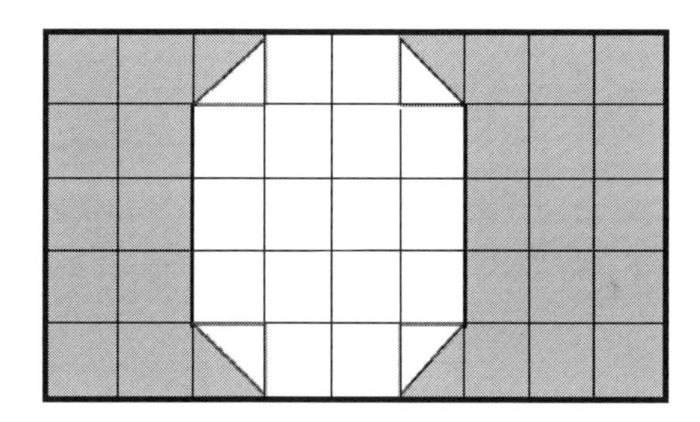

Common Core Standard 3.MD.6 – Measurement & Data

☐ **Which of the figures below represents 12 square inches?**

**A**

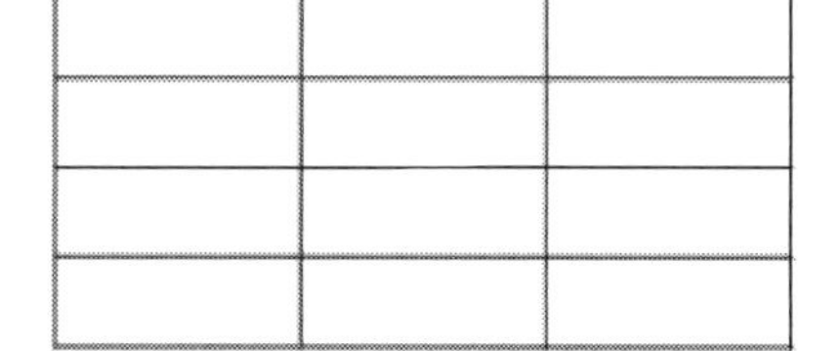

**C**

**B**

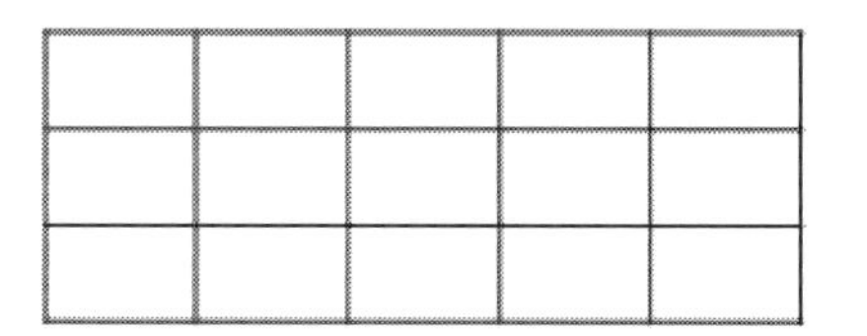

**D**

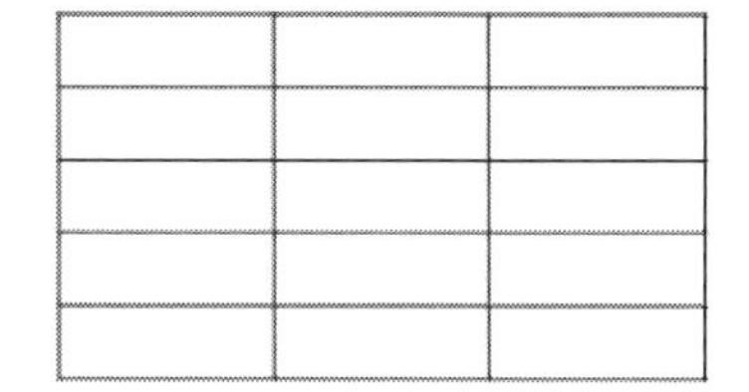

Name ___________________________

**ASSESSMENT**

Common Core Standard 3.MD.6 – Measurement & Data

☐ **What is the area of the square that is NOT shaded? Be sure to show your work.**

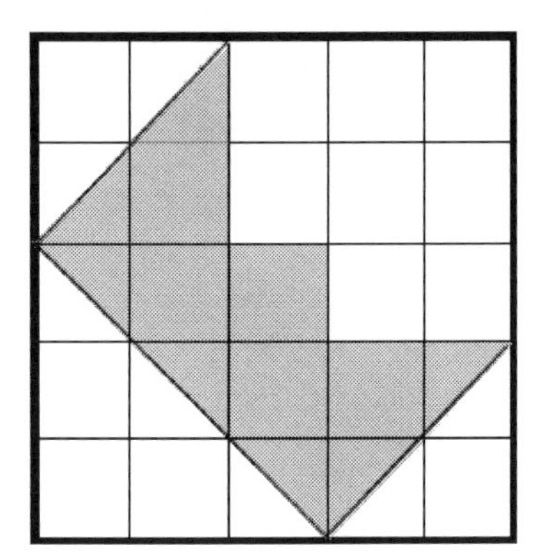

A $8\frac{1}{2}$ square units

B 20 square units

C $16\frac{1}{2}$ square units

D 16 square units

Common Core Standard 3.MD.6 – Measurement & Data

☐ **What is the area of triangle pictured below? Be sure to show your work.**

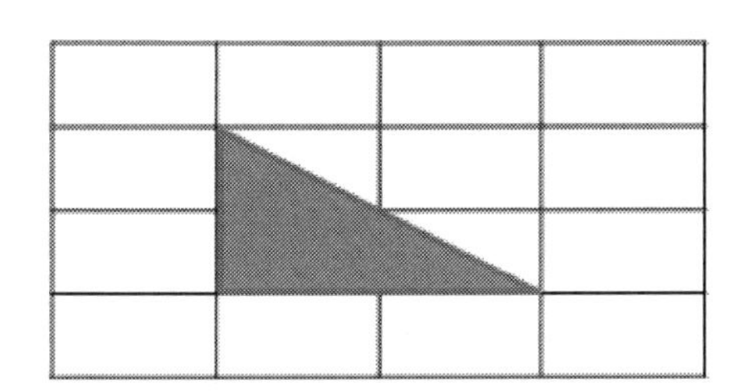

A 5 square units

B 4 square units

C 3 square units

D 2 square units

Common Core Standard 3.MD.6 – Measurement & Data

☐ **What is the area that is NOT shaded? Be sure to show your work.**

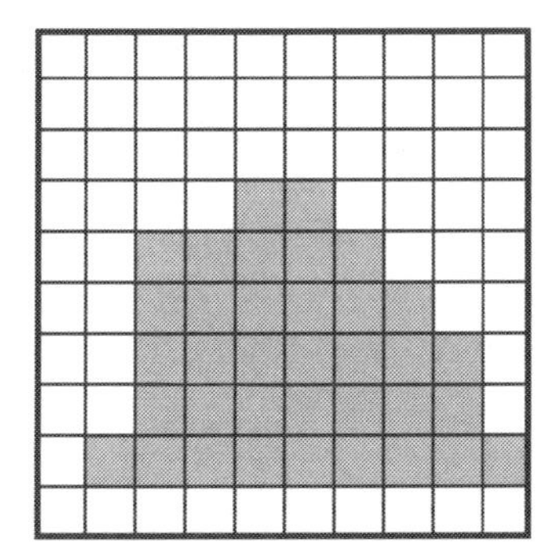

A 62 square units

B 65 square units

C 64 square units

D 63 square units

Name ______________________

**DIAGNOSTIC**

Common Core Standard 3.MD.7 – Measurement & Data

☐ **If each square below is equivalent to** [square: 4 m × 4 m] **. What is the area of the picture below? Be sure to show your work.**

4 m

4 m

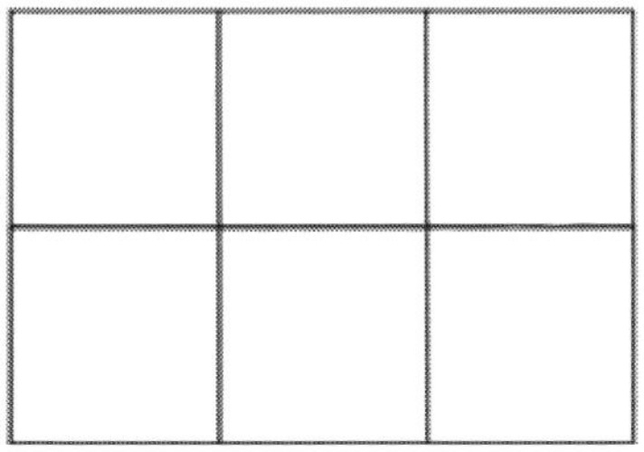

**A** **24 $m^2$**

**B** **48 $m^2$**

**C** **96 $m^2$**

**D** **30 $m^2$**

Common Core Standard 3.MD.7 – Measurement & Data

☐ **Kendrix room is rectangle and measures 5m by 3m. What is the area of his room? Be sure to show your work.**

**A** **15 square meters**

**B** **8 square meters**

**C** **15 square kilometers**

**D** **8 square kilometers**

3m

5m

Common Core Standard 3.MD.7 – Measurement & Data

☐ **The area of the square below is 294 $sq^2$. Find the adjacent sides of each square. Be sure to show your work.**

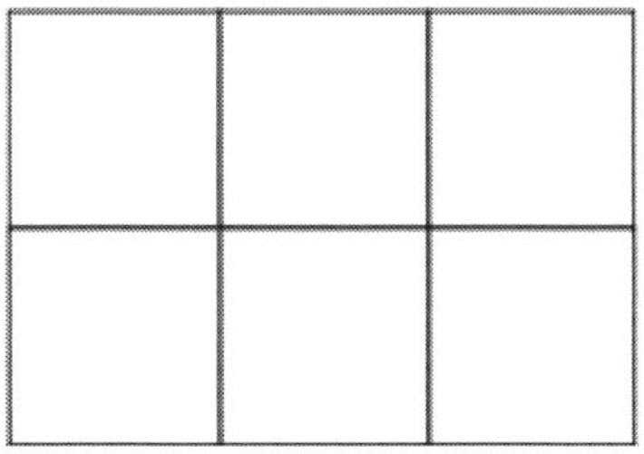

**7 $sq^2$**

**14 $sq^2$**

**6 $sq^2$**

**8 $sq^2$**

Name ____________________

**DIAGNOSTIC**

Common Core Standard 3.MD.7 – Measurement & Data

☐ **Find the area of the figure below. Be sure to show your work.**

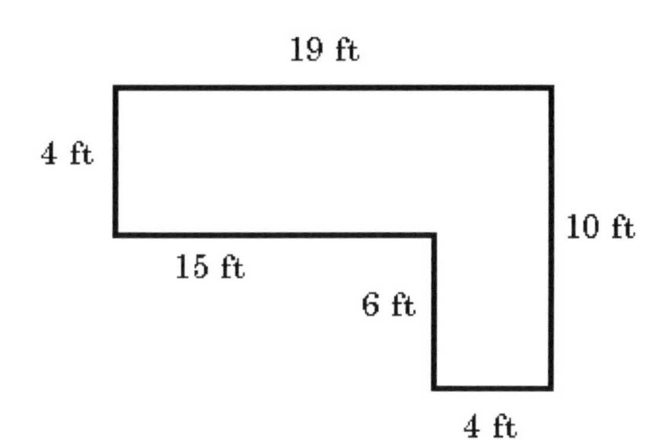


**A** 58 square feet

**B** 33 square feet

**C** 100 square feet

**D** 84 square feet

Common Core Standard 3.MD.7 – Measurement & Data

☐ **A rectangle is 9 meters long and 7 meters wide. What is the area of the rectangle? Be sure to show your work.**

**A** 16 square meters

**B** 16 square feet

**C** 63 square meters

**D** 63 square feet

Common Core Standard 3.MD.7 – Measurement & Data

☐ **Look at the figure below. What would the area of figure if it was three times its size? Be sure to show your work.**

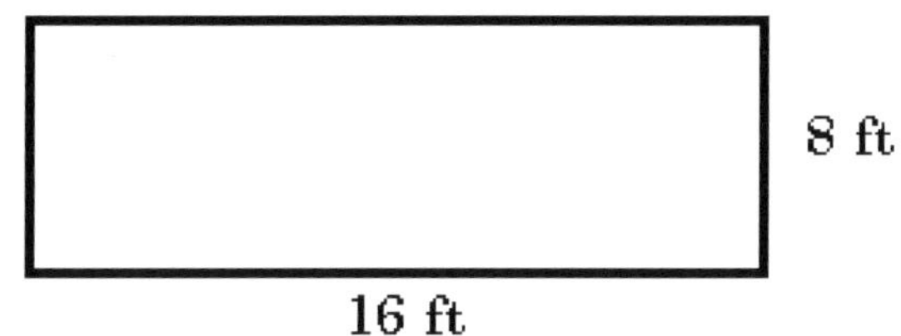


**A** 384 square feet

**B** 128 square feet

**C** 24 square feet

**D** 72 square feet

Name ______________________

**PRACTICE**

Common Core Standard 3.MD.7 – Measurement & Data

☐ **If each square below is equivalent to 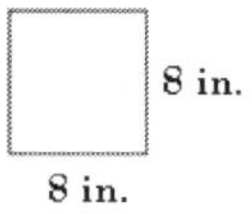**

**. What is the area of the picture below? Be sure to show your work.**

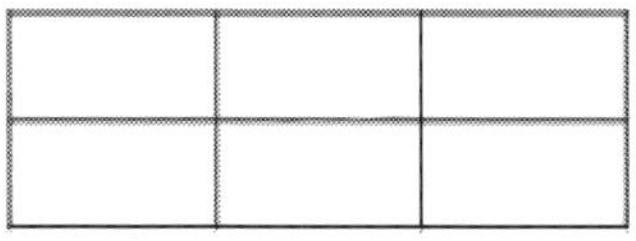

**A** **384 in.²**

**B** **32 in.²**

**C** **96 in.²**

**D** **70 in.²**

Common Core Standard 3.MD.7 – Measurement & Data

☐ **Alexandria's swimming pool is shaped like a rectangle and measures 15 ft. by 9 ft. What is the area of her swimming pool? Be sure to show your work.**

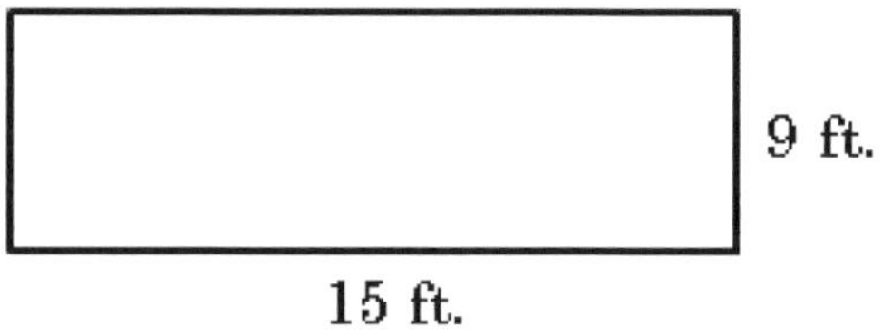


**A** **135 square meters**

**B** **48 square feet**

**C** **24 square feet**

**D** **135 square feet**

Common Core Standard 3.MD.7 – Measurement & Data

☐ **The area of the square below is 200 cm². Find the adjacent sides of each square. Be sure to show your work.**

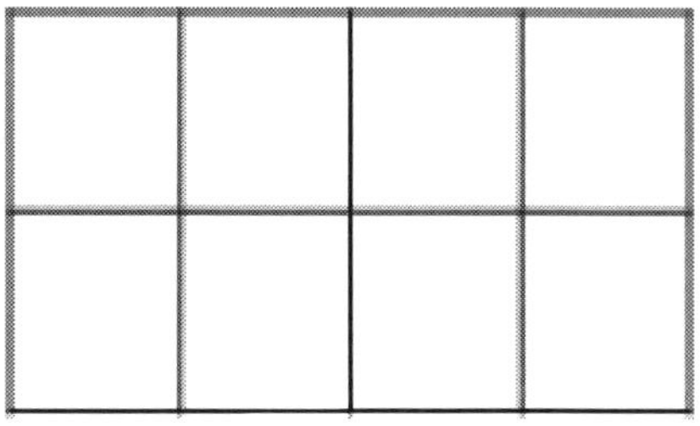

**A** **10 cm**

**B** **25 cm**

**C** **5 cm**

**D** **8 cm**

Name ____________________

PRACTICE

Common Core Standard 3.MD.7 – Measurement & Data

☐ **Find the area of the figure below. Be sure to show your work.**

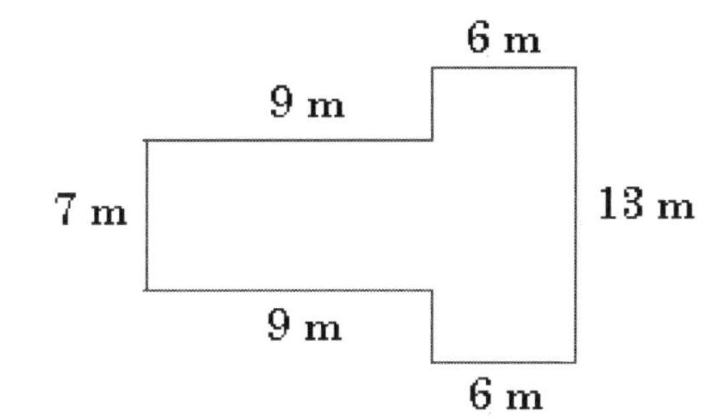


A $70 \text{ m}^2$

B $50 \text{ m}^2$

C $35 \text{ m}^2$

D $141 \text{ m}^2$

Common Core Standard 3.MD.7 – Measurement & Data

☐ **A rectangle is 11 kilometers long and 8 kilometers wide. What is the area of the rectangle? Be sure to show your work.**

A $88 \text{ km}^2$

B $3 \text{ km}^2$

C $80 \text{ km}^2$

D $19 \text{ km}^2$

Common Core Standard 3.MD.7 – Measurement & Data

☐ **Look at the figure below. What would the area of figure if it was 2 times its size?**

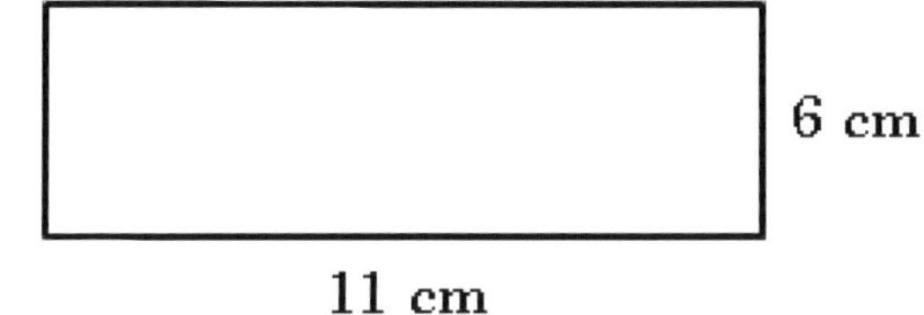


A $66 \text{ cm}^2$

B $132 \text{ cm}^2$

C $34 \text{ cm}^2$

D $17 \text{ cm}^2$

Name ____________________

**PRACTICE**

Common Core Standard 3.MD.7 – Measurement & Data

☐ **If each square below is equivalent to 4 ft. by 3 ft. What is the area of the picture below? Be sure to show your work.**

A 144 $ft.^2$

B 42 $ft.^2$

C 84 $ft.^2$

D 72 $ft.^2$

Common Core Standard 3.MD.7 – Measurement & Data

☐ **Markus needs to rake his front yard. It will take him 4 hours to rake all the leaves. His yard measures 9 meters by 3 meters. What is the area of his yard? Be sure to show your work.**

A 12 square meters

B 144 square meters

C 27 square meters

D 36 square meters

3 m

9 m

Common Core Standard 3.MD.7 – Measurement & Data

☐ **The area of the square below is 192 $cm^2$. Find the adjacent sides of each square. Be sure to show your work.**

A 16 cm

B 32 cm

C 4 cm

D 8 cm

Name 

PRACTICE

Common Core Standard 3.MD.7 – Measurement & Data

☐ Find the area of the figure below. Be sure to show your work.

A 64 $in^2$

B 50 $in^2$

C 32 $in^2$

D 106 $in^2$

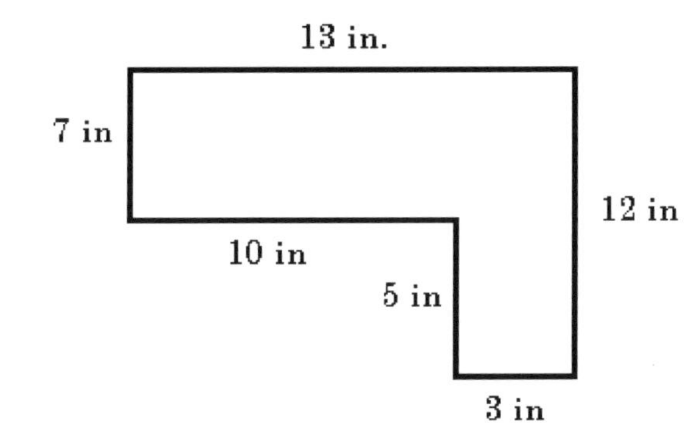


Common Core Standard 3.MD.7 – Measurement & Data

☐ A rectangle on a map is 13 miles long and 4 miles wide. What are the square miles of the rectangle on the map? Be sure to show your work.

A 34 square miles

B 52 square miles

C 17 square miles

D 104 square miles

Common Core Standard 3.MD.7 – Measurement & Data

☐ Look at the figure below. What would the area of figure if it was 4 times its size? Be sure to show your work.

A 200 $m^2$

B 564 $m^2$

C 141$m^2$

D 50 $m^2$

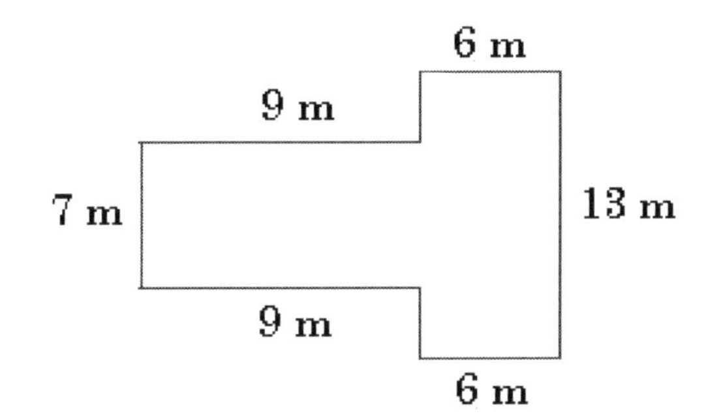

Name ______________________

**ASSESSMENT**

Common Core Standard 3.MD.7 – Measurement & Data

☐ If each square below is equivalent to [square: 6 cm by 6 cm]. What is the area of the picture below? Be sure to show your work.

A 144 $cm^2$

B 48 $cm^2$

C 96 $cm^2$

D 288 $cm^2$

Common Core Standard 3.MD.7 – Measurement & Data

☐ Mrs. Marx's classroom is a rectangle and measures 12 ft by 15 ft. What is the area of her classroom? Be sure to show your work.

A 180 square meters

B 180 square feet

C 27 square feet

D 54 square feet

15 ft

12 ft

Common Core Standard 3.MD.7 – Measurement & Data

☐ The area of the square below is 216 $ft^2$. Find the adjacent sides of each square. Be sure to show your work.

A 7 ft

B 12 ft

C 6 ft

D 8 ft

Name ________________________

**ASSESSMENT**

Common Core Standard 3.MD.7 – Measurement & Data

☐ **Find the area of the figure below. Be sure to show your work.**

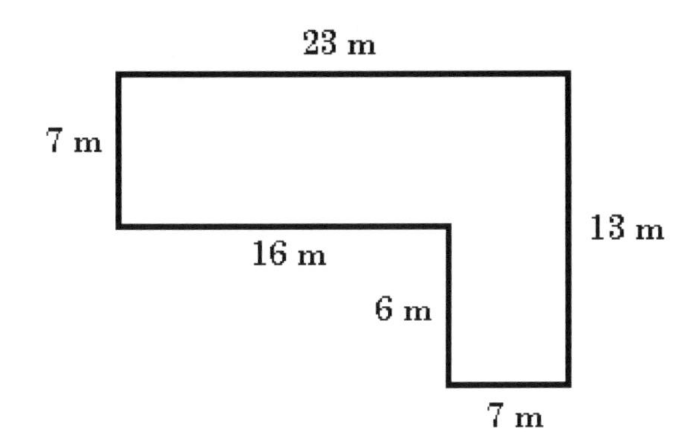

**A** **50 m²**

**B** **203 m²**

**C** **51 m²**

**D** **252 m²**

Common Core Standard 3.MD.7 – Measurement & Data

☐ **A rectangle is 15 meters long and 12 meters wide. What is the area of the rectangle? Be sure to show your work.**

**A** **27 m²**

**B** **54 m²**

**C** **180 m²**

**D** **182 m²**

Common Core Standard 3.MD.7 – Measurement & Data

☐ **Look at the figure below. What would the area of figure if it was four times its size? Be sure to show your work.**

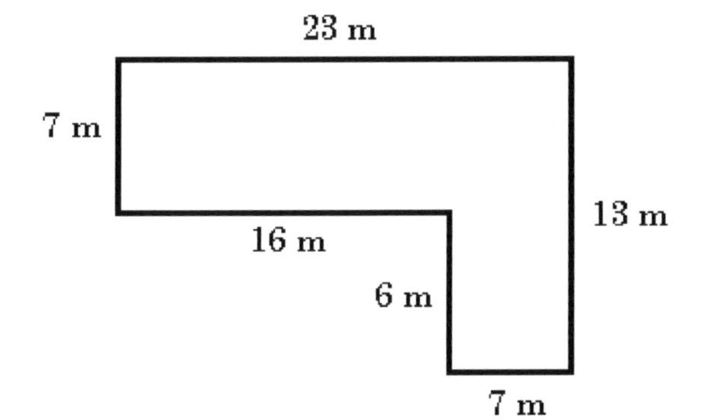


**A** **812 m²**

**B** **200 m²**

**C** **204 m²**

**D** **1008 m²**

Name ________________________

**DIAGNOSTIC**

Common Core Standard 3.MD.8 – Measurement & Data

☐ **One side of a square measures 12 meters. What is the perimeter of the square? Be sure to show your work.**

**A** 24 m

**B** 48 m

**C** 96 m

**D** 36 m

Common Core Standard 3.MD.8 – Measurement & Data

☐ **If the perimeter for the figure below is 22, what is the value for *X*? Be sure to show your work.**

**A** 13 m

**B** 4 m

**C** 2 m

**D** 16 m

$X$

9 m

Common Core Standard 3.MD.8 – Measurement & Data

☐ **Principal Ruiz wants to find the square footage for both Mrs. Grant's and Mr. Leopold's classrooms. Mrs. Grant's classroom measures 20 feet by 11 feet and Mr. Leopold's classroom measures 22 feet by 12 feet. What is the total square footage for both classrooms? Be sure to show your work.**

**A** 65 $ft^2$

**B** 484 $ft^2$

**C** 130 $ft^2$

**D** 1054 $ft^2$

Name ___________________________

DIAGNOSTIC

Common Core Standard 3.MD.8 – Measurement & Data

☐ **What is the perimeter for the figure below? Be sure to show your work.**

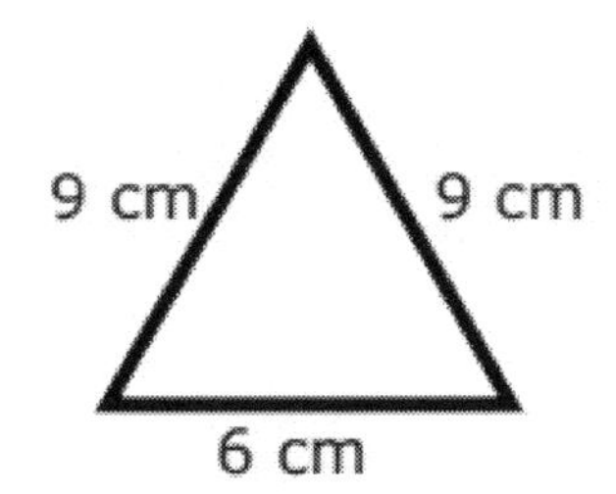


**A 486 cm**

**B 24 cm**

**C 48 cm**

**D 87 cm**

Common Core Standard 3.MD.8 – Measurement & Data

☐ **Marciano wants to find the square footage of his playroom. The dimensions are 12 feet by 11 feet. What is the square footage of the playroom room? Be sure to show your work.**

**A 132 square inches**

**B 23 square feet**

**C 132 square feet**

**D 46 square feet**

Common Core Standard 3.MD.8 – Measurement & Data

☐ **Hank mows yards in the summer. He charges $3.00 per square foot. Mr. Johnson wants him to mow his yard, it measures 10 x 14 ft. How much did Hank charge Mr. Johnson to mow his yard? Be sure to show your work.**

**A $72.00**

**B $144.00**

**C $420.00**

**D $84.00**

Name ___________________________

**PRACTICE**

Common Core Standard 3.MD.8 – Measurement & Data

☐ **What is the length of a rectangle that has a perimeter of 32 meters and a width of 10 meters? Be sure to show your work.**

**A** **22 meters**

**B** **20 meters**

**C** **6 meters**

**D** **4 meters**

Common Core Standard 3.MD.8 – Measurement & Data

☐ **If the perimeter of a square is 48 cm, how long is one side of the square? Be sure to show your work.**

**A** **7 cm**

**B** **4 cm**

**C** **14 cm**

**D** **12 cm**

Common Core Standard 3.MD.8 – Measurement & Data

☐ **If the perimeter for the figure below is 42, what is the value for *X*? Be sure to show your work.**

**A** **2 feet**

**B** **15 feet**

**C** **24 feet**

**D** **36 feet**

6 ft.

$X$

Name ______________________

**PRACTICE**

Common Core Standard 3.MD.8 – Measurement & Data

☐ **What is the perimeter for the figure below? Be sure to show your work.**

**A** **32 km**

**B** **64 km**

**C** **1200 km**

**D** **2880 km**

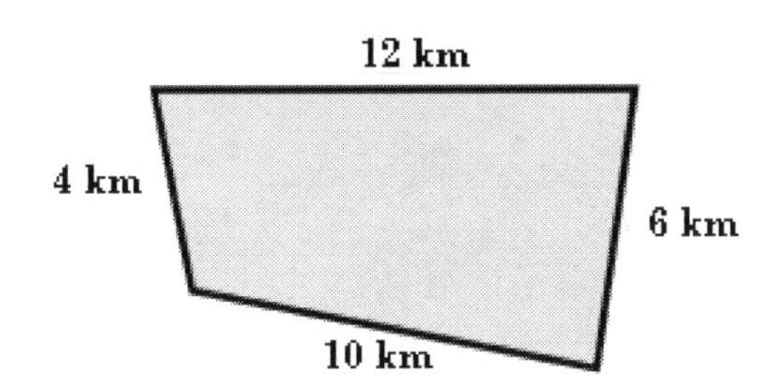


Common Core Standard 3.MD.8 – Measurement & Data

☐ **Hector is hired to paint a room. The room is 12 feet wide by 9 feets long. Hector is paid $7 per square foot that he paints. How much did Hector earn to paint the room? Be sure to show your work.**

**A** **$294**

**B** **$756**

**C** **$147**

**D** **$672**

Common Core Standard 3.MD.8 – Measurement & Data

☐ **Coach Winn needs to know the distance around the football field, so he knows how far is players run during practice. If he knows the length of the field is 100 meters and the perimeter is 350 meters, what is the width of one side of the football field? Be sure to show your work.**

**A** **50 meters**

**B** **250 meters**

**C** **150 meters**

**D** **75 meters**

Name ___________________________

**PRACTICE**

Common Core Standard 3.MD.8 – Measurement & Data

☐ **One side of a square measures 9 cm. What is the perimeter of the square? Be sure to show your work.**

A 18 cm

B 36 cm

C 72 cm

D 28 cm

Common Core Standard 3.MD.8 – Measurement & Data

☐ **If the perimeter for the figure below is 32mm, what is the value for *X*? Be sure to show your work.**

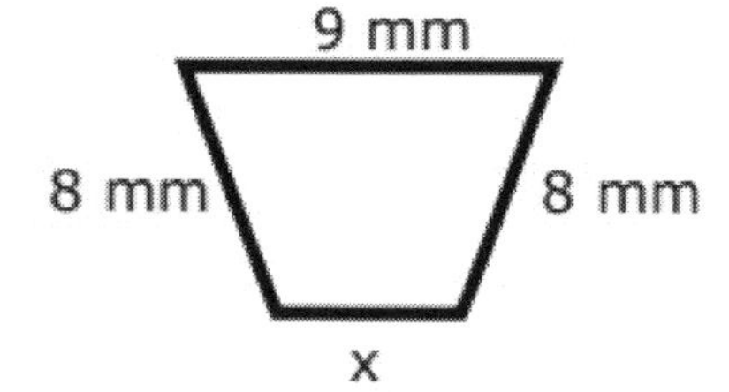


A 16 mm

B 4 mm

C 9 mm

D 7 mm

Common Core Standard 3.MD.8 – Measurement & Data

☐ **Josephine wants to build a fence for her horse. The perimeter of the fence needs to be 144 feet. What is the length of each side of the fence if it is in the shape of a square? Be sure to show your work.**

A 20 ft

B 48 ft

C 36 ft

D 24 ft

Name ________________________

**PRACTICE**

Common Core Standard 3.MD.8 – Measurement & Data

☐ **What is the area for the figure below? Be sure to show your work.**

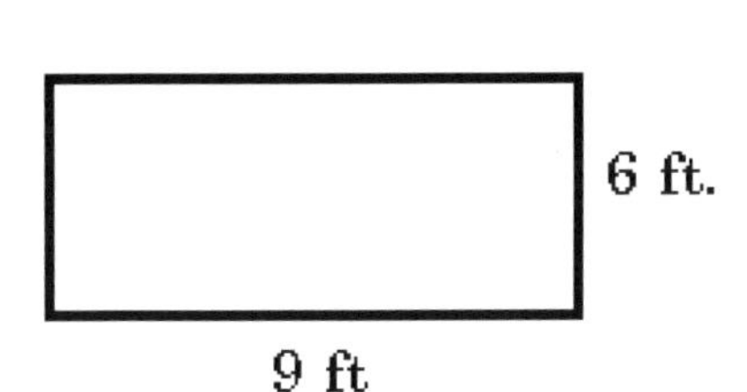


**A** **15 $ft^2$**

**B** **54 $ft^2$**

**C** **30 $ft^2$.**

**D** **2916 $ft^2$**

Common Core Standard 3.MD.8 – Measurement & Data

☐ **What is the perimeter for the figure below? Be sure to show your work.**

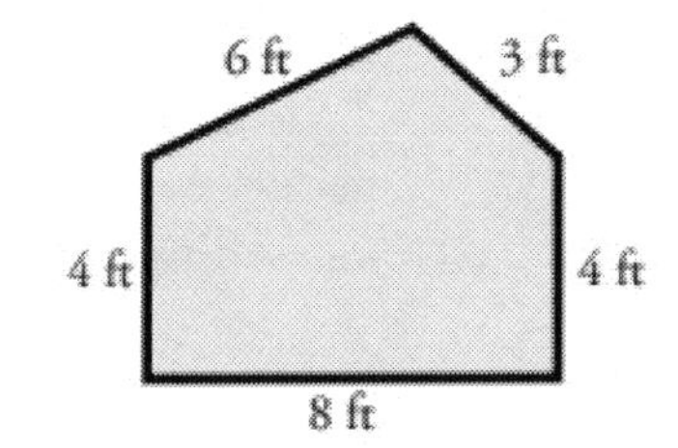


**A** **50 feet**

**B** **2304 feet**

**C** **33 feet**

**D** **25 feet**

Common Core Standard 3.MD.8 – Measurement & Data

☐ **Diane wants to put Christmas lights around her front door. The door has measurement of 3 feet wide by 6 feet high. She has a 3 different strings of Christmas lights, one measures 18 ft, another measures 21 feet, and the final one measures 24 feet. Which string of lights will she use? Be sure to show your work.**

**A** **None of the string fit the door**

**B** **21 feet**

**C** **18 feet**

**D** **24 feet**

Name ___________________________

**ASSESSMENT**

Common Core Standard 3.MD.8 – Measurement & Data

☐ **What is the width of a rectangle that has a perimeter of 28 meters and a length of 9 meters? Be sure to show your work.**

**A** **18 meters**

**B** **5 meters**

**C** **4 meters**

**D** **10 meters**

Common Core Standard 3.MD.8 – Measurement & Data

☐ **If the perimeter of a square is 28 cm. How long is one side of the square? Be sure to show your work.**

**A** **7 cm**

**B** **4 cm**

**C** **14cm**

**D** **12 cm**

Common Core Standard 3.MD.8 – Measurement & Data

☐ **If the perimeter for the figure below is 42, what is the value for *X*? Be sure to show your work.**

**A** **10 m**

**B** **11 m**

**C** **12 m**

**D** **18 m**

$X$

9 m

Name ____________________

**ASSESSMENT**

Common Core Standard 3.MD.8 – Measurement & Data

☐ **What is the perimeter for the figure below? Be sure to show your work.**

**A** 65 in.

**B** 35 in.

**C** 70 in.

**D** 15680 in.

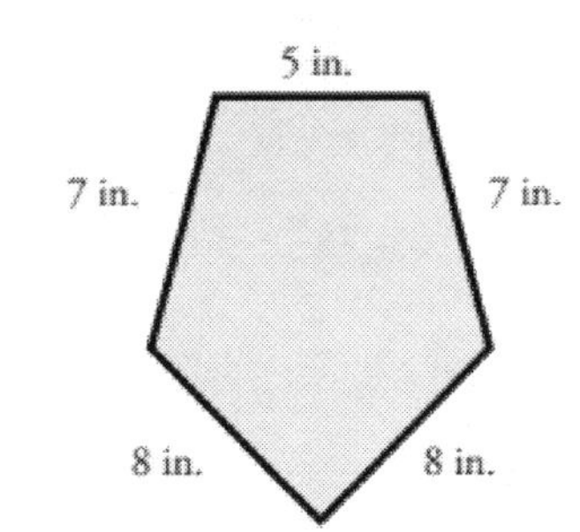


Common Core Standard 3.MD.8 – Measurement & Data

☐ **Ali wants to hang posters in his room. Poster A covers 12 ft.$^2$. Poster B covers 15 ft.$^2$. Poster C covers 9 sq. ft$^2$. He wants to cover the wall behind his bed that measures 3 ft. x 5 ft. Which poster shoud he use? Be sure to show your work.**

**A** Poster A

**B** Poster B

**C** Poster C

**D** No Posters fit

Common Core Standard 3.MD.8 – Measurement & Data

☐ **Hannah is helping her mother put away her winter clothes. The shelves that she is storing her clothes in measures 13 inches high and has 5 shelves. How high is the 4$^{th}$ shelf? Be sure to show your work.**

**A** 65 inches

**B** 18 inches

**C** 52 inches

**D** 17 inches

Name ____________________

DIAGNOSTIC

Common Core Standard 3.G.1 – Geometry

☐ **Which shape has 4 sides, opposite sides are equal and has 4 right angles?**

**A** Square

**B** Parallelogram

**C** Trapezoid

**D** Rectangle

Common Core Standard 3.G.1 – Geometry

☐ **How many sides are there in a square?**

**A** 6

**B** 4

**C** 3

**D** 2

Common Core Standard 3.G.1 – Geometry

☐ **Which of the following describes a right angle?**

**A** 80°

**B** 90°

**C** 45°

**D** 180°

Name ___________________________

**DIAGNOSTIC**

Common Core Standard 3.G.1 – Geometry

☐ **What shape is the figure below?**

**A** **Trapezoid**

**B** **Square**

**C** **Rhombus**

**D** **Pentagon**

Common Core Standard 3.G.1 – Geometry

☐ **How many sides are there in an octagon?**

**A** **7**

**B** **6**

**C** **5**

**D** **8**

Common Core Standard 3.G.1 – Geometry

☐ **Which shape has 4 sides, opposite sides are parallel and does *NOT* have right angles?**

**A** **Square**

**B** **Parallelogram**

**C** **Trapezoid**

**D** **Rectangle**

Name ________________________

PRACTICE

Common Core Standard 3.G.1 – Geometry

☐ **Which of the following are polygons?**

A

C

B

D

Common Core Standard 3.G.1 – Geometry

☐ **How many sides are there in a quadrilateral?**

A 6

B 4

C 3

D 2

Common Core Standard 3.G.1 – Geometry

☐ **Which two angles could be combined to make a right angle?**

A

C

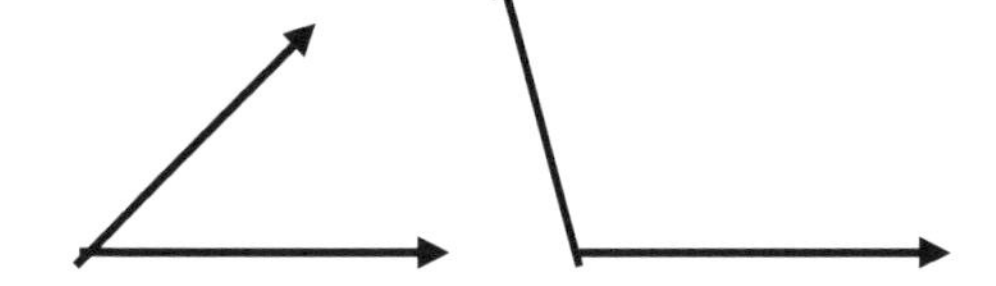

B

D

Name ______________________

PRACTICE

Common Core Standard 3.G.1 – Geometry

☐ What shape is the figure below?

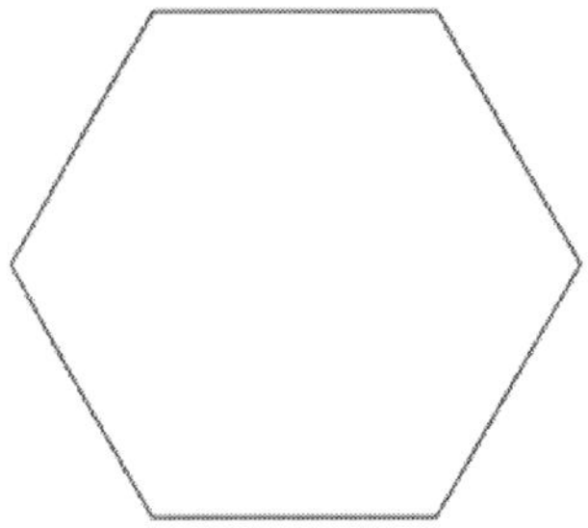

A Trapezoid

B Hexagon

C Octagon

D Pentagon

Common Core Standard 3.G.1 – Geometry

☐ Which shape is a three dimensional shape?

A Rhombus

B Right Triangle

C Equilateral Triangle

D Cone

Common Core Standard 3.G.1 – Geometry

☐ How many sides does a dodecagon have?

A 11

B 6

C 10

D 12

Name ___________________________

**PRACTICE**

Common Core Standard 3.G.1 – Geometry

☐ **Look at the shapes in the box. Which shapes below belong to this group?**

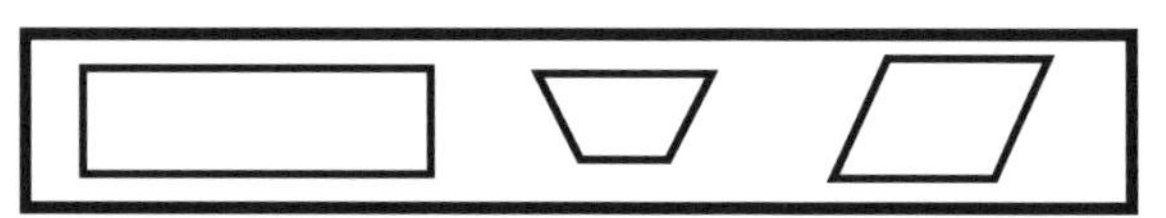

**A** 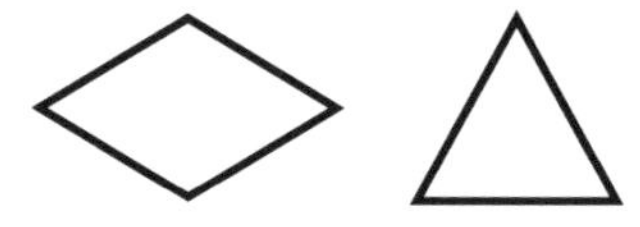

**C** 

**B** 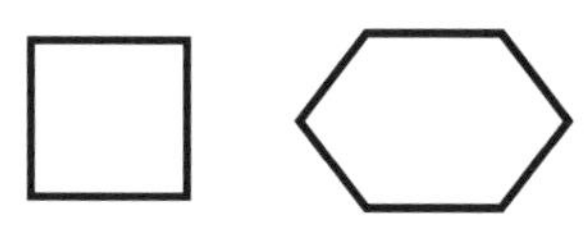

**D** 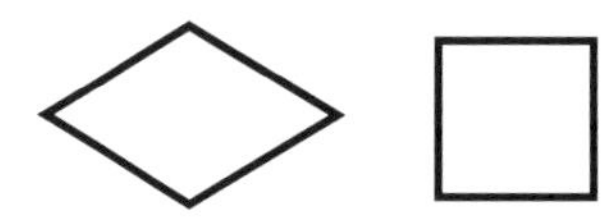

Common Core Standard 3.G.1 – Geometry

☐ **Which of the following has 9 sides?**

**A** **Octagon**

**B** **Dodecagon**

**C** **Nonagon**

**D** **Heptagon**

Common Core Standard 3.G.1 – Geometry

☐ **Which shape below contains a right angle?**

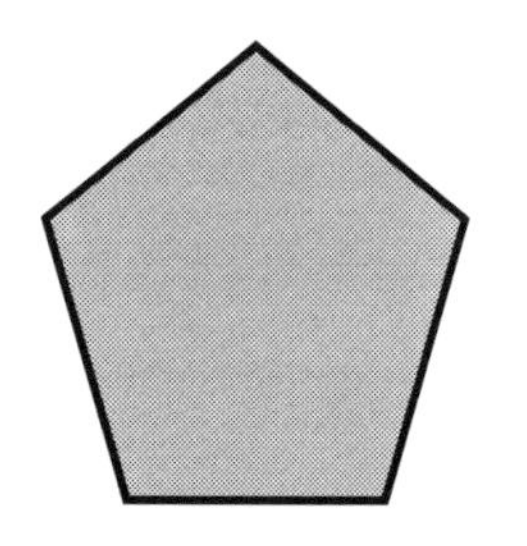

**A**

**B**

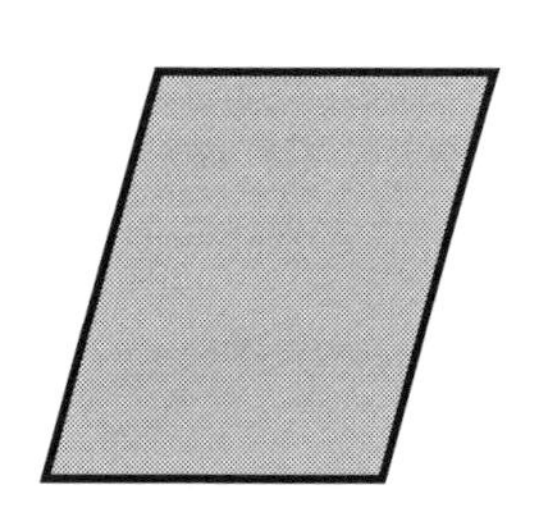

**C**

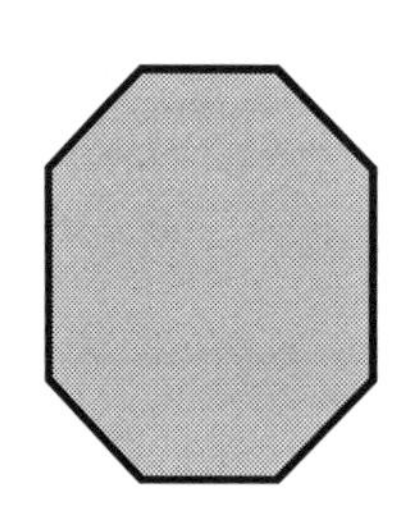

**D**

Name ____________________

**PRACTICE**

Common Core Standard 3.G.1 – Geometry

☐ **What shape is the figure below?**

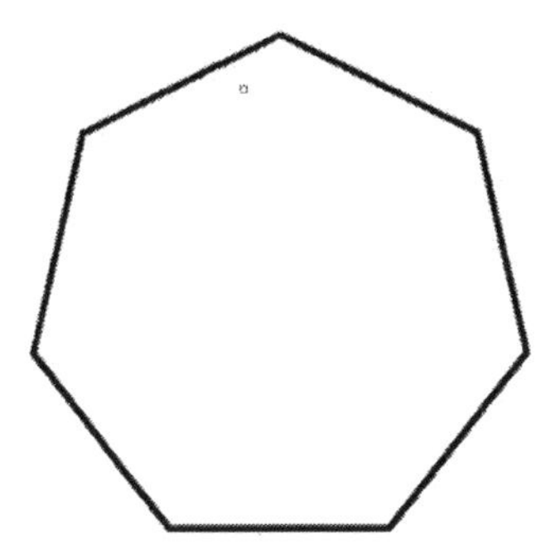

**A** Octagon

**B** Pentagon

**C** Heptagon

**D** Nonagon

Common Core Standard 3.G.1 – Geometry

☐ **How many sides are there in a triangle?**

**A** 4

**B** 3

**C** 5

**D** 2

Common Core Standard 3.G.1 – Geometry

☐ **Which of the following polygons has parallel and perpendicular lines?**

**A** 

**C** 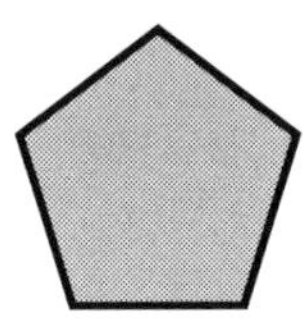

**B** 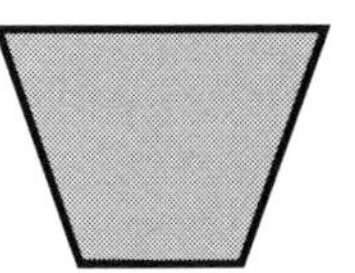

**D** 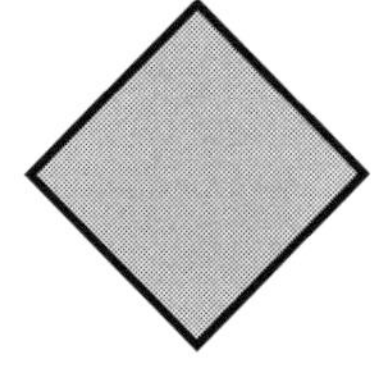

Name ___________________________

**ASSESSMENT**

Common Core Standard 3.G.1 – Geometry

☐ **Which shape has 4 sides and one pair of parallel sides?**

**A** **Square**

**B** **Parallelogram**

**C** **Trapezoid**

**D** **Pentagon**

Common Core Standard 3.G.1 – Geometry

☐ **Which of the following has 7 sides?**

**A** **Octagon**

**B** **Cone**

**C** **Prism**

**D** **Heptagon**

Common Core Standard 3.G.1 – Geometry

☐ **Which angle measures 90°?**

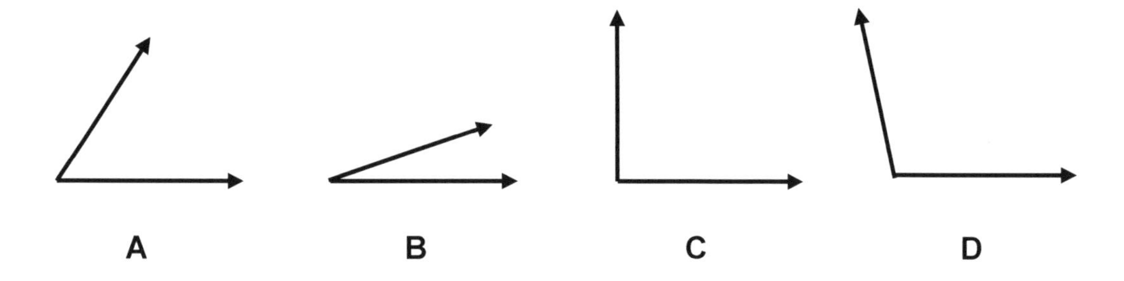

**A** **B** **C** **D**

Name ___________________________

ASSESSMENT

Common Core Standard 3.G.1 – Geometry

☐ **What shape is the figure below?**

A Hexagon

B Heptagon

C Pentagon

D Decagon

Common Core Standard 3.G.1 – Geometry

☐ **How many sides are there in a hexagon?**

A 7

B 6

C 5

D 8

Common Core Standard 3.G.1 – Geometry

☐ **Which shape is a quadrilateral with 4 sides with two pairs of equal-length sides adjacent to each other?**

A Square

B Diamond

C Triangle

D Rectangle

Name ______________________

**DIAGNOSTIC**

Common Core Standard 3.G.2 – Geometry

☐ **Which figure shows the fraction $\frac{4}{7}$?**

**A** 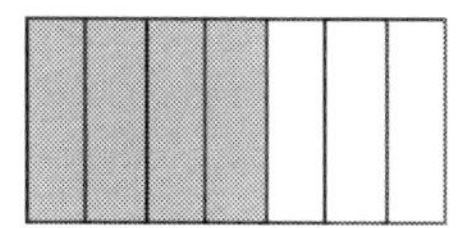

**B** 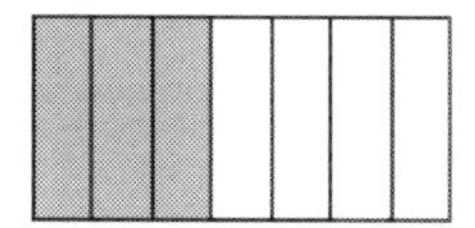

**C** 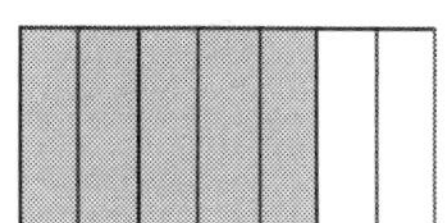

**D** 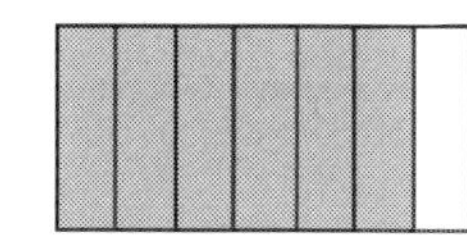

Common Core Standard 3.G.2 – Geometry

☐ **What fraction of the hexagons below are shaded?**

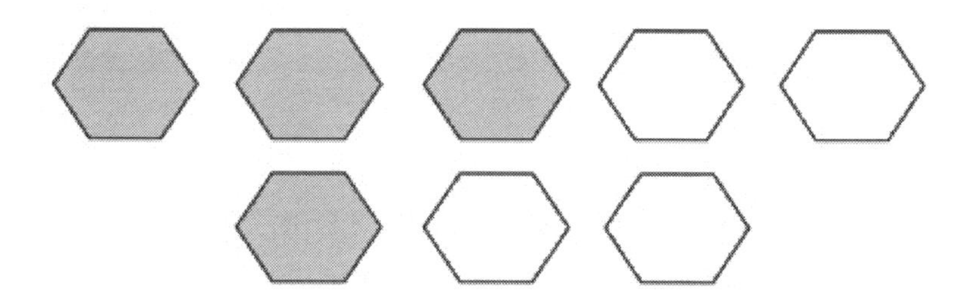

**A** 3/8

**B** 5/8

**C** 4/8

**D** 1/4

Common Core Standard 3.G.2 – Geometry

☐ **What is the fraction for the shape below?**

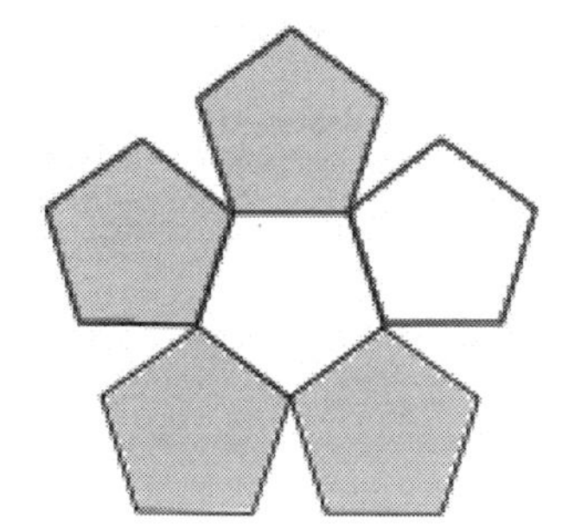

**A** 4/6

**B** 2/6

**C** 5/6

**D** 1/6

Name ____________________

DIAGNOSTIC

Common Core Standard 3.G.2 – Geometry

☐ Which figure shows the fraction $\frac{5}{6}$?

A 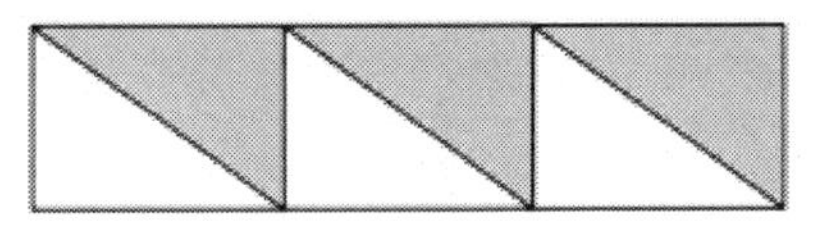

C 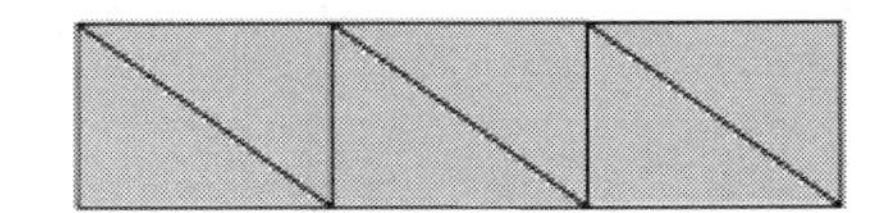

B 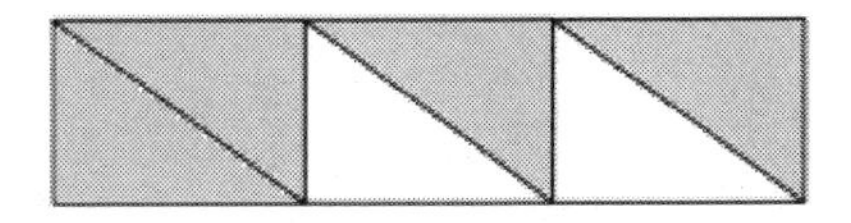

D 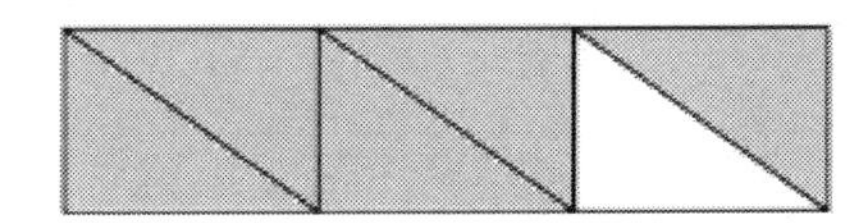

Common Core Standard 3.G.2 – Geometry

☐ What fraction of the triangles below are shaded?

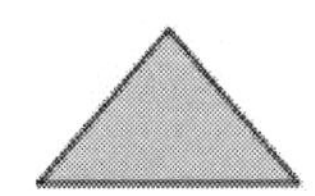 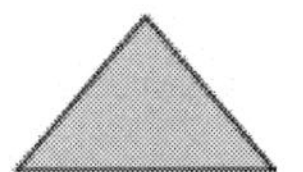 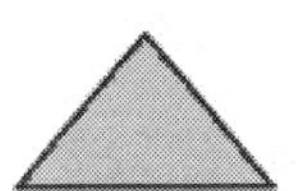 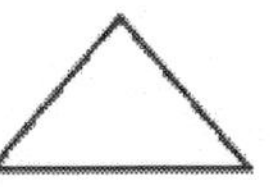 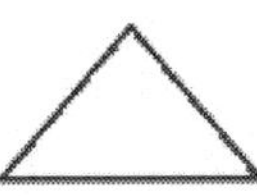  

A 2/7

B 3/7

C 4/7

D 3/8

Common Core Standard 3.G.2 – Geometry

☐ What is the fraction for the shape below?

A 4/6

B 5/6

C 3/6

D 2/6

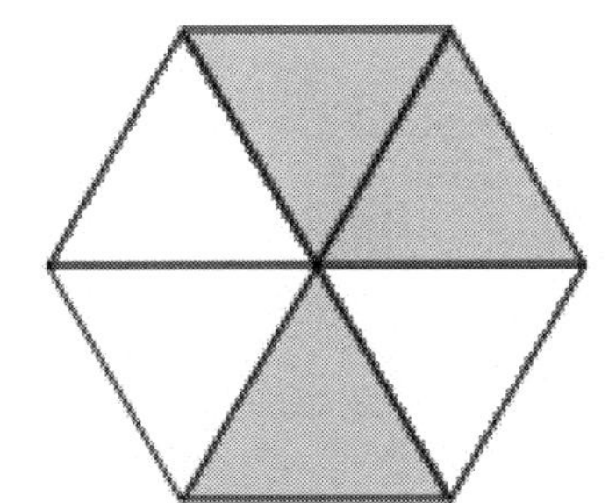

Name ____________________

**PRACTICE**

Common Core Standard 3.G.2 – Geometry

☐ **Which figure shows the fraction $\frac{5}{6}$?**

**A** 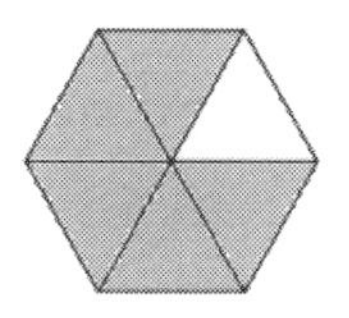

**C** 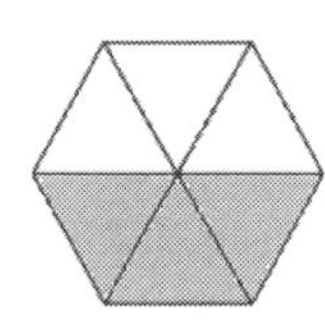

**B** 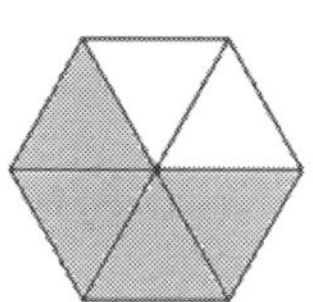

**D** 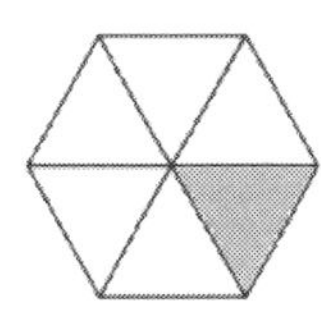

Common Core Standard 3.G.2 – Geometry

☐ **What fraction of the trapezoids below are shaded?**

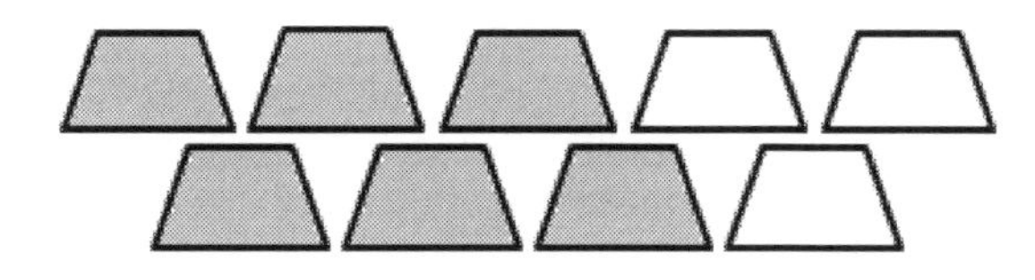

**A** 3/9

**C** 4/9

**B** 5/9

**D** 6/9

Common Core Standard 3.G.2 – Geometry

☐ **What is the fraction for the shape below?**

**A** 6/8

**B** 4/8

**C** 5/8

**D** 3/8

Name ___________________________

**PRACTICE**

Common Core Standard 3.G.2 – Geometry

☐ **Which figure shows the fraction $\frac{1}{4}$?**

A 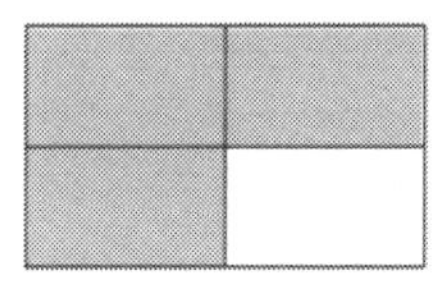

C 

B 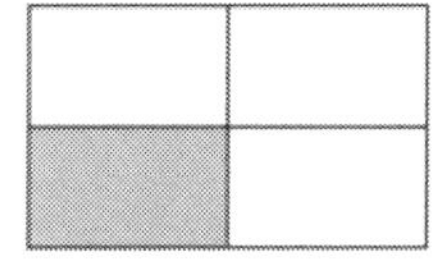

D 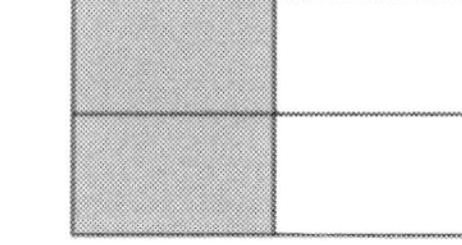

Common Core Standard 3.G.2 – Geometry

☐ **What fraction of the rhombuses below are shaded?**

A 2/6

B 1/6

C 4/6

D 3/6

Common Core Standard 3.G.2 – Geometry

☐ **Which figure shows the fraction $\frac{2}{5}$?**

A 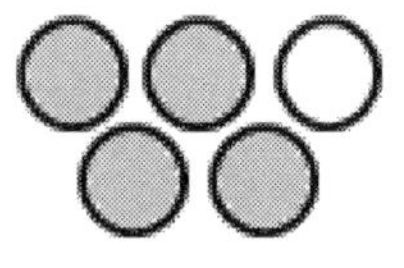

C 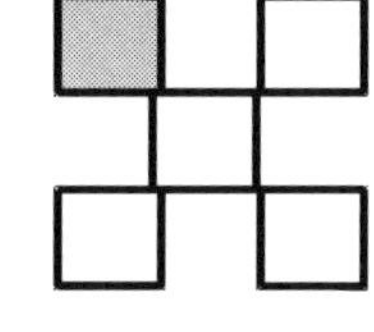

B 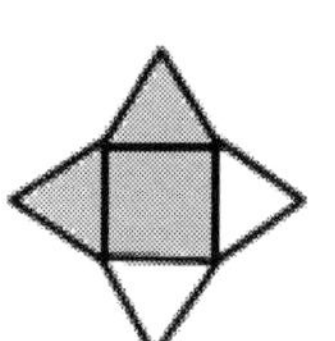

D 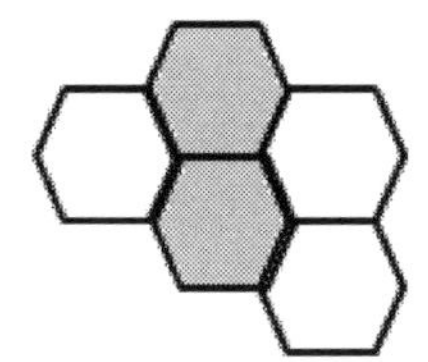

 

Name 

**PRACTICE**

Common Core Standard 3.G.2 – Geometry

☐ **What is the fraction for the shape below?**

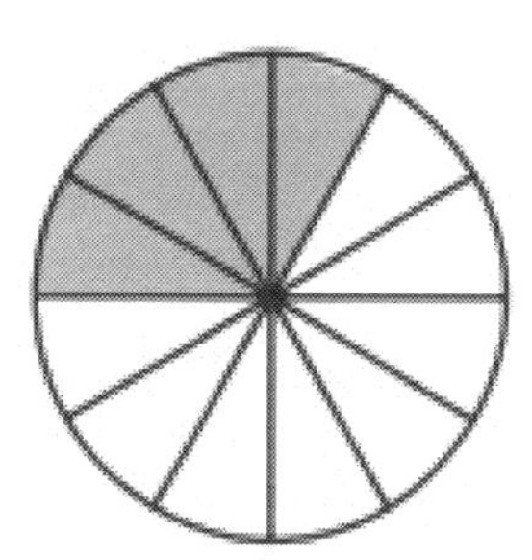

A 6/12

B 8/12

C 5/12

D 4/12

Common Core Standard 3.G.2 – Geometry

☐ **What fraction of the right triangles below are shaded?**

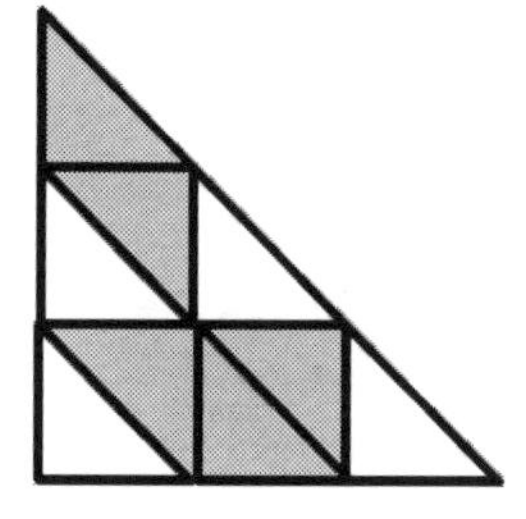

A 3/9

B 5/9

C 4/9

D 6/9

Common Core Standard 3.G.2 – Geometry

☐ **What is the fraction for the shape below?**

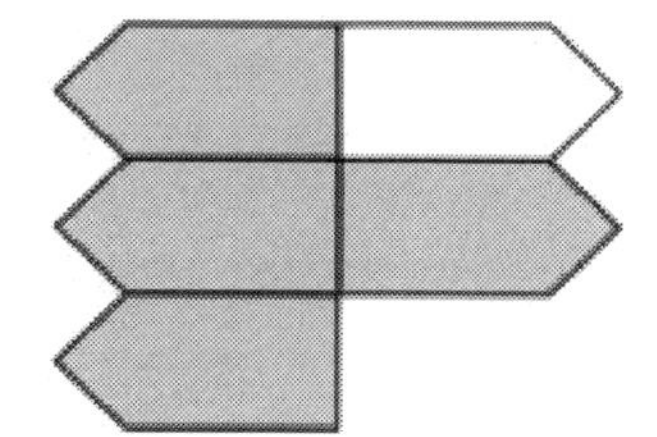

A 4/5

B 3/5

C 2/5

D 1/5

Name ___________________________

**PRACTICE**

Common Core Standard 3.G.2 – Geometry

☐ **Which figure shows the fraction $\frac{7}{11}$ ?**

**A** **C**

**B** **D**

Common Core Standard 3.G.2 – Geometry

☐ **What fraction of the diamonds below are shaded?**

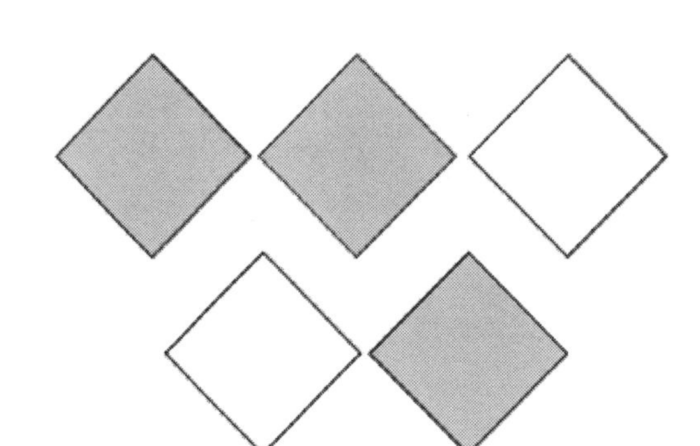

**A** **2/5**

**B** **3/5**

**C** **4/5**

**D** **1/5**

Common Core Standard 3.G.2 – Geometry

☐ **What is the fraction for the shape below?**

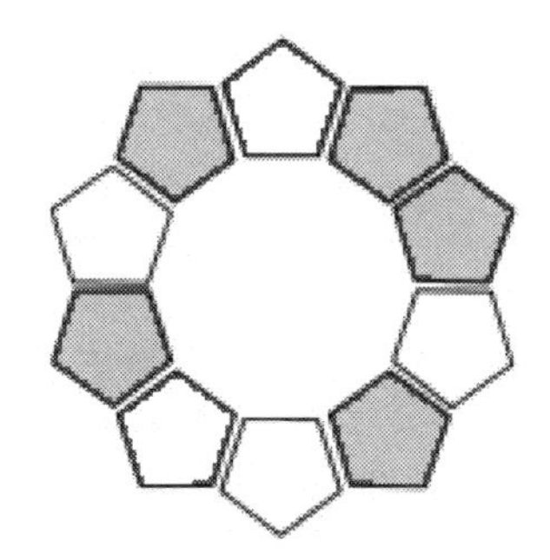

**A** **4/10**

**B** **5/10**

**C** **3/10**

**D** **6/10**

Name ____________________________

**ASSESSMENT**

Common Core Standard 3.G.2 – Geometry

☐ **Which figure shows the fraction $\frac{5}{8}$?**

A 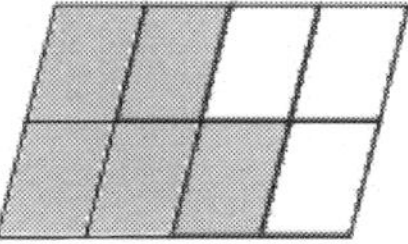

C 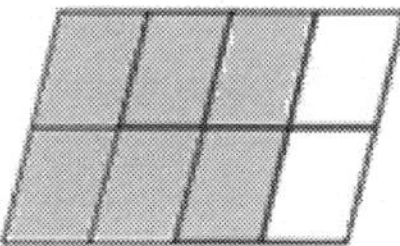

B 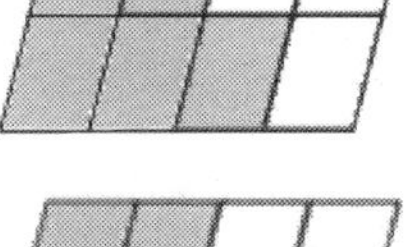

D 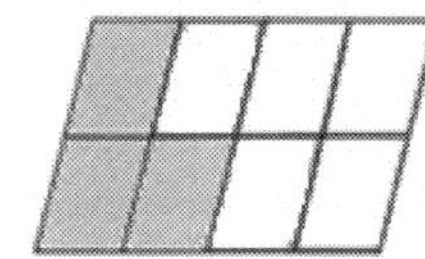

Common Core Standard 3.G.2 – Geometry

☐ **What fraction of the squares below are shaded?**

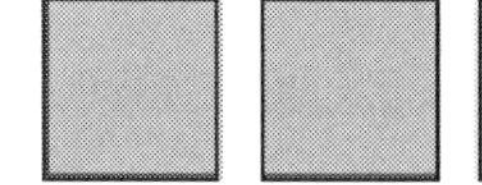 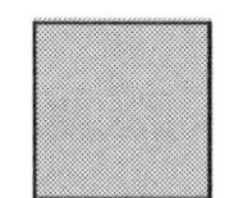     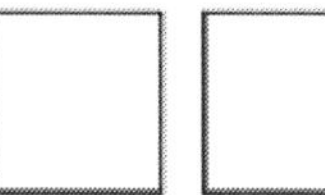

A 3/8

C 4/8

B 5/8

D 1/4

Common Core Standard 3.G.2 – Geometry

☐ **What is the fraction for the shape below?**

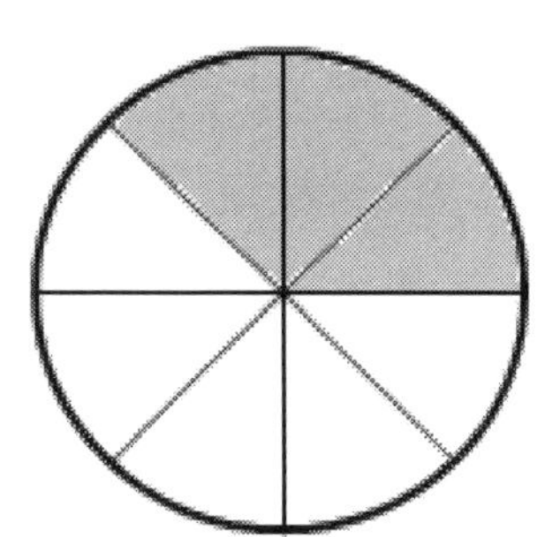

A 6/8

B 4/8

C 5/8

D 3/8

Name ______________________

ASSESSMENT

Common Core Standard 3.G.2 – Geometry

☐ Which figure shows the fraction $\frac{7}{10}$ ?

A 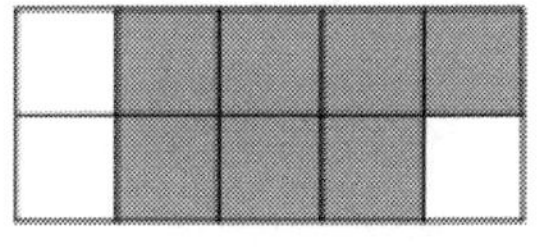

C 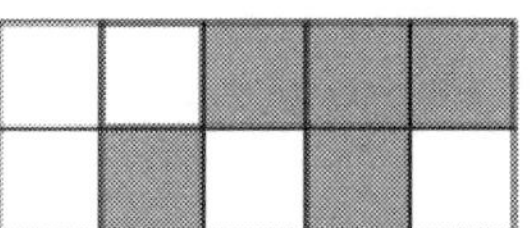

B 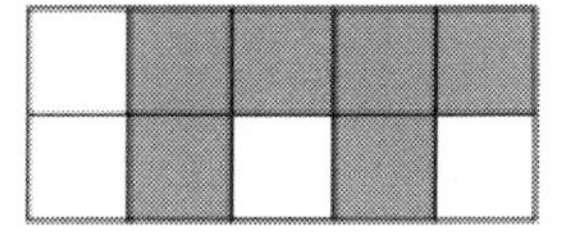

D 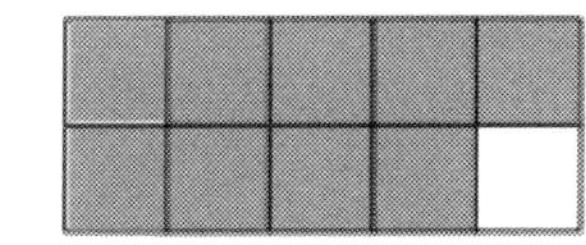

Common Core Standard 3.G.2 – Geometry

☐ What fraction of the circles below are shaded?

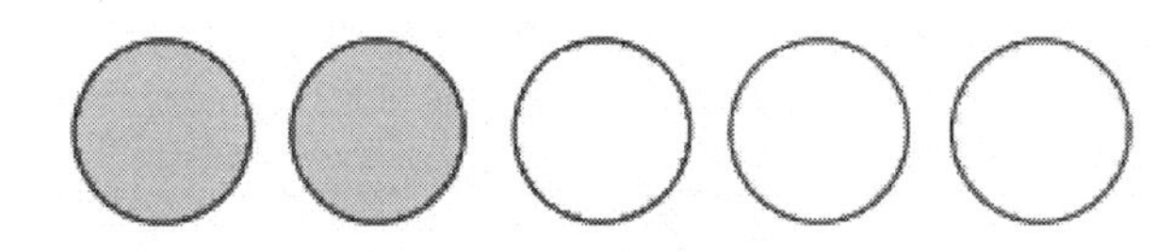

A 2/5

B 3/5

C 4/5

D 3/4

Common Core Standard 3.G.2 – Geometry

☐ Which figure shows the fraction $\frac{3}{4}$ ?

A 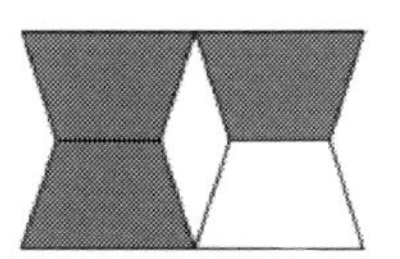

C 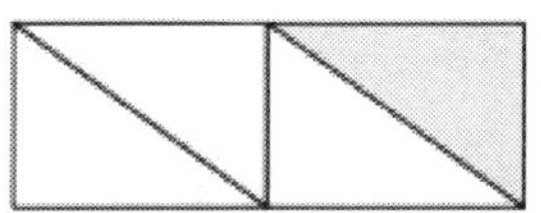

B 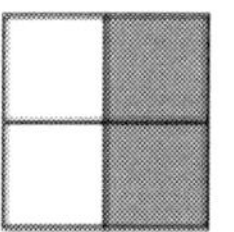

D 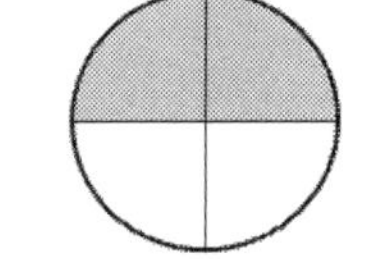

# ANSWER KEY

**3.OA.1**

Page 1 ............ D, C, C
Page 2 ............ B, C, C
Page 3 ............ C, B, C
Page 4 ............ B, C, D
Page 5 ............ C, B, A
Page 6 ............ B, B, C
Page 7 ............ B, A, C
Page 8 ............ D, C, B

**3.OA.2**

Page 9 ............ B, D, A
Page 10 ............ C, C, B
Page 11 ............ C, A, C
Page 12 ............ A, B, C
Page 13 ............ D, C, C
Page 14 ............ A, D, B
Page 15 ............ D, B, A
Page 16 ............ D, B, A

**3.OA.3**

Page 17 .......... B, B, A
Page 18 .......... B, A, A
Page 19 .......... D, B, C
Page 20 .......... B, C, C
Page 21 .......... A, D, B
Page 22 .......... D, D, A
Page 23 .......... C, D, D
Page 24 .......... D, C, B

**3.OA.4**

Page 25 .......... D, A, C
Page 26 .......... C, A, D
Page 27 .......... D, A, D
Page 28 .......... B, B, D
Page 29 .......... B, C, D
Page 30 .......... C, B, D
Page 31 .......... B, C, D
Page 32 .......... B, C, C

**3.OA.5**

Page 33 .......... B, C, B
Page 34 .......... C, B, D
Page 35 .......... D, B, C
Page 36 .......... B, A, B
Page 37 .......... C, B, D
Page 38 .......... C, D, B
Page 39 .......... A, C, D
Page 40 .......... C, B, C

**3.OA.6**

Page 41 .......... A, A, A
Page 42 .......... B, B, B
Page 43 .......... B, A, C
Page 44 .......... D, A, C
Page 45 .......... B, D, A
Page 46 .......... B, D, A
Page 47 .......... D, B, D
Page 48 .......... A, D, B

## ANSWER KEY

**3.OA.7**

Page 49 .......... D, B, A

Page 50 .......... C, C, D

Page 51 .......... A, C, D

Page 52 .......... B, B, D

Page 53 .......... D, D, B

Page 54 .......... B, C, A

Page 55 .......... D, A, B

Page 56 .......... C, A, D

**3.OA.8**

Page 57 .......... B, A, D

Page 58 .......... B, B, A

Page 59 .......... C, A, D

Page 60 .......... C, B, D

Page 61 .......... D, A, B

Page 62 .......... A, B, C

Page 63 .......... D, A, B

Page 64 .......... D, B, B

**3.OA.9**

Page 65 .......... B, C, D

Page 66 .......... C, C, D

Page 67 .......... D, B, B

Page 68 .......... B, D, C

Page 69 .......... B, D, A

Page 70 .......... C, B, D

Page 71 .......... A, C, A

Page 72 .......... C, C, A

**3.NBT.1**

Page 73 .......... A, B, A

Page 74 .......... C, A, B

Page 75 .......... A, B, D

Page 76 .......... B, A, C

Page 77 .......... D, B, A

Page 78 .......... A, C, C

Page 79 .......... B, D, B

Page 80 .......... B, C, A

**3.NBT.2**

Page 81 .......... C, A, D

Page 82 .......... C, B, D

Page 83 .......... A, C, B

Page 84 .......... D, B, D

Page 85 .......... C, D, A

Page 86 .......... B, D, D

Page 87 .......... A, A, C

Page 88 .......... B, D, D

**3.NBT.3**

Page 89 .......... B, A, B

Page 90 .......... D, D, A

Page 91 .......... B, C, B

Page 92 .......... B, B, A

Page 93 .......... A, C, C

Page 94 .......... B, B, C

Page 95 .......... B, C, A

Page 96 .......... C, D, C

# ANSWER KEY

**3.NF.1**

Page 97 .......... D, D, A

Page 98 .......... C, C, C

Page 99 .......... D, C, A

Page 100 .......... B, C, A

Page 101 .......... B, D, C

Page 102 .......... D, A, A

Page 103 .......... B, A, D

Page 104 .......... B, B, D

**3.NF.2**

Page 105 .......... D, B, B

Page 106 .......... B, D, C

Page 107 .......... D, B, C

Page 108 .......... C, B, D

Page 109 .......... D, B, A

Page 110 .......... C, C, A

Page 111 .......... D, B, D

Page 112 .......... A, D, A

**3.NF.3**

Page 113 .......... A, B, A

Page 114 .......... A, B, D

Page 115 .......... A, A, D

Page 116 .......... C, A, D

Page 117 .......... A, B, D

Page 118 .......... B, A, C

Page 119 .......... B, C, D

Page 120 .......... C, A, A

**3.MD.1**

Page 121 .......... D, B, C

Page 122 .......... B, C, B

Page 123 .......... C, B, A

Page 124 .......... D, C, D

Page 125 .......... B, D, A

Page 126 .......... C, B, D

Page 127 .......... D, D, B

Page 128 .......... C, B, D

**3.MD.2**

Page 129 .......... B, B, B

Page 130 .......... D, D, D

Page 131 .......... B, D, C

Page 132 .......... C, A, B

Page 133 .......... C, A, B

Page 134 .......... D, B, B

Page 135 .......... D, C, C

Page 136 .......... C, A, A

**3.MD.3**

Page 137 .......... C, D, B

Page 138 .......... C

Page 139 .......... B, C

Page 140 .......... C

Page 141 .......... D, B, C

Page 142 .......... D

Page 143 .......... C

Page 144 .......... C

Page 145 .......... C, D, A

Page 146 .......... A

# ANSWER KEY

**3.MD.4**

Page 147 ......... B, C, B
Page 148 ......... A, D, B
Page 149 ......... C, C, D
Page 150 ......... B, C, A
Page 151 ......... A, A, B
Page 152 ......... C, B, C
Page 153 ......... C, B, C
Page 154 ......... B, D, D

**3.MD.5**

Page 155 ......... C, C, D
Page 156 ......... C, B, B
Page 157 ......... D, C, B
Page 158 ......... B, D, A
Page 159 ......... C, C, B
Page 160 ......... D, B, D
Page 161 ......... D, B, A
Page 162 ......... A, B, B

**3.MD.6**

Page 163 ......... A, C, D
Page 164 ......... D, D, D
Page 165 ......... B, A, C
Page 166 ......... C, C, A
Page 167 ......... D, D, C
Page 168 ......... B, B, A
Page 169 ......... A, B, A
Page 170 ......... C, D, C

**3.MD.7**

Page 171 ......... C, A, A
Page 172 ......... C, C, A
Page 173 ......... A, D, C
Page 174 ......... D, A, B
Page 175 ......... D, C, C
Page 176 ......... D, B, B
Page 177 ......... D, B, C
Page 178 ......... B, C, A

**3.MD.8**

Page 179 ......... B, C, B
Page 180 ......... B, C, C
Page 181 ......... C, D, B
Page 182 ......... A, B, D
Page 183 ......... B, D, C
Page 184 ......... B, D, C
Page 185 ......... B, A, C
Page 186 ......... B, B, C

**3.G.1**

Page 187 ......... A, B, B
Page 188 ......... C, D, B
Page 189 ......... C, B, B
Page 190 ......... B, D, D
Page 191 ......... D, C, B
Page 192 ......... C, B, D
Page 193 ......... C, D, C
Page 194 ......... D, B, D

## ANSWER KEY

**3.G.2**

**Page 195 .......... A, C, A**

**Page 196 .......... D, B, C**

**Page 197 .......... A, D, D**

**Page 198 .......... B, B, D**

**Page 199 .......... D, B, A**

**Page 200 .......... C, B, B**

**Page 201 .......... A, B, D**

**Page 202 .......... A, A, A**

Made in United States
Troutdale, OR
03/31/2024